W9-ADS-390

Popular Complete Smart Series

Complete
MathSmart®

Grade
11

Proud Sponsor of the Math Team of Canada 2017

Credits

Artwork (Front Cover "3D White Sphere" Senoldo/123RF.com)

 ISBN: 978-1-77149-222-5

COMPLETE MATHSMART (GRADE 11)   ISBN: 978-1-77149-222-5

Overview

Complete MathSmart is our all-time bestselling series. *Complete MathSmart* Grade 11 is designed to strengthen students' math foundation, and allow them to learn the key concepts and demonstrate their understanding by applying their knowledge and skills to solve real-world problems.

This workbook covers the four strands of the Mathematics curriculum:
- Characteristics of Functions
- Exponential Functions
- Discrete Functions
- Trigonometric Functions

This workbook contains eight chapters, with each chapter covering a math topic. Different concepts in the topic are each introduced by a simple example and a "Try This" section to give students an opportunity to check their understanding of the concept. The basic skill questions that follow lead up to application questions that gradually increase in difficulty to help students consolidate the concept they have learned. Useful hints are provided to guide students along and help them grasp the essential math concepts. In addition, a handy reference containing definitions and formulas is included to provide quick and easy access for students whenever needed.

A cumulative review is provided for students to recapitulate the concepts and skills they have learned in the book. The questions are classified into four categories to help students evaluate their own learning. Below are the four categories:
- Knowledge and Understanding
- Application
- Communication
- Thinking

The review is also ideal as testing practice to prepare students for the Math examination in school.

At the end of this workbook is an answer key that provides thorough solutions with the crucial steps clearly presented to help students develop an understanding of the correct strategies and approaches to arrive at the solutions.

Complete MathSmart will undoubtedly reinforce students' math skills and strengthen their conceptual foundation that is a prerequisite for exploring mathematics further in their secondary programs.

Contents

1 Basic Skills

Words TO LEARN

System of linear equations:

a system of two or more linear equations

e.g. $x + y = 1$
          $2x + y = -4$

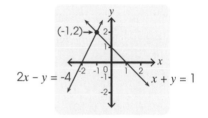

The point of intersection is (-1,2).

Factorization:

a decomposition of a polynomial into a product of other factors, which when multiplied together give back the polynomial

e.g. $x^2 - x - 6$
      $= (x - 3)(x + 2)$

Think
$-3 + 2 = -1$
$-3 \times 2 = -6$

Check by using the distributive property.

$(x - 3)(x + 2) = x^2 + 2x - 3x - 6$
$\qquad\qquad\quad = x^2 - x - 6$

Primary trigonometry ratios:

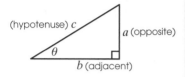

$\sin \theta = \dfrac{\text{opposite}}{\text{hypotenuse}} = \dfrac{a}{c}$

$\cos \theta = \dfrac{\text{adjacent}}{\text{hypotenuse}} = \dfrac{b}{c}$

$\tan \theta = \dfrac{\text{opposite}}{\text{adjacent}} = \dfrac{a}{b}$

1.1 Graphing Systems of Linear Equations

Example

Solve the system of equations by graphing.

$5x - 3y - 3 = 0$
$4x + 3y - 24 = 0$

Solution:

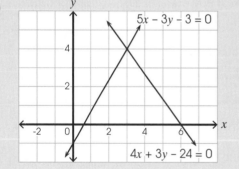

The solution is (3,4).

Try This

Solve by graphing.

$y = x - 4 \qquad x + 2y = 1$

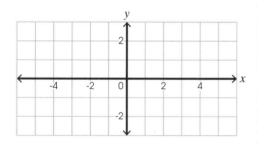

The solution is _____ .

Solve each system of equations by graphing.

① $x + 2y = 6$
   $3x - y = 11$

Solution

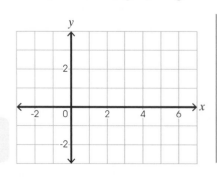

② $x + y - 2 = 0$
   $y = x - 6$

Solution

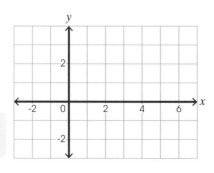

ISBN: 978-1-77149-222-5

③ $\frac{x}{5} - y = -4$

$x - y = 8$

Solution

④ $x - 2y = 12$

$2y + 16 = x$

Solution

⑤ $5x - 2y + 26 = 0$

$3x + 4y = 0$

Solution

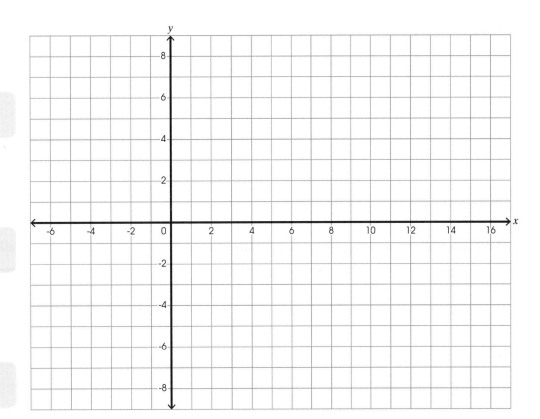

Answer the questions.

⑥

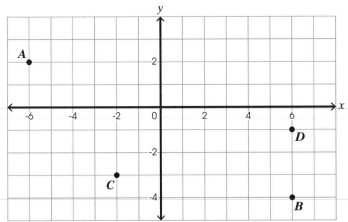

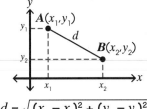

HINT

Distance Formula

distance between two points

$$d = \sqrt{(x_2 - x_1)^2 + (y_2 - y_1)^2}$$

Midpoint Formula

midpoint of two points

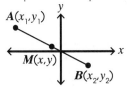

$$M(x,y) = \left(\frac{x_1 + x_2}{2}, \frac{y_1 + y_2}{2}\right)$$

Points A and B and points C and D are the end points of two line segments respectively.

a. Find the lengths of the two line segments.

_____

b. Find the midpoints of AB and CD.

_____

c. Do the midpoints fall on the point of intersection of the two line segments?

_____

Solve each system of equations by substitution.

⑦ $4x - y = 1$
$2x + 3y = 11$

⑧ $7x - 2y = 14$
$5x - 4y = -9$

⑨ $-x + y = 1$
$-0.5x + 0.25y = -1$

Solve each system of equations by elimination.

⑩ $8x + y = -16$
$3x - y = 5$

⑪ $5x + y = 9$
$10x - 7y = -18$

⑫ $-4x + 9y = 9$
$\dfrac{1}{6}x - \dfrac{1}{2}y = -1$

Solve each linear system. Find the number of solutions it has and determine whether the lines have the same slope and *y*-intercept. Then verify your solution by graphing.

⑬ $2x + 8y = 6$
$\dfrac{1}{3}x + \dfrac{4}{3}y = 1$

⑭ $-7x - 8y = 9$
$-4x + 9y = -22$

⑮ $-y = 2x + 4$
$y + 2 = 2x$

_____

_____

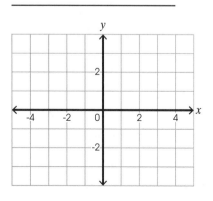

_____

_____

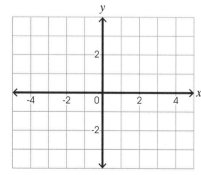

_____

_____

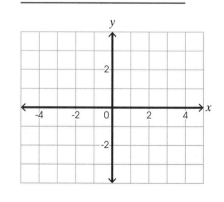

    ISBN: 978-1-77149-222-5

Identify whether each statement is true or false.

⑯ If the slopes of two lines are the same, the lines will never intersect.

    T / F

⑰ The lines $y = ax + k$ and $y = bx + k$ have the same y-intercept, so they will either meet at one point or at infinitely many points.

    T / F

⑱ The midpoint of $A(a, b + 1)$ and $B(1 - a, 2 - b)$ is $(\frac{1}{2}, \frac{3}{2})$.

    T / F

⑲ The vertices of a triangle are at (2,4), (-3,2), and the origin. The perimeter of the triangle is $\sqrt{33}$ units.

    T / F

Solve the problems. Show your work.

⑳ A boat can go 12 km along the water current in 2 hours. The return trip takes 3 hours against the water current. What is the speed of the boat in still water and the speed of the water current?

㉑ Given the diagram shown,

a. what are the coordinates of C?

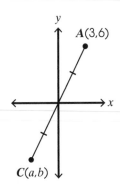

b. what is the perimeter of square $ABCD$ if AC is a diagonal of square $ABCD$?

㉒ A line passes through the point of intersection of the lines l_1: $2x + y = -5$ and l_2: $-x + 3y = 6$. If the line is perpendicular to l_1, what is its equation?

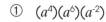

1.2 Exponent Rules and Polynomials

Simplify and write each expression using positive exponents only.

① $(a^4)(a^6)(a^{-2})$

② $(a^6b^3) \div (a^4b^2)$

③ $(ab)^2 \times (ab)^{-5}$

④ $(a^2b^3c^{-2})^2$

⑤ $\left(\dfrac{-3a^2}{b^{-3}}\right)^2 \times (ab^0)^{-2}$

⑥ $\left(\dfrac{2a^0}{3b^3}\right)^4 \div \left(\dfrac{2a}{b^{-2}}\right)^3$

Exponent Rules

$a^m \times a^n = a^{m+n}$

$a^m \div a^n = a^{m-n}$

$(a^m)^n = a^{mn}$

$(ab)^m = a^m b^m$

$\left(\dfrac{a}{b}\right)^m = \dfrac{a^m}{b^m}$

$a^0 = 1$

$a^{-m} = \dfrac{1}{a^m}$

Evaluate each expression. Write the answer as a fraction with positive exponents only.

⑦ $\left(\dfrac{2^2 \times 3^{-2} \times 5^{-1}}{(2 \times 3)^{-2} \times 5^{-2}}\right)^{-1}$

⑧ $\dfrac{(2^3)^{-1}}{(2 \times 3)^{-2}} \times \left(\dfrac{2^{-2}}{2^{-1} \times 3^{-1}}\right)^2$

⑨ $\dfrac{2^2}{(2^{-1} \times 3^{-2})^{-3}} \div \left(\dfrac{2 + 3^0}{3^{-5} \times 3^2}\right)^{-2}$

⑩ $\left(\dfrac{4 \times (2^3)^{-2}}{(2^{-1})^3}\right)^{-1} + \left(\dfrac{3^{-1} \times 9}{3^2}\right)^{-1}$

⑪ $\left(\dfrac{-1}{2}\right)^{-2} \times \left(\dfrac{2^{-2}}{3^2}\right)^{-3} \div \left(\dfrac{3^{-2}}{2}\right)^{-5}$

⑫ $\left(\dfrac{10^{-3}}{2^{-1} \times 5^2}\right)^{-2} \times \left(\dfrac{2 \times 5^6}{10^2 \times 5^3}\right)^2$

ISBN: 978-1-77149-222-5

Expand and simplify.

⑬ $(7x + 2)(2x + 4)$

⑭ $(3x - 1)(-x + 4)$

Distributive Property

$$(a + b)(c + d)$$

$$= ac + ad + bc + bd$$

⑮ $(2y + 5)(y - 6)$

⑯ $(y - 3)(-2y + 1)$

⑰ $(2m - n)(3m + 2n)$

⑱ $(-2m + n)(m - 3n)$

⑲ $(5m - n)(m - 3n)$

Find the GCF of the terms in each polynomial. Then factor it.

⑳ $4x^2 - 8xy$ **GCF**

   $= 4x(\underline{\quad} - \underline{\quad})$

㉑ $-3a^2b^2 + 6ab^2 + 15a^2b$ **GCF**

   $= 3ab(\underline{\quad} + \underline{\quad} + \underline{\quad})$

㉒ $6m^3n^2 - 2m^2n^3 + 4m^3n^3$ **GCF**

㉓ $10abc - 5a^2bc^2 + 15ab^2$ **GCF**

㉔ $9xyz - 3x^2y + 6xyz^2$ **GCF**

㉕ $16m^2n^2 - 8m^2n^4 - 24m^4n^2$ **GCF**

㉖ $3x(x + y) - 4(x + y)$ **GCF**

㉗ $(a + b)(a - b) + 3(a - b)^2$ **GCF**

㉘ $2xy(x - y)^2 - 3(x - y)^2$ **GCF**

㉙ $3a(a + b)^2 - 3(a + b) + 9b(a + b)$ **GCF**

Simplify each polynomial. Then factor it.

㉚ $3p(p + q) - p(p - q)$

㉛ $a(a - b) + b(a + b)$

㉜ $m^2(m + 1) - m(1 - m + m^2)$

㉝ $x^2y(x + y) - xy^2(x - y)$

㉞ $(p + q)^2 - p(p - 3q)$

㉟ $ab(a - b + c) - bc(1 + a)$

㊱ $\dfrac{m(m - n) + n(n - m) - (m + n)^2}{mn}$

㊲ $\dfrac{p^2(q - 3) - pq(p + 4) - p(3p + 2q)}{3p(p - q) + q(p - q)}$

Determine whether the equations in each pair are equivalent.

㊳ $2^{-2}(x + y)^2$ $\qquad$ $(\dfrac{x + y}{2})^2$

㊴ $q(q - 2p)$ $\qquad$ $p^2q^0 - (p + q)^2$

㊵ $(i + j)^2 - (i - j)^2$ $\qquad$ $2i^2 + 2j^2$

㊶ $-4m(m + n)^{-2}$ $\qquad$ $n(\dfrac{m + n}{2})^{-2} - \dfrac{4}{m + n}$

㊷ $p \times p \times p \times p - 3^2 \times p \times p$ $\qquad$ $p^2(p + 3)^2$

㊸ $\dfrac{x^2}{x + y} - x$ $\qquad$ $y - \dfrac{y^2}{x + y}$

ISBN: 978-1-77149-222-5

Solve the problems. Show your work. Write all the answers in factored form.

㊹ Simon has bent a piece of wire to form an isosceles triangle. If he straightens the wire and cuts it into $(p + 1)$ pieces of equal length, how long will each piece be?

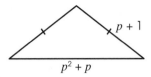

_____

㊺ Kevin has $(y - 1)$ toonies and some quarters in his pocket. If the total amount of the coins is $0.25(8y + 1)(y - 1)$, how many quarters does Kevin have?

_____

㊻ Jason is going to cut a ring out of a square cardboard. The width of the ring is s.

a. What is the area of the ring?

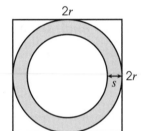

_____

b. If Jason uses a ribbon to decorate the borders of the ring, how much ribbon is needed?

_____

㊼ Figures A and B are similar triangles.

a. What is the ratio of the lengths of Figure B to the lengths of the corresponding sides of Figure A?

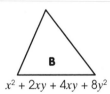

$0.5x + 2y \qquad x^2 + 2xy + 4xy + 8y^2$

_____

b. If one of the sides of Figure B is $(x^2 + 2xy + xy + 2y^2)$, what is the length of the corresponding side of Figure A?

_____

ISBN: 978-1-77149-222-5

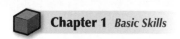

1.3 Factorization

Example

Factor each trinomial.

$x^2 - 5x - 14$ ← coefficient of x: -5
constant: -14

$= (x - 7)(x + 2)$

Think ▮ + ▮ = -5; ▮ × ▮ = -14
-7 + 2 = -5; -7 × 2 = -14

$3x^2 - 7x - 6$ ← coefficient of x: -7
product of coefficient of x^2 and the constant: -18

$= 3x^2 \boxed{-9x} + \boxed{2x} - 6$

$= (3x^2 - 9x) + (2x - 6)$

Think ▮ + ▮ = -7; ▮ × ▮ = -18
-9 + 2 = -7; -9 × 2 = -18

$= 3x(x - 3) + 2(x - 3)$

$= (x - 3)(3x + 2)$

Try This

Factor.

$x^2 + 4x - 21$

$5x^2 - 3x - 14$

Factor each trinomial.

① $6x^2 - x - 40$

② $x^2 - 2x - 15$

③ $3x^2 - 10x + 3$

④ $4x^2 + 11x + 6$

⑤ $x^2 + 2xy - 35y^2$

⑥ $x^2 - 27xy - 90y^2$

⑦ $12x^2 - 5x - 3$

⑧ $11xy + 10x^2 - 6y^2$

⑨ $-20 + 8x + x^2$

Answer the question.

⑩ Katie factored a polynomial as shown. Did she do the work correctly? Give reasons to justify your answer.

$-2x + x^2 + 6$
$= -2x^2 + x + 6$
$= -2x^2 + 4x - 3x + 6$
$= -2x(x - 2) - 3(x - 2)$
$= (x - 2)(-2x - 3)$

ISBN: 978-1-77149-222-5

Factor each perfect-square trinomial.

⑪ $x^2 - 10x + 25$

⑫ $81x^2 - 36xy + 4y^2$

⑬ $4x^2 - 12xy + 9y^2$

⑭ $x^2 + 12x + 36$

⑮ $9x^2 + 24xy^2 + 16y^4$

⑯ $4x^4 - 44x^2y + 121y^2$

Perfect-square Trinomials

$$a^2 + 2ab + b^2 = (a + b)^2$$
$$a^2 - 2ab + b^2 = (a - b)^2$$

e.g. $9x^2 + 6x + 1$
$= (3x + 1)^2$

Think

$a^2 = 9x^2$; so $a = 3x$
$b^2 = 1$; so $b = 1$

$9x^2 - 24xy + 16y^2$
$= (3x - 4y)^2$

Think

$a^2 = 9x^2$; so $a = 3x$
$b^2 = 16y^2$; so $b = 4y$

Determine whether each binomial is a difference of squares. If so, factor it.

⑰ $x^2 + 4$

⑱ $4x^2 - 1$

⑲ $9x^2 + y^2$

⑳ $x^2y^2 - 4$

Difference of Squares

$$a^2 - b^2 = (a + b)(a - b)$$

Think

e.g. $9x^2 - 16y^2$ $a^2 = 9x^2$; so $a = 3x$
$b^2 = 16y^2$; so $b = 4y$

$= (3x + 4y)(3x - 4y)$

㉑ $16x^3 - 1$

㉒ $5y^2 - 16$

㉓ $25x^2 - 36y^2$

㉔ $1 - 49x^2$

Answer the questions.

㉕ Katie wrote a perfect-square trinomial. What are the possible values of k?

$x^2 + kxy + 121y^2$

㉖ Find the shaded area in factored form.

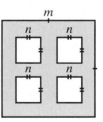

Example

Factor the polynomial.

$-24xy + 8x^2y + 18y$ ← Rearrange.

$= 8x^2y - 24xy + 18y$ ← $2y$ is the GCF.

$= 2y(4x^2 - 12x + 9)$ ← $4x^2 - 12x + 9$ is a
perfect-square trinomial.

$= 2y(2x - 3)^2$

TRY THIS

$3x^3 - 6x + 7x^2$

$= 3x^3 + 7x^2 - \boxed{}$

$= \boxed{} (\boxed{} + \boxed{} - \boxed{})$

$= \boxed{} ( )( )$

Factor the polynomials.

㉗ $18x^2 + 15x - 12$

㉘ $x^2y + 8xy + 15y$

㉙ $x^3 - 7x^2y - 3xy + 21y^2$

㉚ $16x^4 - 1$

㉛ $2x^4 + 12x^2 + 18$

㉜ $256x^4 - 81$

㉝ $-80y^4 + 5x^4$

㉞ $-19xy - 5y + 4x^2y$

㉟ $kx^4 - ky^4$

Solve the problems. Show your work.

㊱ Given $x^5 + kx^3 + 4x$ and $k < 0$, what values of k will make the trinomial factorable? What will the trinomial in factored form be for each possible value of k?

㊲ Taylor said, "Since 8 is not a square number, the binomial $\frac{x^4}{2} - 8$ cannot be factored." Do you agree? Explain your answer.

1.4 Simple Quadratic Equations

Complete the table of values. Graph and describe each quadratic equation.

① **A** $y = x^2$

x	y
-3	
-2	
-1	
0	
1	
2	
3	

B $y = x^2 - 6x + 5$

x	y
0	
1	
2	
3	
4	
5	
6	

Include the following to describe each quadratic equation.

• direction of opening (upward/downward)
• maximum/minimum point
• vertex
• axis of symmetry

A _____

B _____

Complete the table of values. Sketch the graph of each quadratic equation. Then determine whether a compression or a stretch has been applied to $f(x) = x^2$.

②

x	-3	-2	-1	0	1	2	3
$f(x) = x^2$							
$g(x) = \frac{1}{2}x^2$							
$h(x) = 2x^2$							

$g(x) = \frac{1}{2}x^2 = \boxed{} f(x)$ ⟵ This coefficient is between 0 and 1.

$g(x)$: $f(x)$ has been _____ vertically.

$h(x)$: $2x^2 = \boxed{} f(x)$ ⟵ The coefficient is greater than 1.

$h(x)$: $f(x)$ has been _____ vertically.

a. $p(x) = \frac{1}{3}x^2$ b. $q(x) = 5x^2$ c. $t(x) = \frac{3}{2}x^2$

_____   _____   _____

Complete the table of values. Sketch the graph of each quadratic equation. Then determine the direction of opening.

③

x	-3	-2	-1	0	1	2	3
$f(x) = x^2$							
$g(x) = -x^2$							

$f(x) = \boxed{1}\, x^2$ ◄— coefficient > 0

$f(x)$ opens _____ .

$g(x) = \boxed{-1}\, x^2$ ◄— coefficient < 0

$g(x)$ opens _____ .

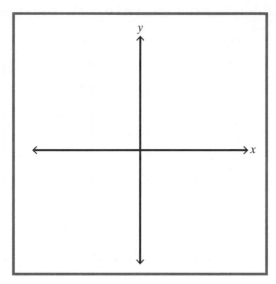

a. $p(x) = -(x + 1)^2$ b. $q(x) = x^2 + 4$ c. $t(x) = -\dfrac{1}{2}x^2 + 2x + 1$

_____   _____   _____

Determine the vertex, the axis of symmetry, and the direction of opening of each quadratic equation in vertex form. Then sketch the graph of the equation.

④ $y = 2(x - 4)^2 + 3$

_____

⑤ $y = -(x + 3)^2 - 6$

_____

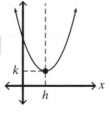

HINT

Vertex Form of a Quadratic Equation

$y = a(x - h)^2 + k$

vertex: (h, k)

axis of symmetry: $x = h$

direction of opening:
$a > 0$ – opens upward
$a < 0$ – opens downward

⑥ $y = -\dfrac{1}{2}(x - 1)^2$

_____

⑦ $y = 3(x - \dfrac{1}{2})^2 + 1$

_____

⑧ $y = x^2 + \dfrac{1}{2}$

_____

⑨ $y = -x^2 - 3$

_____

Use the Pythagorean theorem to find the unknown side lengths. Then determine the primary trigonometric ratios for each of the indicated angles in the triangles.

①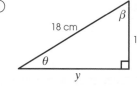

$\sin \theta \ =$

$\cos \theta =$

$\tan \theta =$

$y = \underline{\hspace{2cm}}$

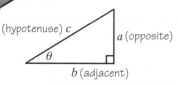

(hypotenuse) c a (opposite)

θ

b (adjacent)

Pythagorean Theorem

$c^2 = a^2 + b^2$

Primary Trigonometric Ratios

$\sin \theta = \dfrac{\text{opposite}}{\text{hypotenuse}} = \dfrac{a}{c}$

$\cos \theta = \dfrac{\text{adjacent}}{\text{hypotenuse}} = \dfrac{b}{c}$

$\tan \theta = \dfrac{\text{opposite}}{\text{adjacent}} = \dfrac{a}{b}$

② 7.7 cm

6 cm

β

y

θ

$y = \underline{\hspace{2cm}}$

Find the value of θ to the nearest degree.

③ $\cos \theta = 0.25$

$\theta \doteq \underline{\hspace{1.5cm}}$

④ $\tan \theta = 0.74$

$\theta \doteq \underline{\hspace{1.5cm}}$

⑤ $\sin \theta = 0.776$

$\theta \doteq \underline{\hspace{1.5cm}}$

⑥ $\cos \theta = 0.5$

$\theta = \underline{\hspace{1.5cm}}$

⑦ $\sin \theta = \dfrac{3}{4}$

$\theta \doteq \underline{\hspace{1.5cm}}$

⑧ $\tan \theta = \dfrac{2}{7}$

$\theta \doteq \underline{\hspace{1.5cm}}$

⑨ $\cos \theta = \dfrac{5}{7}$

$\theta \doteq \underline{\hspace{1.5cm}}$

⑩ $\tan \theta = \dfrac{1}{3}$

$\theta \doteq \underline{\hspace{1.5cm}}$

Evaluate to the nearest hundredth.

⑪ $\sin 32° \doteq \underline{\hspace{1.5cm}}$

⑫ $\cos 45° \doteq \underline{\hspace{1.5cm}}$

⑬ $\tan 28° \doteq \underline{\hspace{1.5cm}}$

⑭ $\sin 76° \doteq \underline{\hspace{1.5cm}}$

⑮ $\cos 15° \doteq \underline{\hspace{1.5cm}}$

⑯ $\tan 39° \doteq \underline{\hspace{1.5cm}}$

⑰

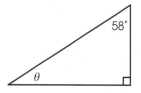

58°

θ

$\sin \theta \doteq \underline{\hspace{1.5cm}}$

$\cos \theta \doteq \underline{\hspace{1.5cm}}$

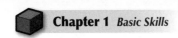

Find the unknowns using the primary trigonometric ratios.

⑱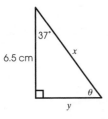

⑲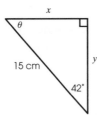

⑳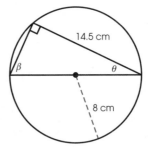

㉑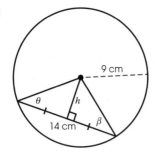

㉒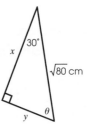

㉓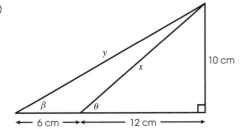

㉔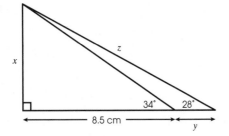

ISBN: 978-1-77149-222-5

Draw to illustrate the situation in each problem. Solve the problem. Show your work.

㉕ A ladder leaning against a wall makes an angle of 60° with the ground. The top of the ladder reaches 2.5 m up the wall.

   a. How long is the ladder?

   _____

   b. How far is the bottom of the ladder away from the wall?

   _____

㉖ A bird is on top of a building. It can view the top of a tower across the street with an angle of elevation of 36° and the bottom of the tower with an angle of depression of 24°.

   a. If the building and the tower is 180 m apart, how tall is the tower?

   _____

   b. What is the shortest distance the bird can travel to the top of the tower?

   _____

㉗ Bird A is on top of a 9-m-tall tree and Bird B is on top of a 7-m-tall tree. An apple which is between the two trees is on the ground. The angles of depression from Bird A and Bird B to the apple are 37° and 54° respectively.

   a. If the birds fly at the same speed, which bird will get the apple first?

   _____

   b. How far apart are the two trees?

   _____

ISBN: 978-1-77149-222-5

2 Equivalent Algebraic Expressions

TO LEARN

Equivalent functions: functions that have the same domain and range, and the values of the functions are equal for every value in the domain

Rational expression: a quotient of polynomials, e.g. $\dfrac{-2x + 1}{3x}$, $x \neq 0$

Rational function: any function that is the ratio of two polynomials, expressed as

$$f(x) = \frac{R(x)}{S(x)}, \text{ where } R \text{ and } S \text{ are polynomials and } S \neq 0$$
$$\text{e.g. } f(x) = \frac{2x^2 + x - 4}{x + 3}, x \neq -3$$

2.1 Adding and Subtracting Polynomials

Example

Simplify the polynomial functions. Then determine whether the functions are equivalent.

$f(x) = (3x^2 - 4x) - (-2x - x^2)$

$g(x) = (-2x^2 - 3x) + (6x^2 + x)$

$f(x) = \underline{3x^2} - \underline{4x} + \underline{2x} + \underline{x^2}$ ← Remove the brackets.
    $= 4x^2 - 2x$ Group the like terms.

$g(x) = \underline{-2x^2} - \underline{3x} + \underline{6x^2} + \underline{x}$
    $= 4x^2 - 2x$

Both $f(x)$ and $g(x)$ simplify to the same function, so $f(x)$ and $g(x)$ are equivalent.

TRY This

$f(x) = (2x^2 - 3x) - (x + x^2 - 1)$

$g(x) = -(x - x^2) - (3x - 1)$

$f(x)$ and $g(x)$ **are / are not** equivalent.

Simplify the polynomial functions. Then determine whether the functions are equivalent.

① $f(x) = 2(x - 1)^2 + 2x - 1$ and $g(x) = (2x^2 - x) + (x^2 - 1)$ _____

② $f(x) = (2x^2 + 7x - 2) - (3x + 7)$ and $g(x) = (x^2 + 12) + (x^2 + 4x - 5)$ _____

③ $f(x) = 2(x^2 + 2x - 3) - (x + 2)^2$ and $g(x) = 2(x^2 + 1) - (x^2 - 8x + 4)$ _____

④ $f(x) = \dfrac{1}{2}(x + 1)^2 - \dfrac{1}{4}(2x + 1)$ and $g(x) = -\dfrac{1}{4}(x - 1) + \dfrac{1}{4}x(2x + 3)$ _____

⑤ $f(x) = 0.5(4 - x) - x(x - 0.5)$ and $g(x) = x(x - 0.5) - 2(x^2 - 0.25x - 1)$ _____

ISBN: 978-1-77149-222-5

Evaluate each pair of polynomial functions using a value of _x_ of your choice. Determine which pair is not equivalent. Write the letter.

⑥ **A** $f(x) = (-1 - x)^2 + (2x + 3)^2$ ◄ ── Substituting 0 for _x_ usually makes the function easy to evaluate.

   $g(x) = 4 - (x + 2)^2 + x$ ◄

B $m(x) = \frac{1}{2}(5x + 3) - (x^2 - x)$

   $n(x) = x(3 - x) + 2(\frac{1}{2}x + 3)$

C $h(x) = 2(2x - 1) - x(2 - 100x)$

   $l(x) = 60x(2 + x) + 40x(x - 2) - 2(1 + 19x)$

D $p(x) = (x^2 - 3x + 1) - 2(2x - 1 - x^2)$

   $q(x) = (x^2 - x) + (-x^2 - 3x) - (2x^2 + 3)$

E $j(x) = 3 - 2(x - 1)^2 + \frac{1}{2}(x + 1)$

   $k(x) = \frac{1}{4}(2x + 1)^2 - 3x(x + 1) + \frac{1}{4}(2x + 5)$

Two polynomial functions/expressions are **not** equivalent* if they result in different values when they are evaluated with the same number substituted for the variables.

────────────

*Note that even if two functions are found equivalent using one value of a variable, it does not mean that they are equivalent.

Evaluating both functions using a single value is sufficient to demonstrate non-equivalence, but it is not enough to demonstrate equivalence.

Functions that are not equivalent:

────────────

Evaluate each pair of polynomial expressions with the given values. If the expressions are not equivalent, put a check mark in the box.

⑦ | $x = 0$ $y = 2$ $z = 1$ | **not equivalent** |
|---|---|
| • $xy + yz + xz$ | |
| • $3xyz$ | |

⑧ | $p = -1$ $q = 1$ $r = \frac{1}{2}$ | **not equivalent** |
|---|---|
| • $(p + q)^2 + (q + r)^2$ | |
| • $p^2 + r^2 + 2q^2 + 2q(p + r)$ | |

⑨ | $a = -1$ $b = 0$ $c = 1$ | **not equivalent** |
|---|---|
| • $a^2 + b^2 + c^2$ | |
| • $(a + b + c)^2 - 2(ab + bc + ac)$ | |

⑩ | $i = 0$ $j = -1$ $k = 1$ | **not equivalent** |
|---|---|
| • $i^2j + j^2k + k^2i$ | |
| • $i^3 + j^3 + k^3$ | |

⑪ | $x = 2$ $y = 1$ $z = -1$ | **not equivalent** |
|---|---|
| • $\frac{1}{2}(x + y)^2 + \frac{1}{2}(y + z)^2$ | |
| • $\frac{1}{2}(x + z)^2 + y(x + z) - xy$ | |

⑫ | $p = 1$ $q = -1$ $r = 1$ | **not equivalent** |
|---|---|
| • $p(q + r) + q(p + r) + r(p + q)$ | |
| • $3(p + q + r)$ | |

ISBN: 978-1-77149-222-5

Answer the questions.

⑬ Use two different methods to show that the two expressions in the box are not equivalent.

$$3x(-5 - x) + 2(3 - x)$$
$$3(x^2 + 5) + x - 9(2x + 1)$$

_____

⑭ If the two expressions below are equivalent, what is m in terms of x?

- $x(2 + x) - 3(x^2 - 1) + 2(-2 - 3x)$
- $-(x + 1)^2 + m$

_____

⑮ Lucy thinks that the two polynomial functions below are equivalent because they have the same value at $x = 0$. Is she correct?

$f(x) = -2(x - 1) + 4x(1 - x)$
$g(x) = x(x - 2) + x(3 - x) + 2$

_____

⑯ Write two non-equivalent polynomials $f(x)$ and $g(x)$ such that $f(1) = g(1)$ and $f(-1) = g(-1)$.

_____

⑰ Each side of a triangle is represented by a polynomial function.
   a. Determine what type of triangle it is.

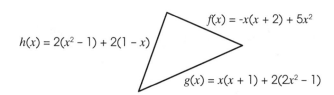

$f(x) = -x(x + 2) + 5x^2$

$h(x) = 2(x^2 - 1) + 2(1 - x)$

$g(x) = x(x + 1) + 2(2x^2 - 1)$

*Not drawn to scale

_____

   b. Write a function for the perimeter of the triangle. What is the perimeter if x is 5?

_____

Solve the problems. Show your work.

⑱ Arya and Simon are hosting a party at a restaurant. Burger Palace has quoted $300 plus $10/person for food, $100 plus $5/person for drinks, and a discount of $7/person if the number of guests is more than 100.

a. Write a function for the quote from Burger Palace.

> * Use two functions to represent the situations of 100 guests or fewer and more than 100 guests.

b. What will the cost be if there are

- 95 guests? _____

- 200 guests? _____

c. The quote from Pizza Time is represented by the function:

$$C(n) = 200 + (150 + 9n) + (50 + 6n)$$

Is this function equivalent to Burger Palace's?

d. Which restaurant should Arya and Simon choose for their party of 200 guests? What will the cost be?

⑲ Tony launched two rockets. The altitude of each rocket was measured when its fuel ran out and when it began to fall. The altitudes of both rockets are represented by the functions below. The altitudes were measured in metres and the time in seconds.

rocket 1: $h_1(t) = -5(t - 10)^2 + 1500$

rocket 2: $h_2(t) = 100(6 - t) - t(5t - 200) + 400$

a. Determine the difference in altitude between the two rockets.

b. Interpret the answer in Question 19a.

c. How long did it take the rockets to reach the ground?

2.2 Multiplying and Factoring Polynomials

Simplify the expressions.

> Multiply each of the three terms in the trinomial by each term in the binomial.

Multiplication of Polynomials

Consider any polynomials a, b, and c.

$ab = ba$ ← commutative
$(ab)c = a(bc)$ ← associative
$a(b + c) = ab + ac$ ← distributive

e.g.
$(x^2 - x + 1)(x + 3)$
$= x^2(x + 3) - x(x + 3) + (x + 3)$
  or
$= (x^2 - x + 1)x + (x^2 - x + 1)3$

① $(2x - 5)(-2x^2 + 3x + 6)$

$= (2x)(-2x^2 + 3x + 6) + (-5)(-2x^2 + 3x + 6)$ ←

$= (-4x^3 + \underline{\qquad} + \underline{\qquad}) + (10x^2 - \underline{\qquad} - \underline{\qquad})$

$= -4x^3 + \underline{\hspace{6cm}}$ ← Group like terms.

$= \underline{\hspace{4cm}}$

② $(x - 4)(3x + 7)(-x - 5)$

③ $6(a - 2)(3 - a) + (a - 2)^2(a - 1)$ _____

④ $3(2b + 5)(b - 4) - (3 - b)^2 + 2(5 - b)$ _____

⑤ $m(m - 1)(m + 1) + (4 - m)(m - 3)$ _____

⑥ $(n - 1)^2(n - 3) - 2(n^3 - 2n - 3)$ _____

Answer the questions.

⑦ Determine whether the expressions in each pair are equivalent.

a. $(2x - 5)(x - 3) + x(x - 1)$ and $(x - 1)(5 - x) + 2(2x - 5)(x - 2)$ _____

b. $(x - 2)^3$ and $(x - 1)(x - 2)x - (1 - x)x^2 - 8(x - 1)$ _____

c. $\frac{1}{2}(2x - 3)^2(x - 3)$ and $(x - 3)(2x^2 - 6x + 9) - \frac{9}{2}(x - 3)$ _____

⑧ The right triangle shown has the given lengths.
a. What is its area?

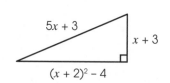

b. What is its perimeter?

ISBN: 978-1-77149-222-5

Factor the polynomials. If the polynomial is not factorable, write "prime".

⑨ by grouping

$x^3 + 2x^2 + 3x + 6$

$= (x^3 + \boxed{}) + (3x + \boxed{})$ ◄——— Separate the expression into two groups.

$= x^2(\boxed{} + \boxed{}) + 3(\boxed{} + \boxed{})$ ◄— Factor each group.

$= (\boxed{} + \boxed{})(x^2 + 3)$

⑩ by recognizing a factorable trinomial

$6x^2 - 25x - 9$ ◄——— Find two numbers whose sum is -25 and whose product is $(6)(-9) = -54$. These numbers are -27 and 2.

$= 6x^2 - \boxed{}x + \boxed{}x - 9$

$= 3x(\boxed{} - \boxed{}) + (\boxed{} - \boxed{})$

$= (\boxed{} - \boxed{})(3x + \boxed{})$

HINT

If there is a GCF, remember to factor it out first.

A polynomial can be factored as:
- a difference of squares
  $a^2 - b^2 = (a + b)(a - b)$

- a perfect-square trinomial
  $a^2 + 2ab + b^2 = (a + b)^2$
  $a^2 - 2ab + b^2 = (a - b)^2$

If the only factors of a polynomial are 1 and itself, that polynomial is prime.

---

⑪ by recognizing the terms in a polynomial

• $50x^2 - 128$

$= 2(\boxed{}x^2 - \boxed{})$ ◄——— Factor the GCF out.

$= 2(\boxed{}x + \boxed{})(\boxed{}x - \boxed{})$ ◄— a difference of squares

• $4x^2 + 28x + 49$ ◄——— 4 and 49 are perfect squares. Their square roots are 2 and 7 respectively. 28 is double the product of 2 and 7.

$= (\boxed{})^2 + 28x + \boxed{}^2$

$= (\boxed{} + \boxed{})^2$ ◄——— a perfect square

• $75x^2 - 90x + 27$

$= 3(\boxed{}x^2 - \boxed{}x + \boxed{})$ ◄——— Factor the GCF out.

$= 3((\boxed{})^2 - \boxed{}x + \boxed{}^2)$ ◄——— The first and last terms are perfect squares.

$= 3(\boxed{} - \boxed{})^2$

• $3x^2 + x + 4$ ◄——— Try finding two numbers whose sum is 1 and whose product is $(3)(4) = 12$.

_____

⑫ $4x^3 - 6x^2 + 2x$

_____

⑬ $8y^2 - 2xy - 21x^2$

_____

⑭ $5x^2 - 45x + 350$

_____

⑮ $48x^2y^2 - 27$

_____

⑯ $m^3 + 3m^2 - 4m - 12$

_____

⑰ $pq - 2p - 3q + 6$

_____

⑱ $9 - x - 20x^2$

_____

⑲ $w^4 - 16$

_____

ISBN: 978-1-77149-222-5

Simplify and factor the polynomials.

⑳ $2x^5 - 2x(13x^2 - 36)$

㉑ $9a^2 - b(b + 2) - 1$

㉒ $(x + 3)(x - 1) - 2x^2 + 27$

㉓ $(x - 1)(x^2 - 2x - 1) - 4$

㉔ $(p - q)(p^2 - 1) - pq(q - p)$

㉕ $-x + x^2(x + 5) - 5$

Answer the questions. Write the answers with factored expressions.

㉖ The dimensions of a rectangle are $(5x^2 + 6x + 2)$ by $2(3x + 1)$.

a. What is its perimeter? _____

b. What is its area? _____

㉗ The height of a triangle is twice as long as its base. Describe how the triangle's area will change if its height is increased by 1 and its base is decreased by 1. Write an expression for the change in area and interpret the result.

_____

㉘ a. Is $(2x - 3y)(4x^2 + 9y^2) = (2x)^3 - (3y)^3$ true? Justify your decision.

_____

b. Write the factored expression of $(2x)^3 - (3y)^3$.

_____

 ISBN: 978-1-77149-222-5

Example

TRY This

Simplify the expression and state any restrictions.

$(4x^2 + 6xy - 28y^2) \div (x^3 - 4xy^2)$

$= (4x^2 + 6xy - 28y^2) \times \dfrac{1}{x^3 - 4xy^2}$ ← Multiply the reciprocal.

$= \dfrac{2(2x + 7y)(x - 2y)}{x(x + 2y)(x - 2y)}$ ← Factor the numerator and the denominator. Divide both by the GCF $(x - 2y)$.

$= \dfrac{2(2x + 7y)}{x(x + 2y)}$

So, $x \neq 0, -2y,$ and $2y.$ ← Determine the restrictions by solving the factored denominator $x(x + 2y)(x - 2y) = 0$. So, $x = 0$, $x + 2y = 0$, and $x - 2y = 0$. The restrictions are 0, $-2y$, and $2y$.

$$\frac{\dfrac{5x^2}{15x^3}}{\dfrac{3 - 9x}{6(x - 1)}}$$

Simplify the expressions and state any restrictions.

① $\dfrac{-12 - 3x}{3x}$

② $\dfrac{(x - 1)^2}{(x + 3)(x - 1)}$

③ $\dfrac{2x^2}{-x^3}$

④ $\dfrac{6x^2 - 6x}{x^2}$

⑤ $\dfrac{3x^2y^2}{9x^2y + 12xy^2}$

⑥ $\dfrac{3xy^2 - 12x}{xy^2 - xy - 2x}$

⑦ $(6x^2y - 9xy^2) \div (8x - 12y)$

⑧ $\dfrac{m + 1}{m^2 - 1} \times \dfrac{m^2 - 3m + 2}{m - 3}$

⑨ $\dfrac{7a^2 - 28a}{a - 4} \div (5a^2)$

⑩ $\dfrac{8n}{4n + 4} \times \dfrac{2(n + 1)}{10}$

Example

Simplify the function and state the domain.

$$f(x) = \frac{9x^2 - 16}{3x^2 - 7x + 4}$$ ← Factor the denominator and the numerator.

$$= \frac{(3x + 4)(3x - 4)}{(3x - 4)(x - 1)}$$ ← Solve $(3x - 4)(x - 1) = 0$

$$= \frac{3x + 4}{x - 1}$$

So, $3x - 4 = 0$ and $x - 1 = 0$. The restrictions are $x \neq \frac{4}{3}$, 1. This means that $f(x)$ is undefined when $x = \frac{4}{3}$ or 1, so they must be excluded from the domain.

Domain: $\{x \in \mathbb{R} \mid x \neq \frac{4}{3}, 1\}$

Try This

$$f(x) = \frac{x^2 - 9x - 10}{x + 1}$$

Simplify each function and state the domain.

⑪ $f(x) = \dfrac{x^3}{x^2 + x}$

⑫ $f(x) = \dfrac{x + 2}{x^2 - 4}$

⑬ $f(x) = \dfrac{x - 3}{15 - 5x}$

⑭ $f(x) = \dfrac{2x^2 + 10x}{-3x - 15}$

Domain:

Domain:

Domain:

Domain:

⑮ $f(x) = (4x^2 - 16) \div (x^2 + x - 6)$

⑯ $f(x) = \dfrac{2x^2 - 2x}{(x - 1)^3}$

⑰ $f(m) = \dfrac{m^2 - 2m + 1}{2m^2 + 16m - 18}$

⑱ $f(t) = (t - 5) \div \dfrac{t^2 - 36}{t^2 - 11t + 30}$

⑲ $f(a) = \dfrac{a^2 - 1}{10a} \times \dfrac{5a^2}{2(a + 1)}$

⑳ $f(w) = \dfrac{w^2 + 2w - 15}{w^2 - 16} \div \dfrac{w + 1}{3w - 12}$

ISBN: 978-1-77149-222-5

Simplify each function and determine the restrictions. State the domain. Then match the function with the sketch of its graph.

㉑ **A** $f(x) = \dfrac{x^2 - 5x + 6}{x - 2}$ **B** $f(x) = \dfrac{2x^2 + 3x - 5}{2x + 5}$ **C** $f(x) = \sqrt{x - 1} \times \dfrac{3x - 18}{x - 6}$

Restrictions: _____   Restrictions: _____   Restrictions: _____

Domain: _____   Domain: _____   Domain: _____

D $f(x) = \dfrac{x^2 - 1}{x^2 - 3x + 2}$ **E** $f(x) = \dfrac{x^2 + 3x + 2}{x^2 - 2x - 3}$ **F** $f(x) = \dfrac{x^4 - 1}{x - 1}$

Restrictions: _____   Restrictions: _____   Restrictions: _____

Domain: _____   Domain: _____   Domain: _____

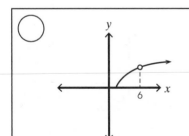
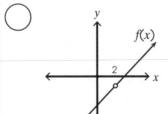
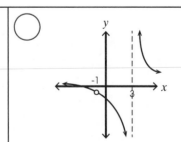

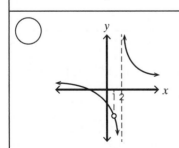
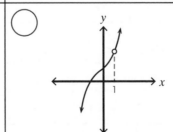
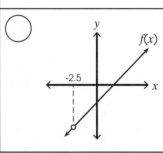

A rational function has a hole (represented by **O** in graphs) when a factor of the denominator is also a factor of the numerator.

ISBN: 978-1-77149-222-5

Determine the measurements of each figure and state any restrictions.

㉒　a. What is the area of the rectangle?

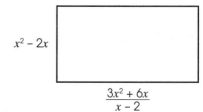

$x^2 - 2x$

$\dfrac{3x^2 + 6x}{x - 2}$

_____

b. What is the ratio of its width to its length?

_____

㉓　a. What is the height of the triangle?

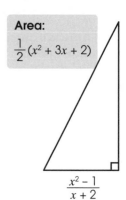

Area:

$\dfrac{1}{2}(x^2 + 3x + 2)$

$\dfrac{x^2 - 1}{x + 2}$

_____

b. The triangle shown is the base of a triangular prism which has a height of $\dfrac{x + 5}{x + 1}$. What is the volume of the triangular prism?

_____

㉔　The volume of the rectangular prism is $x^3 - 6x^2 - 4x + 24$.

a. What is the height of the prism?

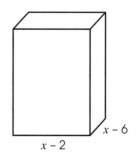

$x - 6$

$x - 2$

_____

b. What is the ratio of its height to its volume?

_____

㉕　The quotient of two polynomials is $y - 4x$. Give two examples of a rational expression equivalent to these polynomials that have the restriction $x \neq 3y$.

_____

㉖　Give two examples of a rational function that have these three restrictions: $x \neq -1, 1, 3$.

_____

ISBN: 978-1-77149-222-5

Simplify the expressions that have common denominators.

① $\dfrac{3m - n}{n} + \dfrac{2n - 5m}{n}$

② $\dfrac{y^2 - y}{3y - 2} - \dfrac{y - 2y^2}{3y - 2}$

③ $\dfrac{4xy}{x + y} + \dfrac{(x - y)^2}{x + y}$

④ $\dfrac{p^2}{p - 9} - \dfrac{3p + 54}{p - 9}$

⑤ $\dfrac{5v^2}{1 - v} - \dfrac{5v}{1 - v}$

⑥ $\dfrac{a^2 - 30}{a + 6} + \dfrac{a}{a + 6}$

⑦ $\dfrac{b}{b^2 + b - 72} - \dfrac{8}{b^2 + b - 72}$

⑧ $\dfrac{x^2}{x - 1} + \dfrac{1}{x - 1} - \dfrac{2x}{x - 1}$

⑨ $\dfrac{y - 5}{y^2 - 3y} + \dfrac{2}{y^2 - 3y}$

⑩ $\dfrac{2 - 5k}{k + 3} - \dfrac{4k - 5}{-3 - k}$

⑪ $\dfrac{5}{x + 5} + \dfrac{2x}{2x + 10}$

⑫ $\dfrac{m - 4n}{9mn} + \dfrac{4(m + n)}{9mn}$

⑬ $\dfrac{1}{(t - 1)^2} - \dfrac{t^2}{(t - 1)^2}$

⑭ Simplify and state any restrictions on the variables.

Ⓐ $\dfrac{49}{x^2 - x - 42} - \dfrac{x^2}{x^2 - x - 42}$

Ⓑ $\dfrac{-y^2}{y - 1} + \dfrac{y^3}{y - 1}$

Ⓒ $\dfrac{xy - x^2}{x^2 - y^2} - \dfrac{y(x - y)}{y^2 - x^2}$

Ⓓ $\dfrac{3x + y}{2x + y} + \dfrac{y}{2x + y} - \dfrac{x}{2x + y}$

Ⓐ _____

Ⓑ _____

Ⓒ _____

Ⓓ _____

Find the least common multiple (LCM) of the unlike denominators. Simplify the expressions and state any restrictions on the variables.

⑮ $\dfrac{2p-3}{p^2-5p+6} - \dfrac{5}{p^2-9}$ ← Factor the denominators.

$= \dfrac{2p-3}{(p-)(p-)} - \dfrac{5}{(p-)(p+)}$ ← the LCM: $(p-)(p-)(p+)$

$= \dfrac{(2p-3)(p+)}{(p-)(p-)(p+)} - \dfrac{5(p-)}{(p-)(p-)(p+)}$ ← Use the LCM to rewrite each term.

$= \dfrac{}{(p-)(p-)(p+)}$ ← Simplify by expanding the numerators.

$= \underline{}$ $; p \neq \underline{}$

⑯ $\dfrac{16}{x^2-16} + \dfrac{2}{x+4}$ **LCM**

⑰ $\dfrac{3m}{(m+3)(m+4)} - \dfrac{4m}{(m+4)(m+1)}$ **LCM**

⑱ $\dfrac{4}{a-3} + \dfrac{a}{a-5}$ **LCM**

⑲ $\dfrac{x+1}{x^2-x-6} + \dfrac{x}{3x^2-8x-3}$ **LCM**

⑳ $\dfrac{4}{a-2} - \dfrac{81}{(a-2)^3}$ **LCM**

㉑ $\dfrac{-3m-1}{(m+2)(m+3)} + \dfrac{m-3}{m+2}$ **LCM**

ISBN: 978-1-77149-222-5

Simplify the expressions using the order of operations. State any restrictions on the variables.

㉒ $\dfrac{3x^2y}{5} \times \dfrac{10}{xy} - \dfrac{4xy}{y}$

㉓ $\dfrac{x^2 - 1}{x + 1} - \dfrac{6x}{x + 1} \div \dfrac{x}{x^2 - 1}$

㉔ $\dfrac{z}{z - 2} - \dfrac{4}{z + 2} \div \dfrac{1}{z^2 + 4z + 4}$

㉕ $\dfrac{b}{b - 2a} - \dfrac{4}{b - 4a} \times \dfrac{3}{b - 2a}$

㉖ $\dfrac{2x^2 + 13x + 20}{2x^2 + 17x + 30} \times \dfrac{x^2 - 16}{x^2 + 8x + 16} \div \dfrac{x - 4}{6x + 30}$

For Your Work

㉗ $\dfrac{5m - 5n}{10} \div \dfrac{m^2 - n^2}{6} + \dfrac{3mn}{m^2 + 2mn + n^2}$

㉘ $\dfrac{4a}{a^2 + 2a + 1} - \dfrac{2a^2 - 7a - 15}{2a^3 - 3a^2 - 2a + 3} \div \dfrac{2a - 10}{3 - 3a}$

㉙ $\dfrac{4p - 16}{5p + 15} \times \dfrac{3p^2 + 10p + 3}{2(p + 2)} \div \dfrac{3p^2 - 11p - 4}{p^2 + 4p + 4}$

㉚ $\dfrac{x^2 + 4x - 12}{x^3 - 4x} \div \dfrac{3x - 6}{x^2 + x - 2} + \dfrac{1}{x} + \dfrac{3x}{x - 2}$

㉛ $\dfrac{2}{n^2 - n - 2} \div \dfrac{10n}{n^2 + 2n - 8} \times \dfrac{n^2 + n}{n^2 + n - 12}$

ISBN: 978-1-77149-222-5

Answer the questions.

③② Andrew simplified the rational function with the following steps. Check his answer to determine whether he did it correctly. If it was done incorrectly, show the correct steps.

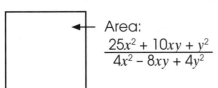

$$f(x) = \frac{x^2 - 2x - 3}{x^2 + 2x - 3} \div \frac{x^2 + 4x + 3}{x^2 - 4x + 3} + \frac{x - 3}{x^2 + 4x + 3}$$

$$= \frac{(x + 1)(x - 3)}{(x + 3)(x - 1)} \times \frac{(x + 3)(x + 1)}{(x - 3)(x - 1)} + \frac{x - 3}{x^2 + 4x + 3}$$

$$= \frac{(x + 1)^2}{(x - 1)^2} + \frac{x - 3}{(x + 1)(x + 3)}$$

$$= \frac{(x + 1)(x - 3)}{(x - 1)^2(x + 3)} \; ; \; x \neq 1$$

③③ What is the perimeter of the square? State any restrictions.

Area:
$$\frac{25x^2 + 10xy + y^2}{4x^2 - 8xy + 4y^2}$$

_____

③④ The trapezoid has the given dimensions.

a. What is the area of the trapezoid?

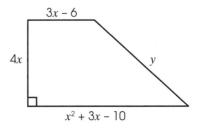

_____

b. What is the side length y in terms of x?

_____

③⑤ Ali drove and covered a distance of $(80x)$ km on a street in $(x + 2)$ hours and a distance of $(60x)$ km on a highway in $(x - 1)$ hours at a higher speed. Write a simplified function to show the difference in Ali's driving speed. State the restrictions on x.

_____

㊱ The volumes of a cylinder and a cone can be calculated using the formulas $V = \pi r^2 h$ and $V = \frac{1}{3}\pi r^2 h$ respectively, where r is the radius and h is the height.

a. Write expressions for the volumes of Solids A and B.

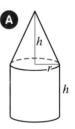

_____

b. What is the ratio of Solid A's volume to Solid B's?

_____

㊲ The total resistance, R, of the parallel circuit shown can be calculated using the formula $\frac{1}{R} = \frac{1}{x} + \frac{1}{y}$, where x and y are the resistances of Resistors X and Y.

a. Write an expression for R if x is increased by 2 and y is decreased by 3. State any restrictions on the variables.

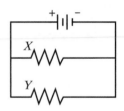

_____

b. For $y = 4x^2 - x$, write the expression for R in terms of x. State the restrictions.

_____

㊳ When an object is moved by a force, energy is transferred and work is done. The relationship among work done, force applied, and distance moved can be determined by the formula W (work done) $= F$ (force) $\times d$ (distance). The work done on an object is $\frac{2(16x^2 - 1)}{x - 1}$ with an applied force of $\frac{8x^2 - 10x - 3}{x - 1}$. Determine the distance moved. State the restrictions.

_____

3 Quadratic Functions

Words TO LEARN

Relation: a set of ordered pairs

Real numbers: numbers that are either rational or irrational; these include all integers, such as 0

Function: a relation where each value of the independent variable corresponds with only one value of the dependent variable

Domain: the set of all values of the independent variable of a relation

Range: the set of all values of the dependent variable of a relation

e.g.

$f(x) = x^2$

↑ function notation

x $f(x)$

5 → 25
9 ⤬ 4
2 → 81

Domain: {2, 5, 9}
Range: {4, 25, 81}

3.1 The Domain and Range of a Function

Example

Determine if the relation is a function. Then state the ordered pairs, domain, and range.

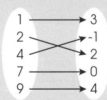

1 → 3
2 ⤬ -1
4 → 2
7 → 0
9 → 4

Since every value in the domain maps to one value in the range, this relation is a function.

Ordered pairs: {(1,3), (2,2), (4,-1), (7,0), (9,4)}
Domain: {1, 2, 4, 7, 9}
Range: {-1, 0, 2, 3, 4}

TRY THIS

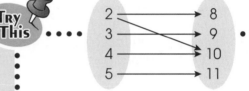

2 → 8
3 → 9
4 → 10
5 → 11

_____

_____

Ordered pairs: _____

Domain: _____

Range: _____

Determine if each relation is a function. Then state the domain and range.

① **A**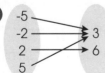

-5
-2
2   3
5   6

Function: _____
        yes / no

Ordered pairs: _____

Domain: _____

Range: _____

B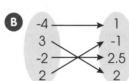

-4 → 1
3   -1
-2 ⤬ 2.5
2   2

Function: _____
        yes / no

Ordered pairs: _____

Domain: _____

Range: _____

ISBN: 978-1-77149-222-5

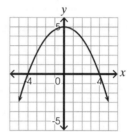

Example

Determine if the relation is a function.

Working Time (h)	0	12	8	4
Earnings ($)	0	180	120	60

Graph it.

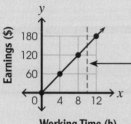

This vertical line intersects the relation at only one point.

This relation is a function.

Hint

Draw a vertical line anywhere on the graph of a relation. If it intersects the graph at only one point, the relation is a function.

Try This

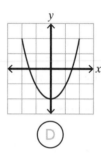

This relation **is** / **is not** a function.

Check if each relation is a function; otherwise, put a cross.

②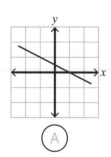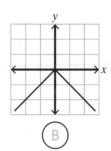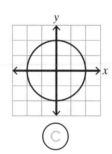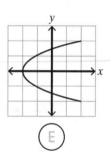

    Ⓐ   Ⓑ   Ⓒ   Ⓓ   Ⓔ

Sketch a graph of each relation and determine if it is a function.

③ the journey of a ball thrown from a cliff

Horizontal Distance (m)	0	15	30	45	60
Vertical Distance (m)	0	-5	-20	-45	-80

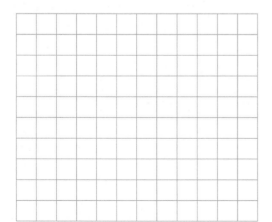

Function: yes / no

④ $x = y^2 + 4$

x	4	8	12	16	20
y					

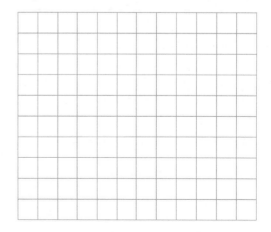

Function: yes / no

Example

Find the domain and range of the data set. Then determine if it is a function.

No. of People	No. of Tickets Sold
5	12
4	24
9	28
7	15
4	21

← "No. of People" is the independent variable.

"No. of Tickets Sold" is the dependent variable.

Domain: {4, 5, 7, 9}

Range: {12, 15, 21, 24, 28}

This is not a function because the element, 4, of the domain maps to two elements, 21 and 24, in the range.

 HINT

Domain: {all values of an independent variable}

Range: {all values of a dependent variable}

TRY This

Age (year)	Weight (kg)
1	10
2	14
5	21
6	28

Domain: _____

Range: _____

_____

_____

Find the domain and range of each data set. Determine if it is a function. Explain your answer.

⑤
Days	2	3	8	11	25
Height of a Plant (cm)	6	9	16	19	33

Domain: _____

Range: _____

Function: _____ ; _____
   Yes / No

⑥
No. of Cakes Sold	5	9	8	5	12
Profit ($)	72	107	96	88	127

Domain: _____

Range: _____

Function: _____ ; _____
   Yes / No

⑦ {(1,4), (2,9), (8,9), (4,7), (2,6)}

Domain: _____

Range: _____

Function: _____ ; _____

_____

⑧ {(-1,-6), (-5,-8), (-4,-9), (-3,0), (2,6)}

Domain: _____

Range: _____

Function: _____ ; _____

_____

ISBN: 978-1-77149-222-5

Example

Determine the domain and range of the equation.

$y = 3x + 4$

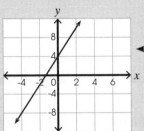

← x can be all real numbers.

y can be all real numbers.

Domain: $\{x \in \mathbb{R}\}$
Range: $\{y \in \mathbb{R}\}$

TRY This

$x^2 + y^2 = 16$

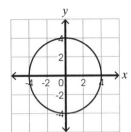

Domain: _____

Range: _____

Match each equation with its domain and range. Write the letter. Then write the domain and range.

⑨ **A** $y = (x + 1)^2 + 2$

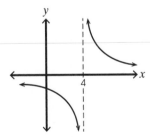

(-1,2)

D $y = \sqrt{x + 2} + 3$

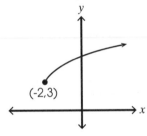

(-2,3)

○ Domain: $\{x \in \mathbb{R} \mid x \geq \text{-}1\}$
Range: $\{y \in \mathbb{R} \mid y \geq \text{-}4\}$

○ Domain: $\{x \in \mathbb{R}\}$
Range: $\{y \in \mathbb{R} \mid y \geq 2\}$

○ Domain: $\{x \in \mathbb{R} \mid x \neq \text{-}7\}$
Range: $\{y \in \mathbb{R} \mid y \neq 0\}$

B $y = \dfrac{1}{x + 7}$

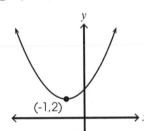

asymptote →
-7

E $y = \dfrac{1}{x - 4}$

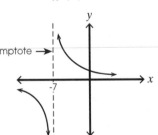

4

D Domain: _____
Range: _____

E Domain: _____
Range: _____

C $y = \sqrt{x + 1} - 4$

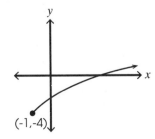

(-1,-4)

F $y = 9 - (x - 1)^2$

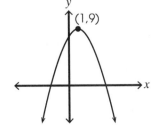

(1,9)

F Domain: _____
Range: _____

Sketch a graph of each function. Then determine the domain and range.

⑩ $y = -x + 7$

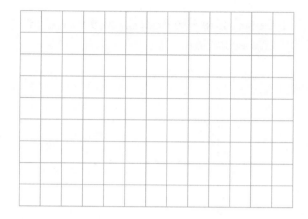

Domain: _____

Range: _____

⑪ $y = -2x^2 + 1$

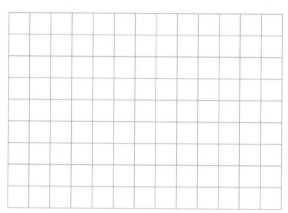

Domain: _____

Range: _____

Sketch a graph of a function or a relation which has the given domain and range. Then write the domain and range using set notation.

⑫ a function that has the set of all real numbers as its domain and all real numbers less than 3 as its range

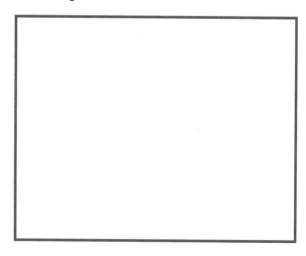

Domain: _____

Range: _____

⑬ a relation that is not a function and has all real numbers greater than -1 as its domain and all real numbers greater than -1 as its range

Domain: _____

Range: _____

ISBN: 978-1-77149-222-5

Example

Determine $f(3)$ for the function below.

$f(x) = 4x + 5$ ← a function

$f(3) = 4(3) + 5$ ← Substitute 3 for x on both sides.

$\quad = 12 + 5$

$\quad = 17$

When x is 3, the function $f(x) = 4x + 5$ has a value of 17.

TRY THIS

Determine $f(-2)$ for the function below.

$$f(x) = 2x^2 + x - 4$$

$$f(\underline{\quad}) = 2(\underline{\quad})^2 + (\underline{\quad}) - 4$$

$$\therefore x = -2, \, f(-2) = \underline{\quad}$$

Determine $f(2)$, $f(0)$, and $f(-\dfrac{1}{3})$ for each function.

① $f(x) = -3x^2 - x + 2$

② $f(x) = (3x - 1)^2 - 1$

③ $f(x) = 1 - \dfrac{1}{x - 1}$

Determine the values of the functions.

④ $f(x) = \dfrac{x}{x + 1}$

a. $f(2) =$ _____

b. $f(-2) =$ _____

c. $f(b) =$ _____

d. $f(b - 1) =$ _____

⑤ $g(x) = x - \dfrac{1}{x + 1}$

a. $g(2) =$ _____

b. $g(-2) =$ _____

c. $g(b) =$ _____

d. $g(b - 1) =$ _____

⑥ Refer to Questions 4 and 5.

a. $f(2) + g(2) =$ _____

b. $f(-2) - g(-2) =$ _____

c. $f(b) + g(b) =$ _____

d. $f(b - 1) - g(b - 1) =$ _____

Create a table of values for the function. Graph it and determine the values of the function using the graph and by evaluation.

⑦ $f(x) = (x - 3)^2 - 4$

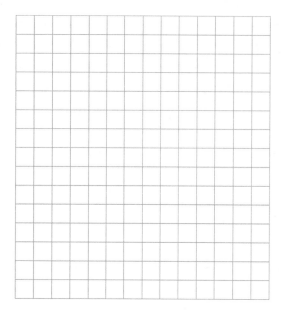

x	y

	from the graph	by evaluation
$f(0)$		
$f(\frac{1}{2})$		
$f(\frac{5}{2})$		
$f(4\frac{1}{2})$		
$f(6)$		

Solve the problems using function notation.

⑧ The average temperature in a river is 15°C. The temperature decreases by 1°C for every 2 m below the surface. What is the water temperature at 18 m below the surface? At what depth is the water temperature 2°C?

Let T represent temperature and d represent depth.

$T(d) = 15 - 1 \times (\frac{d}{2})$

$T(d) = 15 - \frac{d}{2}$ ⟵ This temperature function shows how the temperature changes with the depth.

> **Hint**
>
> When you use function notation to write an equation, remember to state clearly what element each variable represents.

$d = 18$	$T(d) = 2$
$T(18) =$	$2 =$

The temperature is _____ . | The temperature is 2°C at _____ below the surface.

⑨ Alice works at a clothing store. She earns $40 each shift and gets an extra 10% of the sales that she makes. How much will Alice earn if there is a total of $250 in sales per shift? What will the total sales be if Alice earns $58 in a shift?

⑩ The average temperature at the equator is 40°C. As we travel north of the equator, the average temperature decreases by 2°C for every 80 km. What is the average temperature 270 km north of the equator? How far north of the equator is a place if its average temperature is 28°C?

_____

⑪ The value of a new car is $32 000. Its value goes down by $1200 every 6 months. How long will it take for the value of the car to drop to $15 000? What will the value of the car be after 4 years?

_____

⑫ The diameter of the inner circle of a ring is d cm and the width of the ring is also d cm.

a. Write the area of the ring using function notation.

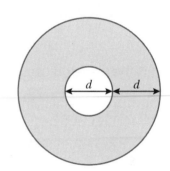

_____

b. Determine the area of the ring when d is 4 cm.

_____

c. Determine the diameter of the inner circle of the ring if the area of the ring is 628 cm².

_____

⑬ The value V of a car in dollars depends on the age a of the car. This value can be determined by $V(a) = \dfrac{19\,000}{a+1} + 1500$.

a. What is the original purchase price of the car?   _____

b. What will the value of the car be after 6 years?   _____

c. How long will it take for the car to be worth $2500?   _____

3.3 Maximum or Minimum Values of Quadratic Functions

Find the vertex by completing the square. Then determine whether the parabola opens up or down and find its maximum or minimum value.

HINT

The vertex can be found by converting the standard form $f(x) = ax^2 + bx + c$ to vertex form $f(x) = a(x - h)^2 + k$ by completing the square.

	parabola	quadratic function
$a > 0$	opens up $\cup$	a minimum value k at $x = h$, $f(h) = k$ vertex (h,k)
$a < 0$	opens down $\cap$	a maximum value k at $x = h$, $f(h) = k$ vertex (h,k)

① $f(x) = 2x^2 + 12x + 17$

Halve the coefficient of x and then square it. Subtract the same amount.

$= 2(x^2 + \boxed{}x) + 17$

$= 2(x^2 + 6x + (\frac{6}{2})^2 - (\frac{6}{2})^2) + 17$

$= 2(x^2 + 6x + \boxed{}^2) - 2 \times \boxed{}^2 + 17$

$= 2(x + \boxed{})^2 - \boxed{} + 17$

$a = \underline{} > 0$,

when $x = -3$,

$= 2(x + \boxed{})^2 - \boxed{}$ $f(-3) = \underline{}$.

The vertex is at _____ . It opens **up** / **down** and has a **min.** / **max.** value of _____ .

② $f(x) = x^2 + 5x + 3$

③ $f(x) = -x^2 + 9x - 20$

④ $f(x) = 3x^2 + 6x + 5$

⑤ $f(x) = 4x - \frac{1}{2}x^2 + 1$

⑥ $f(x) = x^2 - \frac{1}{2}x$

⑦ $f(x) = 3 - 3x - \frac{1}{3}x^2$

ISBN: 978-1-77149-222-5

Find the vertex by partial factoring. Then determine whether the parabola opens up or down and find its maximum or minimum value.

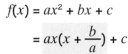

HINT

$f(x) = ax^2 + bx + c$

$$= ax(x + \frac{b}{a}) + c$$

1st Find two points on the parabola that are symmetrically opposite each other.

$$ax(x + \frac{b}{a}) = 0 \longrightarrow x = 0 \text{ or } x = -\frac{b}{a}$$

2nd Average those two points to find the x-coordinate of the vertex.

$$x_{vertex} = \frac{0 + (-\frac{b}{a})}{2} = -\frac{b}{2a}$$

Substitute x_{vertex} into the function to find y_{vertex}.

⑧ $y = 2x^2 - 4x + 5$ ⟵ $a =$ _____ > 0; opens up

$= 2x(\boxed{} - \boxed{}) + 5$

If $2x(x - 2) = 0$, $x = \boxed{}$ or $\boxed{}$.

Average the two x-coordinates $= \dfrac{\boxed{} + \boxed{}}{2} = \boxed{}$
(x-coordinate of the vertex)

Substitute x_{vertex} into the parabola.

$y_{vertex} = 2(\boxed{})^2 - 4(\boxed{}) + 5$

$= \boxed{}$

The vertex is at _____ . It opens **up** / **down** and has a **min.** / **max.** value of _____ .

⑨ $f(x) = 3x^2 - 6x + 1$ ⑩ $f(x) = -2(x + 1)^2 - x + 10$ ⑪ $f(x) = -x^2 - 2 - 3x$

⑫ $f(x) = -4x^2 + 16x + 1$ ⑬ $f(x) = \dfrac{1}{2} + 5x + 2x^2$ ⑭ $f(x) = \dfrac{1}{2}x^2 - 2x$

Find the vertex of each parabola by completing the square and by partial factoring.

⑮ $f(x) = 2x^2 - x + 1$ ⑯ $f(x) = 3x - x^2 + 3$

ISBN: 978-1-77149-222-5

Find the vertex of each parabola by completing the square or by partial factoring. Then graph the parabola and indicate the maximum or minimum value.

⑰ $f(x) = 2x^2 - 4x - 3$

⑱ $f(x) = -2x^2 - 10x - 17$

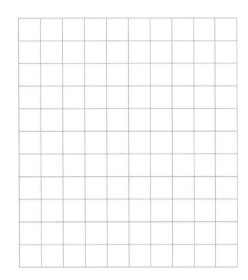

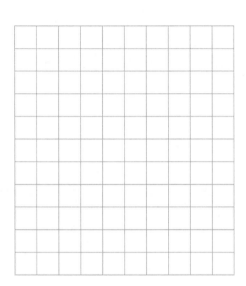

Solve the problems.

⑲ The sum of two numbers is 48. What is their greatest possible product?

Let x be one of the numbers. The other number is _____ .

$f(x) = x($_____$)$

⑳ Sketch the graphs of the functions. Describe how the vertices of the functions are related.

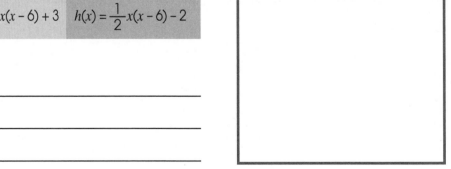

$f(x) = \frac{1}{2}x(x - 6)$ $g(x) = \frac{1}{2}x(x - 6) + 3$ $h(x) = \frac{1}{2}x(x - 6) - 2$

_____

_____

_____

ISBN: 978-1-77149-222-5

㉑ A baseball manufacturer has a daily cost of $C(x) = 2100 - 8x + 0.01x^2$, where C is the total cost in dollars and x is the number of baseballs produced. How many baseballs should be produced each day to yield a minimum cost?

_____

㉒ A shoe company earns a daily profit of P dollars by selling x pairs of shoes, given by $P(x) = -0.5x^2 + 40x - 350$. How many pairs of shoes does the company have to sell each day to maximize the profit?

_____

㉓ What are the dimensions of the rectangle with the greatest area that can be formed with 200 m of fencing? What is the area of the rectangle?

_____

㉔ Mr. Smith had a piece of wire that was 20 m long. He cut the wire into two pieces and bent each piece to form a square. Determine the length of the two pieces so that the sum of the areas of the two squares is a minimum.

_____

㉕ A student council sells school sweatshirts to raise funds. The students sell 600 sweatshirts a year at $50 each. In order to generate more sales, they are planning to decrease the price. The council estimates that for every $1 price drop, an additional 15 sweatshirts will be sold. What will the maximum revenue from sweatshirt sales be? What price will maximize the revenue?

HINT

Revenue = selling price × no. of sweatshirts sold

_____

ISBN: 978-1-77149-222-5

3.4 Operations with Radicals

HINT

Write each as a mixed radical in simplest form.

① $\sqrt{12}$ ← Look for perfect squares in the radicand.

$= \sqrt{\boxed{} \times 3}$

$= \sqrt{\boxed{}} \times \sqrt{3}$

$= \underline{\hspace{2cm}}$

② $\sqrt{32}$

$= \sqrt{\boxed{} \times 2}$

$= \sqrt{\boxed{}} \times \sqrt{2}$

$= \underline{\hspace{2cm}}$

Radical: *a square, cube, or higher root*

a radical symbol

e.g. $\sqrt{64}$ ← a radicand

$= \underline{8}$

Entire Radical	Mixed Radical
a radical with coefficient 1 e.g. $\sqrt{12}$	a radical with coefficient other than 1 e.g. $3\sqrt{2}$

Remember:

- $\sqrt{a} \times \sqrt{b} = \sqrt{ab}$

  e.g. $\sqrt{2} \times \sqrt{3} = \sqrt{2 \times 3} = \sqrt{6}$

- $a\sqrt{b} \times c\sqrt{d} = ac\sqrt{bd}$

  e.g. $2\sqrt{3} \times 4\sqrt{5} = 8\sqrt{15}$

③ $\sqrt{20} \quad = \underline{\hspace{1.5cm}}$

④ $\sqrt{75} \quad = \underline{\hspace{1.5cm}}$

⑤ $\sqrt{112} \quad = \underline{\hspace{1.5cm}}$

⑥ $\sqrt{8} \quad = \underline{\hspace{1.5cm}}$

⑦ $\sqrt{200} \quad = \underline{\hspace{1.5cm}}$

⑧ $\sqrt{24} \quad = \underline{\hspace{1.5cm}}$

⑨ $3\sqrt{40} \quad = \underline{\hspace{1.5cm}}$

⑩ $\frac{4}{9}\sqrt{405} \quad = \underline{\hspace{1.5cm}}$

⑪ $\frac{3}{4}\sqrt{60} \quad = \underline{\hspace{1.5cm}}$

⑫ $-\frac{3}{10}\sqrt{500} \quad = \underline{\hspace{1.5cm}}$

⑬ $(-2\sqrt{5})^3 \quad = \underline{\hspace{1.5cm}}$

⑭ $(3\sqrt{6})^2 \quad = \underline{\hspace{1.5cm}}$

⑮ $(4\sqrt{2})^2 = \underline{\hspace{1.5cm}}$

⑯ $(\frac{1}{2}\sqrt{12})^2 = \underline{\hspace{1.5cm}}$

⑰ $(-\frac{1}{3}\sqrt{18})^3 = \underline{\hspace{1.5cm}}$

⑱ $(\frac{\sqrt{21}}{3})^2 = \underline{\hspace{1.5cm}}$

Simplify.

⑲ $-2\sqrt{5} \times 3\sqrt{10}$

$=$

⑳ $\frac{1}{2}\sqrt{18} \times \frac{2}{3}\sqrt{27}$

$=$

㉑ $3\sqrt{189} \times -\frac{\sqrt{15}}{9}$

$=$

㉒ $2\sqrt{7} \times -6\sqrt{14} \quad = \underline{\hspace{1.5cm}}$

㉓ $-5\sqrt{20} \times \frac{\sqrt{150}}{10} = \underline{\hspace{1.5cm}}$

㉔ $3\sqrt{117} \times \frac{\sqrt{26}}{9} \quad = \underline{\hspace{1.5cm}}$

㉕ $\frac{\sqrt{90}}{2} \times -\sqrt{400} \quad = \underline{\hspace{1.5cm}}$

㉖ $-2\sqrt{192} \times \frac{\sqrt{27}}{4} \quad = \underline{\hspace{1.5cm}}$

㉗ $\sqrt{30} \times \frac{\sqrt{54}}{2} \quad = \underline{\hspace{1.5cm}}$

Simplify.

$$4\sqrt{3} - 2\sqrt{27} \longleftarrow \sqrt{3} \text{ and } \sqrt{27} \text{ are unlike radicals.}$$

$$= 4\sqrt{3} - 2\sqrt{9 \times 3}$$

$$= 4\sqrt{3} - 2 \times 3\sqrt{3}$$

$$= 4\sqrt{3} - 6\sqrt{3} \longleftarrow \text{Only like radicals can be added or subtracted.}$$

$$= -2\sqrt{3}$$

TRY THIS

$$3\sqrt{8} + 5\sqrt{18}$$

$$= 3\sqrt{\boxed{} \times \boxed{}} + 5\sqrt{\boxed{} \times \boxed{}}$$

$$= 3 \times \boxed{}\sqrt{\boxed{}} + 5 \times \boxed{}\sqrt{\boxed{}}$$

$$=$$

Simplify.

㉘ $\sqrt{8} - \sqrt{98}$ = _____

㉙ $2\sqrt{5} + 3\sqrt{80} - \sqrt{180}$ = _____

㉚ $2\sqrt{6} + 3\sqrt{216}$ = _____

㉛ $-5\sqrt{12} + \sqrt{192} - 4\sqrt{75}$ = _____

㉜ $-\sqrt{125} + \dfrac{\sqrt{45}}{2}$ = _____

㉝ $\dfrac{3\sqrt{50}}{2} - 3\sqrt{18} + \dfrac{5\sqrt{32}}{2}$ = _____

㉞ $3\sqrt{54} + 9\sqrt{28} + 4\sqrt{150} + 6\sqrt{7}$

$=$

㉟ $-4\sqrt{3} + 8\sqrt{72} - 7\sqrt{27} - 12\sqrt{8}$

$=$

Simplify the expressions by applying the distributive property.

㊱ $2\sqrt{3}(2 + \sqrt{3})$

$=$ _____ + _____

㊲ $\sqrt{5}(3\sqrt{5} - 2\sqrt{2})$

$=$

㊳ $-3\sqrt{2}(3 - 2\sqrt{5})$

$=$

㊴ $2\sqrt{5}(-2\sqrt{5} + \sqrt{3}) - \sqrt{3}(-\sqrt{5} + \sqrt{3})$ = _____

㊵ $(-\sqrt{2})^2(3 - \sqrt{5}) + \sqrt{5}(-\sqrt{5} + 2)$ = _____

㊶ $(3 + \sqrt{2}) \times 2\sqrt{5} - (\sqrt{20} + \sqrt{45})\sqrt{2}$ = _____

㊷ $(\sqrt{8} + \sqrt{15}) \times -2\sqrt{3} + \sqrt{10}(-\dfrac{\sqrt{2}}{2} + \sqrt{15})$ = _____

Simplify the binomial radical expressions. Write the mixed radicals in simplest form.

㊸ $(5 - \sqrt{12})(3 + \sqrt{3})$ ← Multiply each term in the first pair of brackets
by each term in the second pair of brackets.

$= 5 \times \boxed{} + 5 \times \sqrt{\boxed{}} - \sqrt{12} \times \boxed{} - \sqrt{12} \times \sqrt{\boxed{}}$

$= \underline{} + \underline{} - \underline{} - \underline{}$

$=$

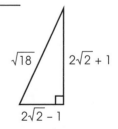

> **HINT**
>
> A mixed radical in simplest form has the smallest possible number written under the radical sign.
>
> e.g. $5\sqrt{12}$ ← not in simplest form
>
> $5\sqrt{12} = 5\sqrt{4 \times 3}$
> $\qquad\quad = 10\sqrt{3}$ ← in simplest form

㊹ $(3 + 2\sqrt{6})(\sqrt{6} - 7)$ $= \underline{}$

㊺ $(6 - 3\sqrt{7})(\sqrt{7} + 5)$ $= \underline{}$

㊻ $(\sqrt{3} + 5)^2$ $= \underline{}$

㊼ $(2\sqrt{2} + 6\sqrt{5})(3\sqrt{5} - \sqrt{2}) = \underline{}$ ㊽ $(3\sqrt{7} - 9)(\sqrt{14} + 3\sqrt{2}) = \underline{}$

㊾ $(\sqrt{2} - 2\sqrt{3})(\sqrt{3} - 2\sqrt{2})$ $= \underline{}$ ㊿ $(-\sqrt{3} - \sqrt{2})(2\sqrt{2} + \sqrt{8}) = \underline{}$

Answer the questions. Write the answers in simplest radical form.

㊱ What is the length of each line segment? What is their difference in length?

- l_1: from (-2,5) to (2,-3)
- l_2: from (10,-2) to (6,-1)

_____

㊲ Find the perimeter and area of the triangle.

_____

㊳ The dimensions of a rectangle are $(\sqrt{k} + 1)$ cm and $(\sqrt{k} - 1)$ cm. What is the length of its diagonal?

On the triangle: $\sqrt{18}$, $2\sqrt{2} + 1$, $2\sqrt{2} - 1$

ISBN: 978-1-77149-222-5

Example

Try This

Solve the quadratic equation by factoring.

$$x^2 + x - 6 = 0$$
$$(x + 3)(x - 2) = 0 \longleftarrow \text{Find the binomial factors.}$$
$$x + 3 = 0 \text{ or } x - 2 = 0$$
$$x = -3 \qquad x = 2 \longleftarrow \text{These are the solutions.}$$

The solutions are $x = -3$ and $x = 2$.

$$x^2 - 6x + 8 = 0$$
$$(x - \boxed{})(x - \boxed{}) = 0$$
$$x - \boxed{} = 0 \quad \text{or} \quad x - \boxed{} = 0$$
$$x = \underline{\qquad} \qquad x = \underline{\qquad}$$

The solutions are _____ and _____ .

Solve the equations by factoring.

① $x^2 + 3x - 10 = 0$

② $3x^2 - 48 = 0$

③ $6x^2 - 8x - 8 = 0$

④ $x^2 + 4x - 12 = 0$

⑤ $28x^2 - 3x - 1 = 0$

⑥ $15x^2 - 8x + 1 = 0$

⑦ $12x^2 + 23x + 10 = 0$

⑧ $12x^2 + 32x + 21 = 0$

⑨ $x^2 + 18x + 77 = 0$

⑩ $7x + x(3x - 9) - 16 = 0$

⑪ $-7x(x - 1) + x(x + 6) - 5 = 0$

⑫ $9(y + 3)^2 - 9(y + 3) - 28 = 0$

⑬ $-6(2y)^2 + 5(2y) + 4 = 0$

Example

Solve the quadratic equation with the quadratic formula.

$3x^2 - 18x + 22 = 0$ ⟵ $a = 3$, $b = -18$, $c = 22$

$x = \dfrac{-(-18) \pm \sqrt{(-18)^2 - 4(3)(22)}}{2(3)}$

$= \dfrac{18 \pm \sqrt{60}}{6}$

$= \dfrac{18 \pm 2\sqrt{15}}{6}$ $\doteq \dfrac{18 \pm 7.75}{6}$

$= \dfrac{9 + \sqrt{15}}{3}$ or $\dfrac{9 - \sqrt{15}}{3}$ $\doteq 4.29$ or 1.71

The solutions are $x = \dfrac{9 + \sqrt{15}}{3}$ or $x = \dfrac{9 - \sqrt{15}}{3}$.

Hint

Quadratic Equation
$ax^2 + bx + c = 0$

Quadratic Formula
$x = \dfrac{-b \pm \sqrt{b^2 - 4ac}}{2a}$

Try This

$5x^2 - 2x - 11 = 0$

$a = \boxed{}$ $b = \boxed{}$ $c = \boxed{}$

$x = \dfrac{-\boxed{} \pm \sqrt{\boxed{}^2 - 4\,\boxed{}\,\boxed{}}}{2\,\boxed{}}$

$= $

Solve the equations with the quadratic formula. Write the answers as radicals in simplest form.

⑭ $2x^2 - 6x - 17 = 0$

⑮ $-x^2 + 13x - 9 = 0$

⑯ $3x^2 - 7x - 8 = 0$

⑰ $2n^2 - n - 4 = 2$ _____

⑱ $9n^2 - 11 = 6n$ _____

⑲ $4y^2 - 2y = 9$ _____

⑳ $-2y^2 = -16 + 5y$ _____

㉑ $3a^2 - a - 6 = a$ _____

㉒ $a(a - 5) = 3a^2 - 5$ _____

㉓ $\dfrac{1 - 4m}{m} = m - 1$ _____

㉔ $m(m - 3) + 1 = \dfrac{2m - 5}{2}$ _____

ISBN: 978-1-77149-222-5

Find the value of the discriminant to determine the number of zeros of each quadratic function.

Quadratic Formula

$$x = \frac{-b \pm \sqrt{b^2 - 4ac}}{2a} \leftarrow \text{discriminant}$$

- $b^2 - 4ac > 0 \leftarrow$ 2 zeros
- $b^2 - 4ac = 0 \leftarrow$ 1 zero
- $b^2 - 4ac < 0 \leftarrow$ 0 zeros

㉕ $f(x) = 5x^2 + 2x - 2$

  $b^2 - 4ac$

  $= \quad ^2 - 4$

  $=$

  _____ zero(s)

㉖ $f(x) = \frac{1}{3}x^2 + 2x - 6$

  _____

㉗ $f(x) = 3x^2 - 3x - 8$ _____

㉘ $f(x) = -2x^2 + x - 12$ _____

㉙ $f(x) = \frac{1}{5}x^2 - 2x + 5$ _____

㉚ $f(x) = 2x^2 - 9x + 5$ _____

㉛ $f(x) = -2.4x^2 + x + 1.2$ _____

㉜ $f(x) = 4x^2 - 12x + 9$ _____

Answer the questions.

㉝ For what value(s) of k will

a. the function $f(x) = \frac{1}{k}x^2 - 2x + 5$ have two zeros? _____

b. the function $f(x) = 3x^2 - kx - k$ have 1 zero? _____

c. the function $f(x) = kx^2 - (2k + 1)x + k$ have no zeros? _____

㉞ The profit P, in dollars, gained by selling x computers is modelled by the function $f(x) = -5x^2 + 520x + 9600$. How many computers are sold to reach a break-even point?

_____

㉟ The height of a ball thrown vertically upward is modelled by $h(t) = -5t^2 + 20t + 1$, where $h(t)$ is the height of the ball from the ground in metres, at a time of t seconds after the throw. When does the ball hit the ground?

_____

ISBN: 978-1-77149-222-5 **COMPLETE MATHSMART (GRADE 11)** **55**

③⑥ The length of a rectangle is 3 cm longer than its width. If its area is 30 cm², what are the dimensions of the rectangle?

Let x be the length of the rectangle.

The dimensions of the rectangle are _____ cm and _____ cm.

Area: (_____) × (_____) = 30

---

③⑦ Kevin walked for x hours at a speed of x km/h and $(x - 1)$ hours at a speed of $(x - 1)$ km/h. He travelled a total distance of 11.5 km. What is the value of x?

---

③⑧ The sum of the squares of two consecutive integers is 545. What could the integers be? List all possibilities.

---

③⑨ A 40-cm piece of wire is cut into two pieces and each piece is bent into a square. If the sum of the areas of these two squares is 68 cm², what are their perimeters?

---

④⓪ Determine the number of zeros of the function $f(x) = k - (x - 2)(-x + 1)$ for different values of k.

ISBN: 978-1-77149-222-5

Example

Find the equation in factored form for a family of quadratic functions with the zeros at -1 and 4. Write the equations of three members of the family and sketch them.

Roots of the equations: -1 and 4

Factors of the functions: $(x + 1)$ and $(x - 4)$

Equation of this family: $f(x) = a(x + 1)(x - 4)$

Equations of three members:

$f(x) = -2(x + 1)(x - 4)$

$f(x) = (x + 1)(x - 4)$

$f(x) = 3(x + 1)(x - 4)$

Try This

zeros at -2 and 3

Roots: _____

Factors: _____

Equation: _____

Three members:

_____

_____

_____

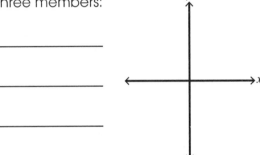

Determine the equations in factored form. Write the equations of three members of the family and sketch their graphs.

①

Zeros at	4 and 7	-4 and 6	-2
Roots			
Factors			
Equation			
Equations and graphs of three members			

Each parabola passes through the given point and has the given zeros. Find its equation in factored form and standard form.

② passes through: (4,-3)
zeros: -2 and 5

$f(x) = a(x -$ ⬚ $)(x -$ ⬚ $)$ ← Write the general form of the equation.

$f(4) =$ _____ ← The equation passes through (4,-3).

⬚ $= a($ ⬚ $+ 2)($ ⬚ $- 5)$ ← Find the value of a.

$f(x) =$ _____
factored form

$f(x) =$ _____
standard form

③ passes through: (2,-6)
zeros: -1 and 4

$f(x) =$ _____
factored form

$f(x) =$ _____
standard form

④ passes through: $(-\frac{1}{2},5)$
zeros: 0 and 1

$f(x) =$ _____
factored form

$f(x) =$ _____
standard form

⑤ passes through: $(0,\sqrt{2})$
zeros: $-\sqrt{2}$ and $\sqrt{2}$

$f(x) =$ _____
factored form

$f(x) =$ _____
standard form

⑥ passes through: (5,-6)
zeros: $1 + \sqrt{10}$ and $1 - \sqrt{10}$

$f(x) =$ _____
factored form

$f(x) =$ _____
standard form

Find the equation of each parabola in vertex form based on the given information.

⑦ passes through: (3,7)
vertex: (4,8)

$f(x) = a(x -$ ⬚ $)^2 +$ ⬚

$f(x) =$ _____

⑧ passes through: (-5,4)
vertex: (-2,-5)

$f(x) =$ _____

⑨ passes through: $(0,-\sqrt{2})$
vertex: $(-\sqrt{2},\sqrt{2})$

$f(x) =$ _____

 ISBN: 978-1-77149-222-5

Answer the questions.

⑩ A Frisbee was tossed from the ground and travelled a horizontal distance of 35 m where it flew over a 3.2-m tall tree and landed 49 m away from where it was tossed.

a. Label the diagram with the correct information.

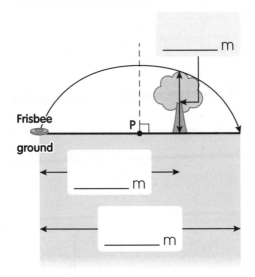

_____ m

Frisbee

ground

P

_____ m

_____ m

b. Determine the equation of the quadratic function to model the Frisbee's path.

zeros = _____ and _____ ← Set the origin at P.

passes through: (_____ , _____) ← location of the tree

$f(x) = a(x -$ _____$)(x -$ _____$)$

c. Determine the maximum height the Frisbee reached.

d. How high would the Frisbee be after it had travelled a horizontal distance of 30 m?

⑪ A bridge has been built in the shape of a parabolic arch. The bridge has a span of 60 m and a maximum height of 42 m.

a. Determine the equation of the quadratic function to model the bridge.

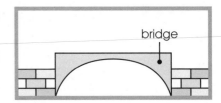

bridge

b. What is the height of the arch when it has a horizontal distance of 8.5 m from one end?

ISBN: 978-1-77149-222-5

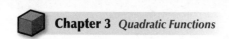

3.7 Solving Linear-quadratic Systems

Determine the points of intersection of each linear-quadratic system of equations using algebra. Then determine the points by graphing.

① $y = x^2 - 7x + 15$ and $y = 2x - 5$

$x^2 - 7x + 15 = $ _____ ◀— Use substitution.

_____ $= 0$ ◀— Group the like terms and rearrange them so that the right side equals 0.

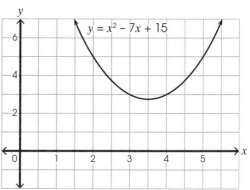

points of intersection: _____ and _____

② $y = -x^2 - 5x - 4$ and $y = -x - 4$

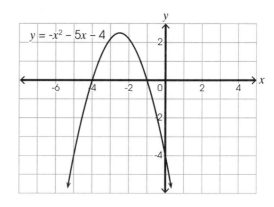

points of intersection: _____

③ $y = -\frac{1}{2}x^2 - 4x - 1$ and $x + y = -\frac{9}{2}$

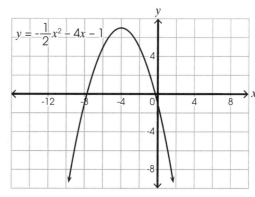

points of intersection: _____

④ $y = -\frac{1}{2}x^2 - 3x + 4$ and $11x + 4y - 10 = 0$

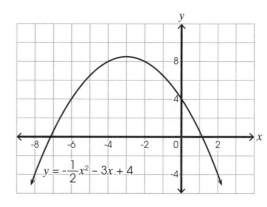

points of intersection: _____

 ISBN: 978-1-77149-222-5

Determine the number of points of intersection (P.O.I.) of the quadratic and linear functions without solving.

⑤ $y = 3x^2 - 2x + 1$ and $y = 5x + 2$

$$3x^2 - 2x + 1 = \text{_____} \longleftarrow \text{Use substitution.}$$

$$3x^2 - \boxed{}\, x - \boxed{} = 0 \longleftarrow a = 3, b = -7, c = -1$$

$$b^2 - 4ac = \text{_____}$$

$$= \text{_____} > 0$$

There will be _____ points of intersection.

Use the **discriminant** to determine the number of points of intersection on the linear and quadratic functions.

	P.O.I.
$b^2 - 4ac > 0$	2
$b^2 - 4ac = 0$	1
$b^2 - 4ac < 0$	0

⑥ $y = x^2 + 3x - 5$ and $y = -x - 1$

P.O.I.: _____

⑦ $y = \frac{1}{2}x^2 + 3x - 14$ and $y = x - 5$

P.O.I.: _____

⑧ $y = 2x^2 - 2x + 1$ and $y = 3x - 5$

P.O.I.: _____

⑨ $y = 3x^2 - 2x - 4$ and $y = 3x + 5$

P.O.I.: _____

⑩ $y + 5x = x^2 + 7$ and $x + y = 3$

P.O.I.: _____

⑪ $y = \frac{1}{3}x^2 + x - 2$ and $y + x = -6$

P.O.I.: _____

⑫ $y = (x + 1)^2 - 5$ and $8x - y = 13$

P.O.I.: _____

⑬ $y = 0.2(x - 1)^2 - 4$ and $0.5x - y - 2 = 0$

P.O.I.: _____

ISBN: 978-1-77149-222-5

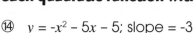

Determine the equation of the tangent line of each quadratic function with the given slope.

⑭ $y = -x^2 - 5x - 5$; slope = -3

The tangent line is _____ .

⑮ $y = -2x^2 + 4x + 3$; slope = 2

The tangent line is _____ .

HINT

A tangent line touches a curve at one point and has the same slope as that of the curve at that point.

e.g. $y = 2x^2 - x + 6$; slope = 3

linear equation: $y = 3x + b$

$2x^2 - x + 6 = 3x + b$ ◄— Substitute.

$2x^2 - 4x + 6 - b = 0$

tangent line: 1 point of intersection

$b^2 - 4ac = 0$

$(-4)^2 - 4(2)(6 - b) = 0$

$8(6 - b) = 16$

$b = 4$

The tangent is $y = 3x + 4$.

Determine the values of the slope of the line k that makes it a tangent to each quadratic function.

⑯ $y = 2x^2 - 3x + 1$
$y = kx - 2$

⑰ $y = -2x^2 - x + 4$
$y = kx + 5$

⑱ $y = 0.5x^2 - 2x - 0.75$
$y = -kx - 2.25$

⑲ $y = (x - 2)^2 - (2x + 1)$
$kx - y + \dfrac{1}{2} = 0$

⑳ $y = 0.3x^2 - (x + 1)^2$
$kx - 2y + 0.5 = 0$

㉑ $y = \sqrt{2}x^2 - 2x + \sqrt{2}$
$y = -kx - \sqrt{2}$

ISBN: 978-1-77149-222-5

Answer the questions.

㉒ What will the value of k be if $g(x) = 2x + k$ intersects the quadratic function $f(x) = -x^2 - x + 1$ at

a. exactly one point? Give one possible answer of $g(x)$.

_____

b. two points? Give one possible answer of $g(x)$.

_____

c. no point? Give one possible answer of $g(x)$.

_____

㉓ The revenue that a company makes and its operating cost in thousands of dollars are projected to be $R = -4x^2 + 30x$ and $C = 24 + 2x$ respectively, where x is the age of the company. When is the company expected to break even?

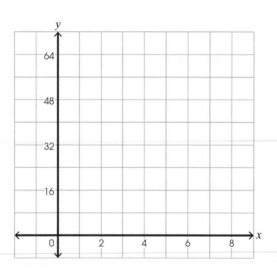

_____

㉔ The path of a rocket is parabolic and represented by $y = -x^2 + 9x$. The path of a flare is a straight line represented by $y = -x + 9$. If the rocket and the flare are launched at the same time, what are the coordinates of the point(s) where the paths intersect? Graph to show the points.

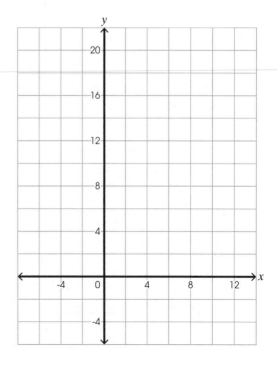

_____

3.8 Transformations

Check the graph that shows a translation.

①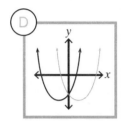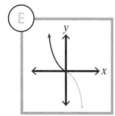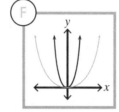

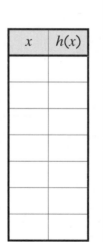 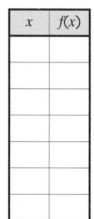 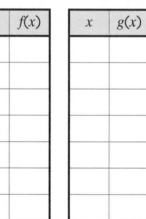

A **translation** is a transformation that has a shift of the parent function but no change in shape.

e.g.

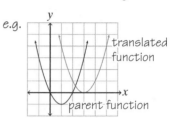

The graph is translated 2 units to the right and 1 unit up.

Complete the table of values. Graph the parent function $f(x)$ and the translated functions. Then describe the translations.

② $f(x) = x^2 + 4$
$g(x) = x^2 + 6 = f(x) + 2$
$h(x) = (x - 3)^2 + 4 = f(x - 3)$

x	$f(x)$

x	$g(x)$

x	$h(x)$

Description: _____

_____

③ $f(x) = |\sqrt{x + 1}|$ ◄— an absolute value function
$g(x) = |\sqrt{x + 1}| + 3 = f(x) + 3$
$h(x) = |\sqrt{x + 4}| = |\sqrt{(x + 3) + 1}| = f(x + 3)$

x	$f(x)$

x	$g(x)$

x	$h(x)$

Description: _____

_____

ISBN: 978-1-77149-222-5

Determine each translated function and its domain and range. Then answer the questions.

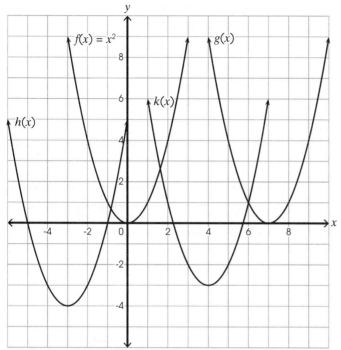

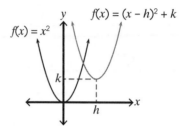
④ $g(x) =$ _____ $h(x) =$ _____ $k(x) =$ _____

domain: {_____}   domain: _____   domain: _____

range: {_____}   range: _____   range: _____

⑤   If the parent function is translated 6 units to the right and 2 units down, what will the translated function, $l(x)$, be? Sketch its graph and find its vertex.

_____

⑥   The point (-12,144) on the parent function $f(x) = x^2$ has been translated to a point on each family member. Determine the equation of each family member.

Parent function			**Family member**
a.	$f(x) = x^2$	(-12,144) → (-7,144)	_____
b.	$f(x) = x^2$	(-12,144) → (-12,154)	_____
c.	$f(x) = x^2$	(-12,144) → (-15,134)	_____
d.	$f(x) = x^2$	(-12,144) → (0,104)	_____
e.	$f(x) = x^2$	(-12,144) → (-12,132)	_____

Identify each type of reflection of the function $f(x) = \sqrt{x}$ to complete the chart.

numerical representation	how to reflect	graphical representation
$(x,y) \longrightarrow (-x,-y)$	in the x-axis	
$(x,y) \longrightarrow (-x,y)$	in the y-axis	
$(x,y) \longrightarrow (x,-y)$	in the x-axis and y-axis	

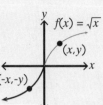 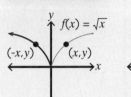 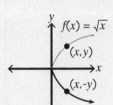

⑦

reflected function	numerical representation	how to reflect	graphical representation
$g(x) = f(-x) = $ _____	$(x,y) \longrightarrow$ _____		
$h(x) = -f(x) = $ _____			
$k(x) = -f(-x) = $ _____			

Reflect the function in the x-axis, y-axis, and the x-axis and y-axis. Sketch the graphs of the reflected functions and label them.

⑧
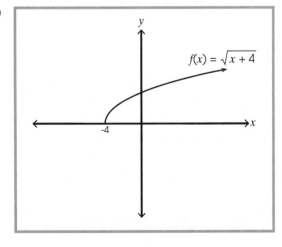

$f(x) = \sqrt{x+4}$

⑨
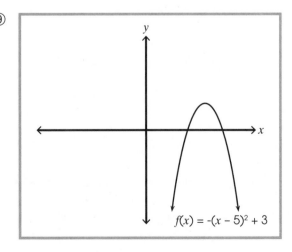

$f(x) = -(x-5)^2 + 3$

ISBN: 978-1-77149-222-5

Determine the transformation applied to the parent function $f(x) = x^2 + 1$. **Then relate the equation of each transformed function to** $f(x)$ **and find the scale factor.**

⑩

vertical / horizontal		stretch / compression	

_____ _____   _____ _____   _____ _____   _____ _____

stretching the graph away from the x-axis	squeezing the graph toward the x-axis	stretching the graph away from the y-axis	squeezing the graph toward the y-axis
$y = af(x),\ |a| > 1$	$y = af(x),\ 0 < |a| < 1$	$y = f(ax),\ 0 < |a| < 1$	$y = f(ax),\ |a| > 1$
scale factor: $|a|$	scale factor: $|a|$	scale factor: $\left|\frac{1}{a}\right|$	scale factor: $\left|\frac{1}{a}\right|$

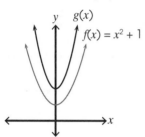 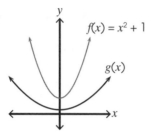 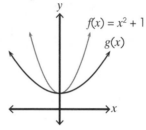 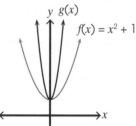

$g(x) = 2(x^2 + 1)$	$g(x) = \frac{1}{5}(x^2 + 1)$	$g(x) = (\frac{1}{2}x)^2 + 1$	$g(x) = (3x)^2 + 1$
= _____	= _____	= _____	= _____
scale factor:	scale factor:	scale factor:	scale factor:
_____	_____	_____	_____

Determine whether each function is a vertical/horizontal stretch/compression. Find the scale factor and the points of the transformed functions. Then answer the question.

⑪

$f(x) = -\dfrac{1}{x} + 2$	transformation	scale factor	a point on $f(x)$	→	a point on $g(x)$
a. $g(x) = \frac{1}{2}f(x)$			$(1,1)$	→	• same x-coordinate • multiply the y-coordinate by the scale factor
b. $g(x) = f(4x)$			$(1,1)$	→	• same y-coordinate • multiply the x-coordinate by the scale factor
c. $g(x) = f(\frac{1}{3}x)$			$(1,1)$	→	• same y-coordinate • multiply the x-coordinate by the scale factor
d. $g(x) = 5f(x)$			$(1,1)$	→	• same x-coordinate • multiply the y-coordinate by the scale factor

⑫   If a function $f(x)$ is stretched horizontally by a scale factor of 2, what will the equation of the transformed function be? If (2,8) is a point on $f(x)$, what will it be after the transformation?

_____

ISBN: 978-1-77149-222-5   **COMPLETE MATHSMART (GRADE 11)**

Example

Describe the transformations applied to the function.

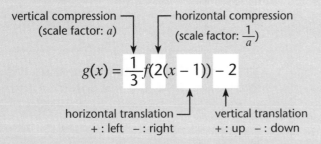

vertical compression (scale factor: a) — horizontal compression (scale factor: $\frac{1}{a}$)

$$g(x) = \frac{1}{3}f(2(x-1)) - 2$$

horizontal translation — $+$: left $-$: right

vertical translation — $+$: up $-$: down

- horizontally compressed by a factor of $\frac{1}{2}$
- vertically compressed by a factor of $\frac{1}{3}$
- translated 2 units down
- translated 1 unit right

Try This

reflection —

$$g(x) = -2f(4(x+1)) + 3$$

- reflection in the _____
- vertically _____
- _____
- _____
- _____

Describe the transformations applied to each function. Then draw all the graphs involved.

⑬ parent function: $f(x) = x^2$

$g(x) = 2f(\frac{1}{3}(x-5))$

- horizontally stretched by a factor of

  _____

- vertically stretched by a factor of

  _____

- translated _____ units **left / right**

Hint

Using transformations to graph functions:

$$y = af(k(x-d)) + c$$

$$f(x) \longrightarrow f(kx) \longrightarrow af(kx) \longrightarrow af(k(x-d)) + c$$

| parent function | horizontal stretch/ compression | vertical stretch/ compression | translation: left/right and up/down |

$f(x)$	$f(\frac{1}{3}x)$	$2f(\frac{1}{3}x)$	$2f(\frac{1}{3}(x-5))$
(-3,9)			
(-2,4)			
(-1,1)			
(0,0)			
(1,1)			
(2,4)			
(3,9)			

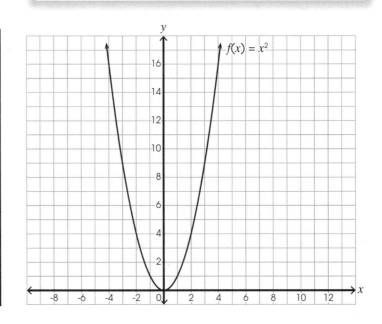

⑭ parent function: $f(x) = \sqrt{x}$

   $g(x) = -\dfrac{1}{2}f(3(x + 6)) - 3$

   * _____

   * _____

   * _____

   * _____

$f(x)$	$f(3x)$	$\dfrac{1}{2}f(3x)$	$-\dfrac{1}{2}f(3x)$	$-\dfrac{1}{2}f(3(x+6))-3$
(0,0)				
(1,1)				
(4,2)				
(9,3)				

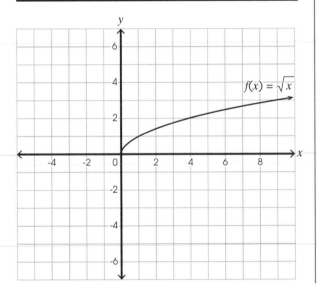

⑮ parent function: $f(x) = \dfrac{1}{x}$

   $g(x) = 2f(5x) + 1$

   * _____

   * _____

   * _____

$f(x)$	$f(5x)$	$2f(5x)$	$2f(5x) + 1$
$(-10,-\dfrac{1}{10})$			
$(-5,-\dfrac{1}{5})$			
$(5,\dfrac{1}{5})$			
$(10,\dfrac{1}{10})$			

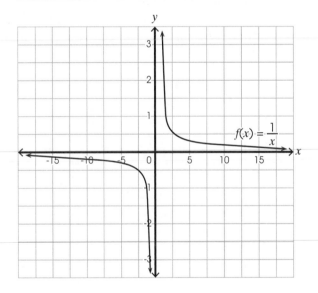

Answer the question.

⑯ Two balls are dropped from a building. The distance travelled by Ball A follows the function $d_A(t) = 150 - 3(t + 6)^2$ and Ball B follows $d_B(t) = 150 - 3t^2$, where the distance d is measured in metres and the time t in seconds. Graph the two functions and state their domains and ranges. Determine whether they will meet before reaching the ground.

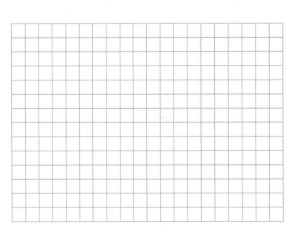

_____

3.9 The Inverse of a Function

Determine the ordered pairs. Then graph each function and its inverse.

①

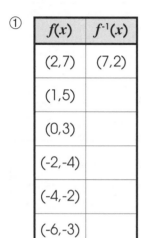

$f(x)$	$f^{-1}(x)$
(2,7)	(7,2)
(1,5)	
(0,3)	
(-2,-4)	
(-4,-2)	
(-6,-3)	

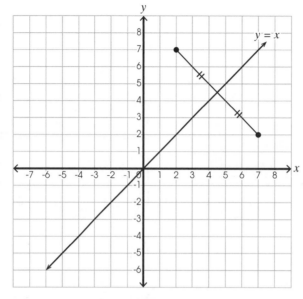

The inverse of a function is the reverse of the original function.

The x-values and y-values of the inverse of a function are the reverse of those of the original function. The inverse of function $f(x)$ is written as $f^{-1}(x)$.

e.g.

$f(x)$	$f^{-1}(x)$
(3,5)	(5,3)
(7,13)	(13,7)

The inverse of the function is its reflection in the line $y = x$. Therefore, the points on the functions and their corresponding points on the inverse have the same distance from the line $y = x$.

② **A** $\quad f(x) = x^2$ **B** $\quad f(x) = -x^2 - x$

$f(x)$	$f^{-1}(x)$
(-4,)	
(-3,)	
(-2,)	
(-1,)	
(0,)	
(1,)	
(2,)	
(3,)	

$f(x)$	$f^{-1}(x)$
(-4,)	
(-3,)	
(-2,)	
(-1,)	
(0,)	
(1,)	
(2,)	
(3,)	

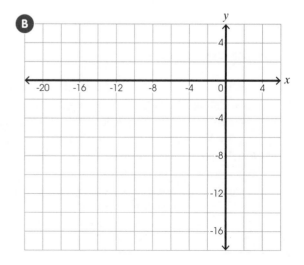

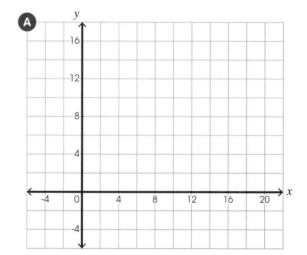

ISBN: 978-1-77149-222-5

Graph the inverse of each function. Then determine whether the inverse is a function. Check the circle if it is.

③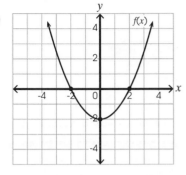

$f^{-1}(x)$: a function ◯

④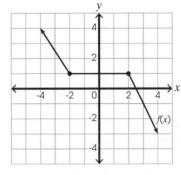

$f^{-1}(x)$: a function ◯

⑤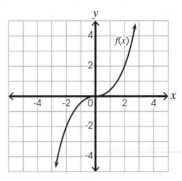

$f^{-1}(x)$: a function ◯

⑥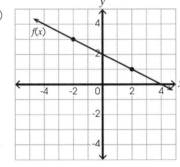

$f^{-1}(x)$: a function ◯

⑦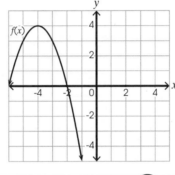

$f^{-1}(x)$: a function ◯

⑧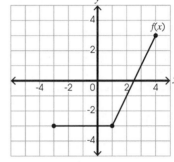

$f^{-1}(x)$: a function ◯

Determine the inverse of each function.

⑨ $f(x) = x^2 + 6$

　　$y = x^2 + 6$

　　$x = y^2 + 6$

　　$y =$ _____

　　$f^{-1}(x) =$ _____

⑩ $f(x) = 3x + 7$

> **HINT**
>
> Steps to finding the inverse of a function:
>
> **1st** Interchange x and y in the original function.
>
> **2nd** Solve for y.

⑪ $f(x) = 5x^2 - 3$

_____

⑫ $f(x) = 10 - 2x$

_____

⑬ $f(x) = -(x + 1)^2 - 1$

_____

⑭ $f(x) = \sqrt{x} + 1$

_____

⑮ $f(x) = \frac{1}{2}(x - 1)^2$

_____

⑯ $f(x) = 4 + 5x$

_____

ISBN: 978-1-77149-222-5

Determine the inverse of each quadratic function. Find its domain and range. Write each inverse as a function with the restricted domain of the quadratic function. Then find the domain and range of each inverse.

⑰ $f(x) = x^2 - 10x + 15$

$y = (x - \underline{\hspace{1cm}})^2 - \underline{\hspace{1cm}}$ ⟵ Write the quadratic function in vertex form.

$x = (y - \underline{\hspace{1cm}})^2 - \underline{\hspace{1cm}}$ ⟵ Interchange x and y.

$y = \underline{\hspace{3cm}}$ ⟵ Solve for y.

$f(x) = x^2 - 10x + 15 = (x - \underline{\hspace{1cm}})^2 - \underline{\hspace{1cm}}$

domain: _____

range: _____

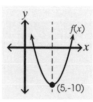

Remember to write the quadratic function in vertex form first by completing the square before interchanging x and y.

_____

If the inverse is a function,

• the range of the inverse is equal to the restricted domain of the original function.

• the domain of the inverse is equal to the range of the original function.

For $f(x)$ restricted to $x \geq 5$,	For $f(x)$ restricted to $x < 5$,
$f^{-1}(x) = \underline{\hspace{2.5cm}}$	$f^{-1}(x) = \underline{\hspace{2.5cm}}$
domain: _____	domain: _____
range: _____	range: _____

⑱ $f(x) = x^2 + 5x + 1$

$f(x) = \underline{\hspace{3cm}}$

domain: _____ range: _____

For $f(x)$ restricted to _____,	For $f(x)$ restricted to _____,
$f^{-1}(x) = \underline{\hspace{2.5cm}}$	$f^{-1}(x) = \underline{\hspace{2.5cm}}$
domain: _____	domain: _____
range: _____	range: _____

⑲ $f(x) = -x^2 - 2x - 4$

$f(x) = \underline{\hspace{3cm}}$

domain: _____ range: _____

For $f(x)$ restricted to _____,	For $f(x)$ restricted to _____,
$f^{-1}(x) = \underline{\hspace{2.5cm}}$	$f^{-1}(x) = \underline{\hspace{2.5cm}}$
domain: _____	domain: _____
range: _____	range: _____

ISBN: 978-1-77149-222-5

Answer the questions.

⑳ For $f(x) = -\frac{1}{2}x^2 - 3x$ and $x \le 0$, determine

a. the vertex form, domain, and range of $f(x)$.

_____

_____

_____

b. the restricted domain of $f(x)$ to make the inverse $f^{-1}(x)$ a function. State the domain and range of $f^{-1}(x)$.

_____

㉑ The distance travelled by an arrow from a bow can be modelled by the function $d(x) = \frac{x^2}{8}$, where $d(x)$ is the distance travelled in metres and x is the force exerted on the arrow measured in newtons (N), where $x \ge 0$.

a. Complete the table of values. Graph the distance function.

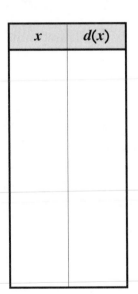

x	$d(x)$

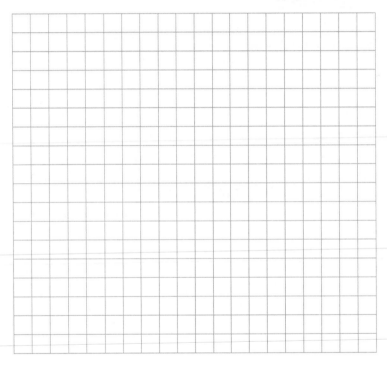

b. State the range of $f(x)$ and explain your answer.

_____

c. Determine the model that describes force in terms of distance.

_____

d. Is the new model a function? _____

ISBN: 978-1-77149-222-5

4 Exponential Functions

TO LEARN

Asymptote: a line that a graph approaches closely but never touches

Half-life: the time taken for a quantity to reduce to half of its original value

y $f(x) = 2^x - 3$

x

asymptote: $y = -3$

4.1 Exponents

Example

Evaluate the exponents.

3^{-2}

$= \dfrac{1}{3^2}$

$= \dfrac{1}{9}$

$\left(\dfrac{1}{3}\right)^{-2}$

$= \left(\dfrac{3}{1}\right)^2$

$= 9$

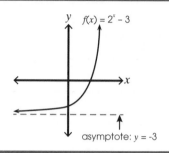

Try This

5^{-2} $\left(\dfrac{2}{3}\right)^{-3}$

$=$ $=$

$=$ $=$

Hint

$a^{-n} = \dfrac{1}{a^n}$

$\left(\dfrac{a}{b}\right)^{-n} = \left(\dfrac{b}{a}\right)^n$

Evaluate.

① 2^{-2}

② 4^{-3}

③ -3^{-3}

④ $(-5)^{-2}$

⑤ $\left(\dfrac{1}{4}\right)^{-2}$

⑥ $\left(\dfrac{3}{2}\right)^{-3}$

⑦ $\left(-\dfrac{4}{5}\right)^{-1}$

⑧ $-\left(\dfrac{3}{4}\right)^{-2}$

⑨ $\dfrac{2^{-1}}{8}$

⑩ $\dfrac{2}{8^{-1}}$

⑪ $\dfrac{3^{-2}}{2^{-3}}$

⑫ $\dfrac{2^3}{2^{-1}}$

   ISBN: 978-1-77149-222-5

Example

Simplify. Express the answer in rational form.

$$2^{-2} \times 2^{-3} \times 2^{6}$$
$$= 2^{-2 + (-3) + 6}$$
$$= 2^{1}$$
$$= 2$$

Try This

$$3^4 \times 3^{-1} \qquad\qquad \frac{4^2 \times 4^3}{4^4}$$

Simplify. Write your answers in rational form.

⑬ $2^5 \times 2^{-1} \times 2^{-2}$

⑭ $8^{-9} \times 8^{8} \times 8^{-2}$

Hint

$$a^m \times a^n = a^{m+n}$$
$$a^m \div a^n = a^{m-n}$$
$$(a^m)^n = a^{mn}$$

⑮ $\dfrac{10^2}{10^3 \times 10^{-1}}$

⑯ $\dfrac{9^3 \times 9^{-1}}{9^{-2} \times 9^3}$

⑰ $\dfrac{(3^{-1})(3^4)(3^{-3})}{(3^{-2})(3^3)}$

⑱ $\dfrac{(14^{10})(14^{-5})}{(14^{-2})(14^7)(14)}$

⑲ $2^{-2} + 4^{-2}$

⑳ $\dfrac{1}{3^{-2}} - 3^{-1}$

㉑ $(3^{-2} + 6^{-1}) \times \dfrac{1}{6^{-2}}$

㉒ $\left(\dfrac{16^2}{2^{-1}}\right)(2^{-5})\left(\dfrac{1}{2^4}\right)$

㉓ $\left(\dfrac{1}{5}\right)^{-1}(5^{-2}) + 5^{-1}$

Evaluate the expressions with the given values.

㉔ $\dfrac{a^{-1} \times a^{3}}{a}$ $a = 4$

㉕ $\dfrac{(x^{-4})^{-2}}{x^{3}}$ $x = 2$

㉖ $\dfrac{b^{2} \times (-b^{-1})^{2}}{b^{-1} + b}$ $b = 8$

㉗ $(x^{-3}y^{-4})(xy)^{2}$ $x = 2$ $y = 3$

㉘ $(cd)^{-3}\left(\dfrac{c^{-1}}{d^{2}}\right)^{-1}$ $c = 2$ $d = -1$

㉙ $\left(\dfrac{m^{-1}}{n}\right)^{2}\left(\dfrac{1}{m}\right)^{-1}$ $m = -2$ $n = 3$

㉚ $x^{a-b}\left(\dfrac{1}{x}\right)^{b}$ $x = 10$ $a = 6$ $b = 3$

㉛ $\dfrac{a^{3x + 2y}}{a^{-x + y}}$ $a = -3$ $x = -2$ $y = 7$

㉜ $(m^{2}n)^{x}(-mn)^{-2x}$ $m = -2$ $n = 3$ $x = 1$

Answer the questions.

㉝ Are $(5^{2})^{-1}$ and $5^{2} \times 5^{-1}$ equal? Evaluate them.

㉞ Lucas thinks that $\left(\dfrac{2}{5}\right)^{-2}$ and $\left(\left(\dfrac{5}{2}\right)^{-1}\right)^{-2}$ are the same. Is he correct? Show your work.

㉟ Look at Kyle's solution. Describe what was done incorrectly. Find the correct solution.

$$2x^{-2} \times \dfrac{1}{x^{2}}$$

$$= 2x^{2} \times \dfrac{1}{x^{2}}$$

$$= 2$$

㊱ Look at Carrie's solution. Was it done correctly? Explain.

$$\left(\dfrac{1}{y^{-2}}\right)(y^{-1})^{0}$$

$$= \left(\dfrac{y^{-1}}{y^{-2}}\right)^{0}$$

$$= 1$$

Example

TRY This

Evaluate.

$8^{\frac{1}{3}}$ $8^{\frac{2}{3}}$

$= \sqrt[3]{8}$ $= (\sqrt[3]{8})^2$

$= 2$ $= 2^2$

       $= 4$

$81^{\frac{1}{4}}$ $32^{\frac{4}{5}}$

$=$ $=$

$=$ $=$

          $=$

HINT

$a^{\frac{1}{n}} = \sqrt[n]{a}$

$a^{\frac{m}{n}} = (\sqrt[n]{a})^m = (\sqrt[n]{a^m})$

Evaluate without using a calculator.

① $\left(\dfrac{1}{10\,000}\right)^{\frac{1}{4}}$

② $(-8)^{\frac{1}{3}}$

③ $16^{-\frac{1}{2}}$

④ $(-27)^{-\frac{1}{3}}$

⑤ $49^{0.5}$

⑥ $(-32)^{0.2}$

⑦ $\sqrt[4]{256^2}$

⑧ $(\sqrt[3]{729})^{0.5}$

⑨ $\sqrt[3]{-\dfrac{64}{125}}$

⑩ $\dfrac{36^{0.5}}{(\sqrt[3]{-216})^2}$

⑪ $\left(-\dfrac{27}{64}\right)^{-\frac{2}{3}}$

⑫ $\left(\left(\dfrac{16}{81}\right)^{-0.5}\right)^{0.5}$

⑬ $\dfrac{(-8)^{-\frac{4}{3}}}{(-128)^{-\frac{3}{7}}}$

⑭ $\dfrac{(\sqrt[7]{-1})^4(9^{2.5})}{(3^5)^{0.8}\sqrt{9}}$

⑮ $\dfrac{(\sqrt[5]{25})^{\frac{15}{2}}}{81^{0.5} - 16^{\frac{1}{2}}}$

⑯ $\dfrac{(8^{\frac{1}{2}})^{\frac{2}{3}} + (\sqrt{4})^2}{16^{-0.25}}$

Example

Simplify and write each as a simple power.

$(4^{\frac{1}{2}})(4^{\frac{1}{2}})$ $3^{\frac{3}{4}} \div \sqrt{3}$

$= 4^{\frac{1}{2}+\frac{1}{2}}$ $= 3^{\frac{3}{4}} \div 3^{\frac{1}{2}}$

$= 4$ $= 3^{\frac{3}{4}-\frac{1}{2}}$

$= 3^{\frac{1}{4}}$

Try **This**

$(5^{\frac{1}{3}})^2(5^{-2})$ $(\sqrt[3]{6})^2 \div 6^{-1}$

Simplify and write the answers with positive exponents.

⑰ $\dfrac{10^{\frac{1}{4}}}{10^{-1}}$

⑱ $(8^{\frac{5}{2}})(8^{-\frac{3}{5}})$

⑲ $(\sqrt{-5})^{-3}(-5)^{\frac{1}{3}}$

⑳ $(7^2)^{-3}\left(\dfrac{1}{7^{-1}}\right)$

㉑ $\left(\dfrac{1}{\sqrt{-6}}\right)^3 (-6)^{-\frac{1}{5}}$

㉒ $\left(\sqrt[4]{\dfrac{16}{81}}\right)^3 \left(\sqrt{\left(\dfrac{4}{9}\right)^3}\right)$

㉓ $(32^{-\frac{1}{5}})^3(\sqrt{-8})^2$

㉔ $\dfrac{(\sqrt[6]{64})^{12}(125^{\frac{1}{2}})}{\sqrt{20}}$

㉕ $\dfrac{3^2(81^{0.25})}{(-27^{\frac{1}{3}})^2}$

㉖ $\dfrac{4^2(4^{0.5})(4^{-3.5})}{(\sqrt[4]{16})^{-2}}$

㉗ $(\sqrt[3]{27})^2 + 9^{\frac{3}{2}} - 81^{0.25}$

㉘ $\dfrac{6.25^{\frac{3}{2}}}{\sqrt{100} + (2.25)^{0.5}}$

Evaluate each expression with the given values.

㉙
$a = 9$	$b = 16$

a. $\left(a^{\frac{1}{2}} b^{\frac{1}{4}}\right)^2$

b. $\left(\dfrac{a}{b}\right)^2\left(\left(\dfrac{a}{b}\right)^{-1}\right)^{0.5}$

c. $\left(\dfrac{1}{a^{-1}}\right)^{0.5}(\sqrt{ab})^{\frac{1}{2}}$

㉚
$x = 4$	$y = -3$

a. $\left(\dfrac{xy}{\sqrt{x}}\right)^{0.5}(2y)^{\frac{1}{2}}$

b. $2^{2-y}x^y\left(\dfrac{x}{y^2}\right)^{\frac{1}{2}}$

c. $\sqrt{4}x^{0.5}y^2\left(\dfrac{x^2y}{2^{-1}}\right)^{-1}$

㉛
$m = 27$	$n = -1$

a. $\dfrac{\sqrt[3]{mn}}{(mn^2)^{-\frac{1}{3}}}$

b. $\sqrt[4]{\left(\dfrac{m}{3n^2}\right)^2}\left(\sqrt{\dfrac{1}{3}m}\right)^{-3}$

c. $\dfrac{\left(\dfrac{n}{m}\right)^{\frac{2}{3}}\left(\dfrac{m}{n}\right)^{-\frac{1}{3}}}{(\sqrt{m+2n})^{-1}}$

Answer the questions.

㉜ Justin evaluated $\sqrt{25^3}$ as shown.

$$\sqrt{25^3}$$
$$= \sqrt{15\,625}$$
$$= 125$$

Can it be evaluated more efficiently? Show your work.

㉝ If there is a cube root of an integer n, then n can be a negative integer. Is this true? Explain.

㉞ Audrey thinks that $(\sqrt[3]{4})^{\frac{3}{2}}$ is not an integer because $\sqrt[3]{4}$ is not an integer. Is she correct? Explain.

㉟ Kyle says, "Even roots can have negative bases." Is this true? Explain.

ISBN: 978-1-77149-222-5

4.3 Algebraic Expressions Involving Exponents

Example

TRY This

Simplify the algebraic expressions.

$(x^{\frac{1}{2}})(x^{\frac{1}{4}})$

$= x^{\frac{1}{2}+\frac{1}{4}}$ ← apply the exponent rule
$a^m \times a^n = a^{m+n}$

$= x^{\frac{3}{4}}$

$(x^3)^{\frac{1}{2}}$

$= x^{3 \times \frac{1}{2}}$ ← apply the exponent rule
$(a^m)^n = a^{mn}$

$= x^{\frac{3}{2}}$

Simplify. Write the answers with positive exponents.

$(y^{-1})(y^{\frac{1}{2}})$ 　　　　　　　　$(m^{-2})^{\frac{3}{4}}$

Simplify the algebraic expressions. Write the answers with positive exponents.

① $(x^{-2})(x^{\frac{1}{3}})(x^{\frac{3}{4}})$

② $(y^{-3})^{\frac{1}{4}}(y^2)$

HINT

It is common practice to express answers with positive exponents.

e.g. $(b^{-1})^2 = b^{-2} = \dfrac{1}{b^2}$

③ $\left(\dfrac{1}{k^2}\right)^3$

④ $\left(\dfrac{x^{-2}}{x^3}\right)^{-\frac{1}{2}}$

⑤ $\dfrac{(m^{-2})(m^{\frac{3}{2}})}{m^{-1}}$

⑥ $\dfrac{(a^4)(a^{-0.75})}{(a^{-2})^3}$

⑦ $\left(\dfrac{b^{-3}}{b^2}\right)^{0.5}\left(\dfrac{b^4}{b^{-1}}\right)^{0.2}$

⑧ $\left(\dfrac{(d^{0.5})(d^{-3})}{d^{-1}}\right)^{\frac{5}{3}}$

⑨ $\left(\dfrac{1}{n^{-3}}\right)^2\left(\dfrac{n^2}{(n^{-0.25})(n^{\frac{1}{4}})}\right)^{-1}$

⑩ $x^{-1}\left(\dfrac{x(x^{-0.2})}{x^{-2}}\right)^2$

Simplify the algebraic expressions.

⑪ $\dfrac{(3x^{-2}y)^2}{x^{-1}y^3}$

⑫ $\dfrac{(5a)^2b^{-1}}{5(a^2b)^{-1}}$

⑬ $\dfrac{(-2m^2)(3m^{-2}n)^2}{(mn)^{-2}}$

⑭ $\dfrac{(x^{-2n})^{0.5}(x^{-3})}{x^{-n}}$

⑮ $\left(\dfrac{i^{0.25}}{i^{n+1}}\right)\left(\dfrac{1}{i^{-n}}\right)^{0.5}$

⑯ $\left(\dfrac{(b^{\frac{1}{3}n})^2(b^{-n})}{b^{0.2n}}\right)^2$

Example

Simplify.

$\dfrac{(\sqrt[10]{a^4})^5}{(\sqrt[3]{a^6})^{-\frac{1}{2}}}$ ← remove the radical sign by changing the expression to exponential form

$= \dfrac{(a^{\frac{4}{10}})^5}{(a^{\frac{6}{3}})^{-\frac{1}{2}}}$ ← simplify using exponent rules

$= \dfrac{a^2}{a^{-1}}$

$= a^3$

Try This

Simplify.

$\left(\dfrac{\sqrt[4]{b^3}}{\sqrt[3]{b^2}}\right)^6$

$\dfrac{(\sqrt{x^4})^{-1}}{(\sqrt[4]{x^2})^{-2}}$

---

⑰ $(\sqrt{x^5})^3(\sqrt{x^3})^2$

⑱ $\dfrac{y^{-1.5}\sqrt{y}}{(\sqrt[4]{y})^{-2}}$

⑲ $\dfrac{(a^{-0.3})(a^{\frac{4}{5}})}{(\sqrt{a})^2}$

⑳ $\left(\dfrac{1}{\sqrt{-x}}\right)^3(-x^{-\frac{1}{5}})$

㉑ $\left(\sqrt{\left(\dfrac{a}{b}\right)^3}\right)\left(\sqrt[4]{\dfrac{4a}{3b}}\right)^3$

㉒ $\dfrac{(m^3)^{0.5}(\sqrt[6]{n^3})^{12}}{\sqrt{mn}}$

ISBN: 978-1-77149-222-5

Simplify and evaluate.

㉓ $(a^{\frac{1}{4}} b^{-\frac{1}{2}})^2$

㉔ $\dfrac{(xy)^3 (x^{-\frac{3}{4}})}{(x^{\frac{1}{2}})^{\frac{1}{2}}}$

It is usually a good idea to simplify an algebraic expression before evaluating it to avoid unnecessary calculations.

evaluate

$a = 9$
$b = 16$

evaluate

$x = 4$
$y = -1$

㉕ $\left(\dfrac{m^4}{m^{-1}}\right)^{0.2}\left(\dfrac{n^2}{n^{-3}}\right)^{0.5}$

㉖ $\dfrac{(\sqrt[8]{d^3})^4}{(\sqrt[5]{e^{10}})^{\frac{1}{2}}}$

㉗ $\sqrt[10]{\dfrac{(p^6 q^8)^{0.5}}{p^{-2}(q^{-3})^2}}$

evaluate

$m = -1$
$n = 8$

evaluate

$d = 9$
$e = -5$

evaluate

$p = 25$
$q = -\dfrac{1}{2}$

Answer the questions.

㉘ What values of x and/or y will make each expression undefined? Show your work.

0^0 is undefined.

a. $(x+y)^2\left(\dfrac{1}{x-y}\right)^2$

b. $(\sqrt{x})^x(\sqrt{x})^y$

c. $(xy)^x(\sqrt[3]{xy})^6$

ISBN: 978-1-77149-222-5

Sketch the graph of each function using the table of values. Then answer the questions.

①

$y = 2x$

x	y
-3	
-2	
-1	
0	
1	
2	
3	

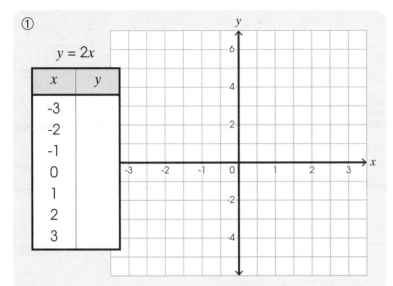

$y = x^2$

x	y
-3	
-2	
-1	
0	
1	
2	
3	

$y = 2^x$

x	y
-3	
-2	
-1	
0	
1	
2	
3	

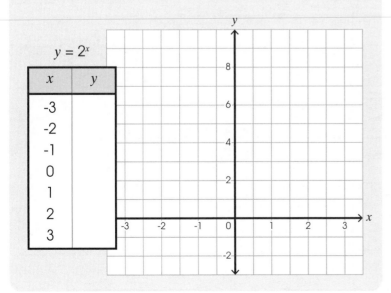

② Identify whether each function is linear, quadratic, or exponential.

$y = 2x$

_____ function

$y = x^2$

$y = 2^x$

③ Find the first differences. Which function has first differences that are

a. all the same?

_____

b. related by addition?

_____

c. related by multiplication?

_____

④ Check the ones that represent exponential functions.

Ⓐ
x	y
-2	-4
-1	-1
0	0
1	-1
2	-4

Ⓑ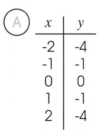

Ⓒ
x	y
-2	4
-1	2
0	1
1	0.5
2	0.25

Ⓓ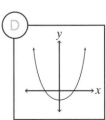

ISBN: 978-1-77149-222-5

Fill in the blanks about exponential functions. Then identify whether each graph represents an exponential growth or decay. Then do the matching and answer the question.

⑤

Exponential Functions

Consider $y = b^x$.

- y can never be 0 for any value of x. Therefore, the function has a _____
  horizontal/vertical
  asymptote at $y = $ _____ .

- When $x = 0$, $y = $ _____ . Therefore, the function has a y-intercept of _____ .

Exponential Growth

- b must be _____ than 1.
  greater/less

- The greater the value of b is, the

  _____ the growth is.
  faster/slower

Exponential Decay

- b must be _____ than 0 but
  greater/less

  _____ than 1.
  greater/less

- The lesser the value of b is, the _____
  faster/slower
  the decay is.

⑥ $f(x) = 4^x$ •

$f(x) = (\frac{1}{5})^x$ •

$f(x) = 0.25^x$ •

$f(x) = 5^x$ •

• Exponential Growth

• Exponential Decay

⑦ Does the exponential function $f(x) = 2^{-x}$ represent an exponential growth or decay? Explain.

_____

Match and label the graphs with the given functions.

$f(x) = 3^x$ $f(x) = (\frac{1}{10})^x$ $f(x) = 2^x$ $f(x) = (\frac{1}{3})^x$ $f(x) = (\frac{1}{2})^x$ $f(x) = 10^x$

⑧
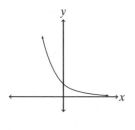
_____

⑨
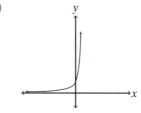
_____

⑩
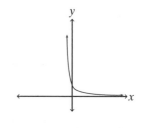
_____

⑪
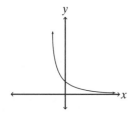
_____

⑫
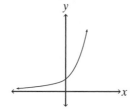
_____

⑬
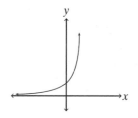
_____

    ISBN: 978-1-77149-222-5

Sketch the graph of each function. Then identify the properties of the function and answer the question.

⑭ $f(x) = 4^x$

$f(x) = (\frac{1}{2})^x$ $f(x) = 2^x$

exponential **growth** / **decay**

domain: _____

range: _____

y-intercept: _____

asymptote: _____

⑮ $f(x) = (\frac{1}{4})^x$

$f(x) = (\frac{1}{2})^x$ $f(x) = 2^x$

exponential **growth** / **decay**

domain: _____

range: _____

y-intercept: _____

asymptote: _____

⑯ $f(x) = 4^{-x}$

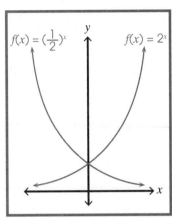

$f(x) = (\frac{1}{2})^x$ $f(x) = 2^x$

exponential **growth** / **decay**

domain: _____

range: _____

y-intercept: _____

asymptote: _____

⑰ Do all exponential functions in the form $f(x) = b^x$ have the same domain, range, y-intercept, and asymptote? Explain.

_____

_____

Answer the questions.

⑱ Laura says, "For $y = (\frac{1}{n})^x$, the function must be an exponential decay for any positive value of n." Is she correct? Explain.

⑲ Annette says, "If $y = (\frac{1}{a})^x$ and $a > 1$, then the function is an exponential decay only for $x < 0$." Is she correct? Explain.

⑳ Consider $y = 2^x$.

a. What will the value of y be as x gets very big?

b. What will the value of y be as x gets very small?

4.5 Transformations of Exponential Functions

Complete the table and sketch the graph of each function. Then fill in the blanks.

①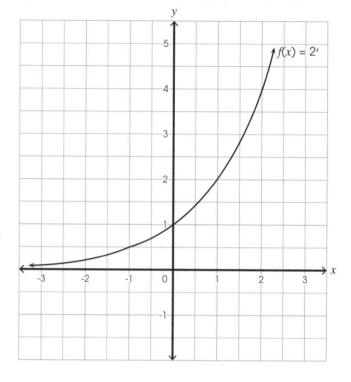

$f(x) = 2^x$	$f(x) = 2^x + 1$	$f(x) = 2^x - 1$
$(-2, \frac{1}{4})$	$(-2, \underline{\quad})$	$(-2, \underline{\quad})$
$(-1, \frac{1}{2})$	$(-1, \underline{\quad})$	$(-1, \underline{\quad})$
$(0, 1)$	$(0, \underline{\quad})$	$(0, \underline{\quad})$
$(1, 2)$	$(1, \underline{\quad})$	$(1, \underline{\quad})$
$(2, 4)$	$(2, \underline{\quad})$	$(2, \underline{\quad})$

Consider $f(x) = b^x + c$. Describe the transformation applied to $f(x) = b^x$ when

a. $c > 0$: a translation of c units _____ .
   up/down

b. $c < 0$: a translation of c units _____ .
   up/down

Describe the transformations the functions have on $f(x) = 3^x$ and identify their y-intercepts. Then match the functions with their graphs.

②

	transformation applied to $f(x) = 3^x$	y-intercept
$f(x) = 3^x + 3$		
$f(x) = 3^x - 1$		
$f(x) = 3^x - 2$		
$f(x) = 3^x + 1$		

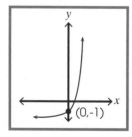
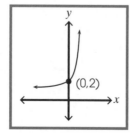
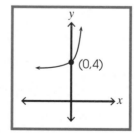
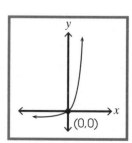

_____   _____   _____   _____

ISBN: 978-1-77149-222-5

Complete the table and sketch the graph of each function. Then answer the questions.

③

$f(x) = 2^x$	$f(x) = 2^{(x-1)}$	$f(x) = 2^{(x+1)}$
$(-2, \frac{1}{4})$	$(-2, \underline{\quad})$	$(-2, \underline{\quad})$
$(-1, \frac{1}{2})$	$(-1, \underline{\quad})$	$(-1, \underline{\quad})$
$(0, 1)$	$(0, \underline{\quad})$	$(0, \underline{\quad})$
$(1, 2)$	$(1, \underline{\quad})$	$(1, \underline{\quad})$
$(2, 4)$	$(2, \underline{\quad})$	$(2, \underline{\quad})$

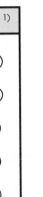

$f(x) = 2^x$

Consider $f(x) = b^{(x-d)} + c$.

a. Describe the transformation applied to $f(x) = b^x$ when

$d > 0$	$d < 0$
a translation of d units to the **left / right**	a translation of d units to the **left / right**

b. State the horizontal asymptotes.

- $f(x) = 2^x$ _____

- $f(x) = 2^{(x-1)}$ _____

- $f(x) = 2^{(x+1)}$ _____

c. Does translating $f(x) = b^x$ horizontally change the horizontal asymptote? Explain.

_____

_____

Describe the transformation each function has on $f(x) = 3^x$. Then match the functions with their graphs.

④ transformation applied to $f(x) = 3^x$

$f(x) = 3^{x+1}$ •

$f(x) = 3^{x-2}$ •

$f(x) = 3^{x-1}$ •

$f(x) = 3^{x+3}$ •

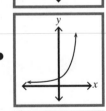

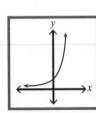

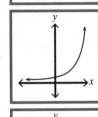

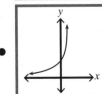

ISBN: 978-1-77149-222-5

Given the graphs of the exponential functions, complete the descriptions of the transformations.

⑤ The graphs of the exponential functions in the form $f(x) = ab^{x-d} + c$ are given. Fill in the blanks to describe the transformations applied to $f(x) = b^x$ when

a. $|a| > 1$:

a vertical ＿＿＿＿＿＿＿＿＿ by
<u>stretch/compression</u>
a factor of $|a|$

b. $0 < |a| < 1$:

a vertical ＿＿＿＿＿＿＿＿＿ by
<u>stretch/compression</u>
a factor of $|a|$

c. $a < 0$:

a ＿＿＿＿＿＿＿＿＿ in the x-axis
<u>reflection/rotation</u>

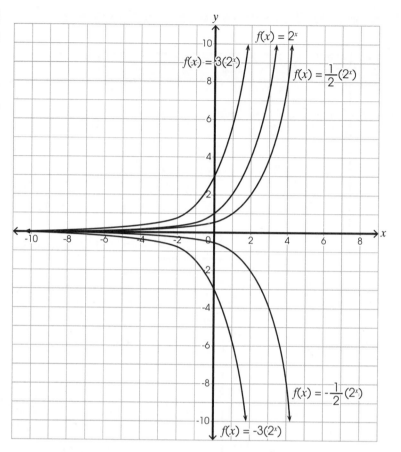

$f(x) = 2^x$

$f(x) = 3(2^x)$

$f(x) = \frac{1}{2}(2^x)$

$f(x) = -\frac{1}{2}(2^x)$

$f(x) = -3(2^x)$

Sketch the graph of each exponential function with the given graph of $f(x) = 4^x$. Describe the transformations. Then answer the question.

⑥ **A** $f(x) = 3(4^x)$ **B** $f(x) = \frac{1}{2}(4^x)$

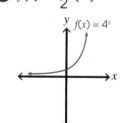

$f(x) = 4^x$

$f(x) = 4^x$

C $f(x) = -3(4^x)$ **D** $f(x) = -\frac{1}{2}(4^x)$

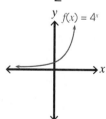

$f(x) = 4^x$

$f(x) = 4^x$

Transformations

A ＿＿＿＿＿＿＿＿＿＿＿＿＿＿＿＿＿

＿＿＿＿＿＿＿＿＿＿＿＿＿＿＿＿＿＿

B ＿＿＿＿＿＿＿＿＿＿＿＿＿＿＿＿＿

＿＿＿＿＿＿＿＿＿＿＿＿＿＿＿＿＿＿

C ＿＿＿＿＿＿＿＿＿＿＿＿＿＿＿＿＿

＿＿＿＿＿＿＿＿＿＿＿＿＿＿＿＿＿＿

D ＿＿＿＿＿＿＿＿＿＿＿＿＿＿＿＿＿

＿＿＿＿＿＿＿＿＿＿＿＿＿＿＿＿＿＿

⑦ Lawrence thinks that $f(x) = 4^x$ and $g(x) = 2^{2x}$ are the same. Is he correct? Explain.

＿＿＿＿＿＿＿＿＿＿＿＿＿＿＿＿＿＿＿＿＿＿＿＿＿＿＿＿＿＿＿＿＿＿＿＿＿＿

＿＿＿＿＿＿＿＿＿＿＿＿＿＿＿＿＿＿＿＿＿＿＿＿＿＿＿＿＿＿＿＿＿＿＿＿＿＿

Given the sketches of the graphs, describe the transformations. Then answer the questions.

⑧

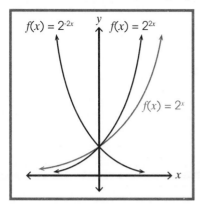

$f(x) = 2^{2x}$

_____

_____

$f(x) = 2^{-2x}$

_____

_____

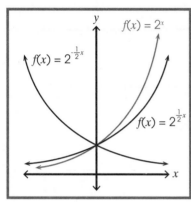

$f(x) = 2^{\frac{1}{2}x}$

_____

_____

$f(x) = 2^{-\frac{1}{2}x}$

_____

_____

⑨ Consider $f(x) = ab^{k(x-d)} + c$. Describe the transformation applied to $f(x) = b^x$ when

a. $|k| > 1$: a horizontal _____ by a factor of $\left|\frac{1}{k}\right|$
   <u>stretch/compression</u>

b. $0 < |k| < 1$: a horizontal _____ by a factor of $\left|\frac{1}{k}\right|$
   <u>stretch/compression</u>

c. $k < 0$: a reflection in the _____
   <u>x-axis/y-axis</u>

Describe the transformations the functions have on $f(x) = 3^x$. Then sketch the graph of each function.

⑩ $f(x) = 3^{2x}$

_____

$f(x) = 3^{-\frac{1}{3}x}$

_____

$f(x) = 3^{-2x}$

_____

$f(x) = 3^{\frac{1}{3}x}$

_____

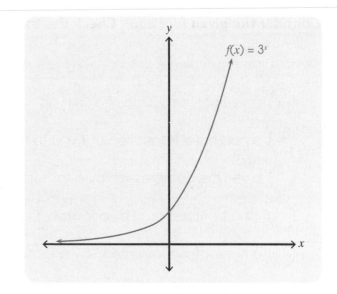

Describe the roles of the parameters c, d, a, and k of exponential functions. Then answer the question.

$$f(x) = ab^{k(x-d)} + c$$

⑪ **Parameter c**

- $c > 0$: _____

  _____

- $c < 0$: _____

  _____

Parameter d

- $d > 0$: _____

  _____

- $d < 0$: _____

  _____

Parameter a

- $|a| > 1$: _____

  _____

- $0 < |a| < 1$: _____

  _____

- $a < 0$: _____

  _____

Parameter k

- $|k| > 1$: _____

  _____

- $0 < |k| < 1$: _____

  _____

- $k < 0$: _____

  _____

⑫ Changing which parameter will change the asymptote of an exponential function? Explain.

_____

_____

Consider the given function. Check the transformations that are applied to $f(x) = 2^x$.

⑬ The given function is $f(x) = (\frac{1}{10})2^{2(x+1)} + 6$.

Ⓐ a vertical translation of 6 units up

Ⓑ a horizontal translation of 1 unit to the right

Ⓒ a vertical compression by a factor of $\frac{1}{10}$

Ⓓ a horizontal stretch by a factor of $\frac{1}{2}$

Ⓔ a horizontal compression by a factor of 2

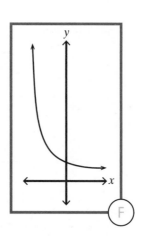

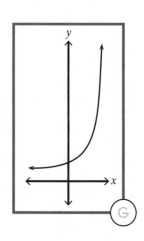

Write an exponential function with the given transformations applied to the given base functions.

⑭ $f(x) = 5^x$

- a translation of 2 units to the left and 3 units up
- a vertical compression by a factor of $\frac{1}{3}$
- a horizontal stretch by a factor of 4

_____

⑮ $f(x) = 3^x$

- a vertical stretch by a factor of 4
- a horizontal compression by a factor of $\frac{1}{2}$
- a translation of 1 unit to the right and 4 units down

_____

⑯ $f(x) = 2^x$

- a translation of 3 units to the left
- a reflection in the x-axis
- a vertical stretch by a factor of 4

_____

⑰ $f(x) = 4^x$

- a translation of 2 units up
- a horizontal compression by a factor of $\frac{1}{3}$
- a reflection in the y-axis

_____

Perform the combined transformations and sketch the graph of each function. Find the characteristics of each function and answer the question.

⑱ $f(x) = \frac{1}{3}(2^{x+1}) + 2$

domain: _____ range: _____

y-intercept: _____ asymptote: _____

⑲ $f(x) = 5(2^{x-1}) - 4$

domain: _____ range: _____

y-intercept: _____ asymptote: _____

⑳ Consider two transformations applied to $f(x) = \sqrt{x}$: a reflection in the x-axis and a translation of 2 units up. Does the order of the transformations affect the result of the transformed function? If it does, describe the correct order.

_____

_____

ISBN: 978-1-77149-222-5

Solve for each unknown.

① $y = 150(2^5)$

② $k = 20(1.05)^3$

③ $p = 96(3.01)^{2.5}$

④ $13.44 = i(0.4^3)$

⑤ $25 = a(5^4)$

⑥ $12.15 = h(3^4)$

Complete the table. Then write the exponential equations and solve for the unknowns.

⑦

Exponential Functions $f(x) = ab^x$

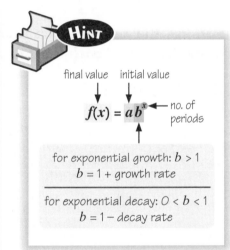

	$g = 2(1.5)^4$	$84 = 0.5(3)^t$	$16 = n(\frac{4}{5})^2$
exponential growth/decay			
initial value			
growth/decay rate			
number of periods			
final value			

HINT

final value   initial value

$f(x) = a\,b^x$ ← no. of periods

for exponential growth: $b > 1$
$b = 1 + $ growth rate
_____
for exponential decay: $0 < b < 1$
$b = 1 - $ decay rate

⑧ initial value: 5
growth rate: 20%
no. of periods: 3
final value: y

equation

$y = $ _____

⑨ initial value: m
growth rate: 100%
no. of periods: 5
final value: 96

equation

$m = $ _____

⑩ initial value: 4
decay rate: 25%
no. of periods: 2
final value: d

equation

$d = $ _____

ISBN: 978-1-77149-222-5

Study each scenario. Identify the characteristics of each scenario. Then write an exponential equation that models the scenario.

⑪ In an experiment, there are 20 of a species of bacterium. It doubles its number every hour. What will its population be after 3 hours?

- exponential _____
  growth / decay

- initial value: _____

- rate: _____

- no. of periods: _____

  equation

⑫ Cecilia bought a boat 5 years ago at $90 000. The boat depreciates by 25% each year. What is the current value of the boat?

- exponential _____

- initial value: _____

- rate: _____

- no. of periods: _____

  equation

⑬ Due to a recently implemented hunting law, it is predicted that the deer population will increase by 6% each year. If there were 210 deer when the law was first put into effect, how many deer will there be after 78 months?

- exponential _____

- initial value: _____

- rate: _____

- no. of periods: _____

  equation

⑭ A 300 g sample of tungsten-176 has a half-life of 2.5 hours, meaning that the amount of it left will be reduced by half every 2.5 hours. How long will it take for this sample to decay to 75 g?

- exponential _____

- initial value: _____

- rate: _____

- final value: _____

  equation

⑮ A group of cells grows by 25% every 2 hours. If the initial population was 180, what will the population be after 5 hours?

- exponential _____

- initial value: _____

- rate: _____

- no. of periods: _____

  equation

⑯ The temperature of a cup of hot water drops at the same rate from 100°C every minute after being left at room temperature. After 8 min, it is predicted that its temperature will be 42°C. What is the rate?

- exponential _____

- initial value: _____

- no. of periods: _____

- final value: _____

  equation

Answer the questions.

⑰ Each year, the number of people P who vote in a small town's municipal election is represented by $P(n) = 1425(1.04)^n$, where n is the number of elections for $n \geq 1$.

a. How many people voted initially?

b. What is the growth rate? What does the growth rate imply?

c. How many people will vote in the 5th election?

⑱ The temperature T of a freezie in Celsius depends on the time t in minutes that the freezie has been in the freezer for. It is represented by the equation $T(t) = 25(0.94)^t - 4$.

a. What is the temperature of the freezie at room temperature?

b. What will the temperature of the freezie be after 15 minutes?

c. What will the lowest temperature of the freezie be?

⑲ The goose population of a rural area in hundreds is given as $P(t) = 115\left(\frac{5}{8}\right)^t$, where t is the number of weeks after fall begins.

a. Is this an exponential growth or decay?

b. What will the goose population be 5 weeks after fall begins?

⑳ The value of an investment in dollars is modelled by $I(t) = 2500(1.08)^{2t}$, where t is the number of years of the investment.

a. What are the initial investment and the interest rate?

b. What will the value of the investment be after 3 years?

ISBN: 978-1-77149-222-5

Solve the problems. Show your work.

㉑ A petri dish has two species of yeast. Yeast A has an initial population of 200 and doubles every day while Yeast B has an initial population of 50 and triples every day.

a. Write an exponential equation that models the growth of each species of yeast.

_____

b. What will the population of each species of yeast be after 3 days?

_____

c. Will the population of Yeast B be greater than that of Yeast A within 5 days?

_____

㉒ An investor invested $15 000 at 6% per year compounded semi-annually. What will the value of the investment be after 10 years?

_____

㉓ The half-life of silicon-33 is 6 seconds. If there was 31.25 g left in the sample after 24 seconds, what was the initial amount in the sample?

_____

㉔ A car was bought at $35 000. It depreciates at a rate of 20% each year. What will the value of the car be after 5 years?

_____

5 Trigonometry

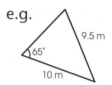
Identity: a statement of two expressions that are equivalent for all possible values of the variables except for the stated restrictions

Bearing: a clockwise angle between the magnetic North and the object

Ambiguous case of the sine law: occurs when more than one triangle can exist with given measures of two sides and one angle opposite one of the sides

e.g.

two triangles with measures of 9.5 m, 10 m, and 65°

9.5 m 65° 10 m 9.5 m 10 m 65°

5.1 Reciprocal Trigonometric Ratios

Evaluate the trigonometric ratios and their reciprocals. Round your answers to 2 decimal places.

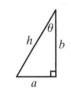

HINT

Reciprocals of Trigonometric Ratios

① **Trigonometric Ratios** | **Corresponding Reciprocals**

$\sin 18° \doteq$ _____ | $\csc 18° = \dfrac{1}{\sin 18°} \doteq$ _____

$\cos 18° \doteq$ _____ | $\sec 18° = \dfrac{1}{\cos 18°} \doteq$ _____

$\tan 18° \doteq$ _____ | $\cot 18° = \dfrac{1}{\tan 18°} \doteq$ _____

$$\csc \theta = \frac{1}{\sin \theta} = \frac{h}{a}$$

$$\sec \theta = \frac{1}{\cos \theta} = \frac{h}{b}$$

$$\cot \theta = \frac{1}{\tan \theta} = \frac{b}{a}$$

Calculators have no buttons for evaluating cosecant (csc), secant (sec), or cotangent (cot). To evaluate them, divide 1 by their corresponding trigonometric ratios.

$$\text{e.g. } \csc 30° = \frac{1}{\sin 30°} = 2$$

② $\cos 76° \doteq$ _____

$\sec 76° \doteq$ _____

③ $\tan 8° \doteq$ _____

$\cot 8° \doteq$ _____

④ $\sin 52° \doteq$ _____

$\csc 52° \doteq$ _____

⑤ $\cos 29° \doteq$ _____

$\sec 29° \doteq$ _____

⑥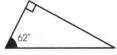

62°

cosecant

$\csc 62° \doteq$ _____

cotangent

⑦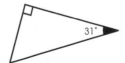

31°

secant

cosecant

⑧

43°

cotangent

secant

State the reciprocal of each trigonometric ratio and evaluate it.

⑨ **cos 28°**

$\sec 28° \doteq$ _____

⑩ **sin 63°**

⑪ **tan 47°**

⑫ **sin 61°**

⑬ **tan 72°**

⑭ **cos 15°**

⑮ **cos 7°**

⑯ **tan 22°**

⑰ **sin 86°**

Find the measures of the angles.

⑱ $\csc \theta = \dfrac{11}{4}$

$\sin \theta =$ _____

$\theta \doteq$ _____

⑲ $\cot \beta = \dfrac{4}{9}$

⑳ $\sec \alpha = \dfrac{7}{5}$

㉑ $\cot \theta = \dfrac{2}{7}$

㉒ $\sec \alpha = \dfrac{8}{5}$

㉓ $\csc \beta = \dfrac{5}{3}$

Find the unknown of each triangle in two different ways.

㉔   **Way 1** **Way 2**

8 cm, 55°, x

㉕ **Way 1** **Way 2**

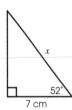

x, 52°, 7 cm

㉖ 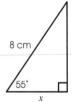 **Way 1** **Way 2**

60°, 1.5 cm, x

㉗ **Way 1** **Way 2**

x, 43°, 5 cm

ISBN: 978-1-77149-222-5

Circle T for true and F for false.

㉘ The cosecant and secant must always be greater than or equal to 1.   T / F

㉙ The cotangent cannot be 1.   T / F

㉚ If the tangent ratio is 0, then its cotangent is undefined.   T / F

㉛ $\sin^{-1} \theta$ and csc θ are the same.   T / F

㉜ The measure of an angle θ can be found if the value of cot θ is given.   T / F

Draw a diagram for each problem and solve it using reciprocal trigonometric ratios. Show your work.

㉝ A 30-m ladder is leaning against a wall, making a 65° angle with the ground. Determine how far away the base of the ladder is from the wall.

㉞ The top of a 1.3-m-tall tent is tethered to the ground by a cable. The cable makes a 37° angle with the ground. How long is the cable?

㉟ From the ground, Jason sees his two friends waving at him from a building. He sees Toby at an angle of elevation of 30° and he sees Kate at 65°. Jason is 20 m away from the base of the building. How far apart are his friends?

Find the missing lengths. Then find the exact values of the trigonometric ratios of the special angles.

 HINT

Special Angles

The angles 30°, 45°, and 60° give exact values for the primary trigonometric ratios.

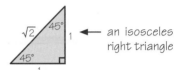

← an isosceles right triangle

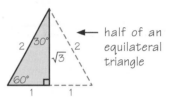

← half of an equilateral triangle

①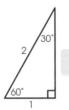

sin 45° = ☐

cos 45° = ☐

tan 45° = ☐

②

sin 30° = ☐   sin 60° = ☐

cos 30° = ☐   cos 60° = ☐

tan 30° = ☐   tan 60° = ☐

Find the exact values of the trigonometric ratios. Then answer the questions.

③

sin 45° = _____

cos 45° = _____

tan 45° = _____

Are the triangles in Questions 1 and 3 similar? Do they have the same trigonometric ratios?

_____

④

sin 30° = _____   sin 60° = _____

cos 30° = _____   cos 60° = _____

tan 30° = _____   tan 60° = _____

Are the triangles in Questions 2 and 4 similar? Do they have the same trigonometric ratios?

_____

⑤ Make an inference about the angles of a triangle and the exact values of its trigonometric ratios.

_____

_____

Find the exact values of the trigonometric ratios.

⑥ cos 45° = _____

sin 60° = _____

cos 30° = _____

sin 45° = _____

tan 45° = _____

⑦

sin θ = _____

cos α = _____

tan θ = _____

⑧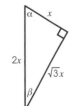

sin β = _____

cos α = _____

tan α = _____

Example

Find the exact value of the expression.

$$\sin 60° \times \tan 30° - \cos 60°$$

$$= \frac{\sqrt{3}}{2} \times \frac{1}{\sqrt{3}} - \frac{1}{2} \quad \longleftarrow \quad \text{exact values of the trigonometric ratios}$$

$$= \frac{1}{2} - \frac{1}{2}$$

$$= 0$$

$$\sin 30° \times \cos 60°$$

Find the exact values of the trigonometric expressions.

⑨ $\sin 45° + \cos 45°$

⑩ $\dfrac{\cos 30°}{\tan 30°} + \tan 45°$

HINT

$\sin^2 \theta = \sin \theta \times \sin \theta$

e.g. $\sin^2 30°$
$\quad = \sin 30° \times \sin 30°$

⑪ $\tan 45° + \sin 45° \times \cos 45°$

⑫ $\sin^2 45° + \sin 30°$

⑬ $\cos^2 30° + \dfrac{1}{\sin^2 60°}$

Determine whether or not the expressions in each pair are equivalent.

⑭ $\sin 45° \cos 45°$ $\sin 30° \tan 45°$

⑮ $\tan 30° \tan 60°$ $\sin 60° \cos 30°$

_____
equivalent/not equivalent

_____

⑯ $(\tan^2 60°)(\cos 60°)$ $\sin 60° \tan 30°$

⑰ $\dfrac{\sin 30°}{\sin 60° \tan 30°}$ $\tan^2 30°$

_____

_____

Find the exact values of the unknowns with the given trigonometric ratios.

 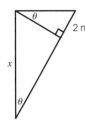

Given: $\sin\theta = \dfrac{1}{2}$

Solve for x.

 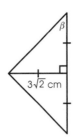 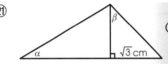

Given: $\cos\beta = \dfrac{\sqrt{2}}{2}$

Find the perimeter.

 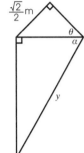

Given: $\sin\theta = \dfrac{\sqrt{2}}{2}$

$\tan\alpha = \sqrt{3}$

Solve for y.

Given: $\tan\beta = 1$

$\tan\alpha = \dfrac{\sqrt{3}}{3}$

Find the area.

Solve the problems. Show your work. Express your answers in exact values.

㉒ A forest ranger spots a bear from the top of a tower. The tower is 25 m tall and the angle of depression to the bear is 60°. How far away is the bear from the base of the tower?

_____

㉓ A lightning rod is installed to a building. Standing 10 m away from the bottom of the building, the angle of elevation to the top of the building is 30°.

a. How tall is the building?

_____

b. The angle of elevation to the top of the lightning rod is 45°. What is the height of the rod?

_____

5.3 Angles in the Cartesian Plane

Find the trigonometric ratios of θ (for θ = 45°) that the terminal arm makes in each quadrant using a calculator. Fill in the boxes with "=" or "≠". Then check the correct set of relationships.

①

Quadrant 1

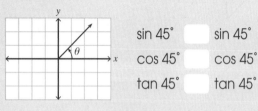

sin 45° ☐ sin 45°

cos 45° ☐ cos 45°

tan 45° ☐ tan 45°

sin θ = sin θ
cos θ = cos θ
tan θ = tan θ

Ⓐ

sin θ = -sin θ
cos θ = -cos θ
tan θ = -tan θ

Ⓑ

 **HINT**

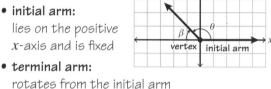

- **initial arm:**
  lies on the positive
  x-axis and is fixed
- **terminal arm:**
  rotates from the initial arm
- **principal angle (θ):**
  the angle measured counterclockwise from the
  initial arm to the terminal arm
- **related acute angle (β):**
  the acute angle between the terminal arm of
  an angle and the *x*-axis

Quadrant 2

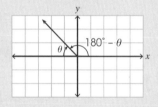

sin (180° – 45°) ☐ sin 45°

cos (180° – 45°) ☐ -cos 45°

tan (180° – 45°) ☐ -tan 45°

sin (180° – θ) = -sin θ
cos (180° – θ) = cos θ
tan (180° – θ) = tan θ

Ⓐ

sin (180° – θ) = sin θ
cos (180° – θ) = -cos θ
tan (180° – θ) = -tan θ

Ⓑ

Quadrant 3

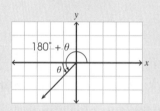

sin (180° + 45°) ☐ -sin 45°

cos (180° + 45°) ☐ -cos 45°

tan (180° + 45°) ☐ tan 45°

sin (180° + θ) = -sin θ
cos (180° + θ) = -cos θ
tan (180° + θ) = tan θ

Ⓐ

sin (180° + θ) = sin θ
cos (180° + θ) = cos θ
tan (180° + θ) = -tan θ

Ⓑ

Quadrant 4

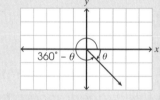

sin (360° – 45°) ☐ -sin 45°

cos (360° – 45°) ☐ cos 45°

tan (360° – 45°) ☐ -tan 45°

sin (360° – θ) = sin θ
cos (360° – θ) = cos θ
tan (360° – θ) = tan θ

Ⓐ

sin (360° – θ) = -sin θ
cos (360° – θ) = cos θ
tan (360° – θ) = -tan θ

Ⓑ

② In which quadrants does each trigonometric ratio always stay positive?

sine

cosine

tangent

ISBN: 978-1-77149-222-5

Check the trigonometric ratios that are equivalent to the ones given.

 HINT

Refer to p. 102 to complete this activity.

e.g. $\sin(180° - \theta) = \sin\theta$
So, $\sin 135° = \sin 45°$.

③ **sin 38°**
- Ⓐ -sin 142°
- Ⓑ sin 142°
- Ⓒ -sin 322°

④ **tan 110°**
- Ⓐ tan 290°
- Ⓑ tan 70°
- Ⓒ -tan 250°

⑤ **cos 85°**
- Ⓐ -cos 265°
- Ⓑ cos 275°
- Ⓒ cos 95°

⑥ **cos 150°**
- Ⓐ cos 210°
- Ⓑ -cos 30°
- Ⓒ cos 30°

⑦ **sin 210°**
- Ⓐ sin (-30°)
- Ⓑ sin 30°
- Ⓒ -sin 150°

⑧ **tan 190°**
- Ⓐ -tan 170°
- Ⓑ tan (-10°)
- Ⓒ tan 170°

⑨ **sin 25°**
- Ⓐ -sin 205°
- Ⓑ -sin 155°
- Ⓒ sin 335°

Example

The point (-2,3) lies on the terminal arm of angle θ in standard position. Find the primary trigonometric ratios for θ.

HINT
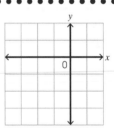

$\sin\theta = \dfrac{y}{r}$

$\cos\theta = \dfrac{x}{r}$

$\tan\theta = \dfrac{y}{x}$

Solution:

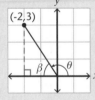

$r = \sqrt{(-2)^2 + 3^2} \doteq 3.61$

$\sin\beta = \dfrac{3}{3.61}$ $\cos\beta = \dfrac{2}{3.61}$ $\tan\beta = \dfrac{3}{2}$

According to the relationship among the trigonometric ratios of θ and β in quadrant 2, the sine ratio is positive while the cosine and tangent ratios are negative.

$\sin\theta = \dfrac{3}{3.61}$ $\cos\theta = -\dfrac{2}{3.61}$ $\tan\theta = -\dfrac{3}{2}$

TRY THIS

(-3,-4)

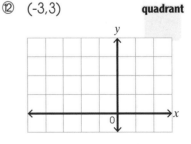

For each given point that lies on the terminal arm of angle θ in standard position, make a sketch of angle θ and find its trigonometric ratios.

⑩ (-5,3)   quadrant

⑪ (4,-2)   quadrant

⑫ (-3,3)   quadrant

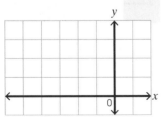
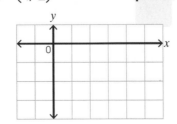

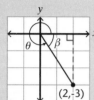

Example

The point (2,-3) lies on the terminal arm of angle θ. Find the values of θ in both a counterclockwise rotation and a clockwise rotation.

Solution:

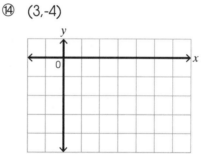

$r = \sqrt{2^2 + (-3)^2} \doteq 3.61$

$\sin \beta = \dfrac{3}{3.61}$

$\beta \doteq 56°$

$\theta = 360° - 56° = 304°$ ← counterclockwise

$\theta = -56°$ ← clockwise

Try This

(-5,-3)

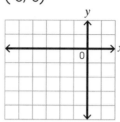

(-4,3)

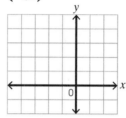

The given points lie on the terminal arm of angle θ. Find the values of θ in both a counterclockwise rotation and a clockwise rotation.

⑬ (-2,-3)

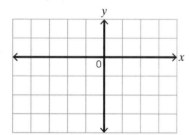

⑭ (3,-4)

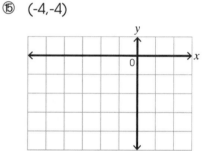

⑮ (-4,-4)

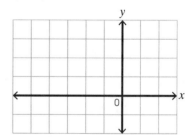

⑯ (5,-2)

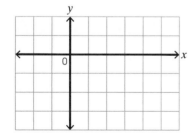

⑰ (-4,-1)

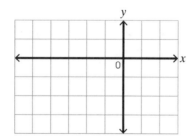

⑱ (-3,2)

ISBN: 978-1-77149-222-5

Example

Determine the value of θ with the given trigonometric ratio, for $0° \le \theta \le 360°$.

$$\sin \theta = 0.5446$$

Solution:

The sine ratio is positive. This implies that the terminal arm can be in quadrant 1 or 2.

The value of θ in

- quadrant 1:

  $\theta = \sin^{-1} 0.5446$

  $\theta \doteq 33°$

- quadrant 2:

  $\theta = 180° - 33°$

  $\theta = 147°$

θ can be either $33°$ or $147°$.

HINT

CAST Rule

This is a way to remember which trigonometric ratios are positive in each quadrant.

S	A
only **s**ine is positive	**a**ll ratios are positive
T	C
only **t**angent is positive	only **c**osine is positive

TRY THIS

$$\cos \theta = 0.866$$

Find all values of θ if $0° \le \theta \le 360°$. Then answer the question.

⑲ $\sin \theta = 0.8192$

⑳ $\tan \theta = 2.4751$

㉑ $\cos \theta = 0.766$

㉒ $\cos \theta = -0.9135$

㉓ $\csc \theta = 1.1547$

㉔ $\sin \theta = -0.5736$

㉕ $\tan \theta = -0.4663$

㉖ $\cot \theta = -0.0875$

㉗ $\sec \theta = 1.0154$

㉘ In finding the values of θ, why is it necessary to determine in which quadrants the terminal arms lie first?

_____

_____

5.4   Trigonometric Identities

Simplify each expression.

① $\sin \theta \sec \theta$

② $\cot \theta \sin \theta \sec \theta$

③ $\dfrac{1}{\csc^2 \theta} - \tan^2 \theta \cos^2 \theta$

④ $\dfrac{\tan \theta \cos \theta}{\csc \theta \sin \theta}$

⑤ $\dfrac{\sin^2 \theta}{\cos^2 \theta} \cdot \cot \theta$

⑥ $(2 \cos \theta - \dfrac{1}{\sec \theta})(\dfrac{\tan \theta}{\sin \theta})$

Example

Prove that sec θ sin θ cos θ = sin θ for all angles θ where $0° \leq \theta \leq 360°$ except 90° and 270°. Prove in terms of x, y, and r.

Solution:

$\text{LS} = \sec \theta \sin \theta \cos \theta \qquad \text{RS} = \sin \theta$

$\quad = \dfrac{r}{x} \cdot \dfrac{y}{r} \cdot \dfrac{x}{r} \qquad\qquad\quad = \dfrac{y}{r}$

$\quad = \dfrac{y}{r} \qquad\qquad\qquad\qquad\quad = \text{LS}$

$\therefore$ sec θ sin θ cos θ = sin θ for all angles θ where $0° \leq \theta \leq 360°$ except 90° and 270°.

Try This

Prove that sec θ = csc θ tan θ for all angles θ where $0° \leq \theta \leq 360°$ except 0°, 90°, 180°, 270°, and 360°. Prove in terms of x, y, and r.

Prove each identity in terms of x, y, and r.

⑦
$\sin^2 \theta + \cos^2 \theta = 1$

for all angles θ where $0° \leq \theta \leq 360°$

⑧ $1 + \tan^2 \theta = \sec^2 \theta$

for all angles θ where $0° \leq \theta \leq 360°$ except 90° and 270°

⑨ $1 + \cot^2 \theta = \csc^2 \theta$

for all angles θ where $0° \leq \theta \leq 360°$ except 0°, 180°, and 360°

ISBN: 978-1-77149-222-5

Example

Prove the identity. State the restrictions on θ.

$$\tan \theta \cos \theta \csc \theta = 1$$

Solution:

$LS = \tan \theta \cos \theta \csc \theta$

$= \dfrac{\sin \theta}{\cos \theta} \cdot \cos \theta \cdot \dfrac{1}{\sin \theta}$

$= 1$

$= RS$

When $\cos \theta = 0$, $\tan \theta$ is undefined. This occurs when $\theta = 90°$ or $270°$.

When $\sin \theta = 0$, $\csc \theta$ is undefined. This occurs when $\theta = 0°$, $180°$, or $360°$.

$\therefore \tan \theta \cos \theta \csc \theta = 1$ for all angles θ where $0° \leq \theta \leq 360°$ except $0°$, $90°$, $180°$, $270°$, and $360°$.

HINT

Some Trigonometric Identities

Reciprocal Identities

$$\csc \theta = \dfrac{1}{\sin \theta} \qquad \sec \theta = \dfrac{1}{\cos \theta} \qquad \cot \theta = \dfrac{1}{\tan \theta}$$

Quotient Identities

$$\tan \theta = \dfrac{\sin \theta}{\cos \theta} \qquad \cot \theta = \dfrac{\cos \theta}{\sin \theta}$$

Pythagorean Identities

$$\sin^2 \theta + \cos^2 \theta = 1 \qquad 1 + \tan^2 \theta = \sec^2 \theta \qquad 1 + \cot^2 \theta = \csc^2 \theta$$

Try This

Prove the identity. State the restrictions on θ.

$$\csc \theta = \sec \theta \cot \theta$$

Prove each identity. State the restrictions on θ.

⑩ $\sin \theta (1 + \csc \theta) = \sin \theta + 1$

⑪ $\csc^2 \theta = \cot^2 \theta (1 + \tan^2 \theta)$

⑫ $\cot^2 \theta + 1 = \csc^2 \theta$

⑬ $\dfrac{\sec \theta}{\sin \theta} = \cot \theta + \tan \theta$

Example

Prove that $\cos^2 \beta \csc^2 \beta = \csc^2 \beta - 1$.

State any restrictions on the variables.

Solution:

$LS = \cos^2 \beta \csc^2 \beta$

$= \cos^2 \beta \cdot \dfrac{1}{\sin^2 \beta}$

$= \dfrac{\cos^2 \beta}{\sin^2 \beta}$

$RS = \csc^2 \beta - 1$

$= \dfrac{1}{\sin^2 \beta} - \dfrac{\sin^2 \beta}{\sin^2 \beta}$

$= \dfrac{1 - \sin^2 \beta}{\sin^2 \beta}$

$= \dfrac{\cos^2 \beta}{\sin^2 \beta}$

$= LS$

When $\sin \beta = 0$, $\csc^2 \beta$ is undefined.

$\therefore \cos^2 \beta \csc^2 \beta = \csc^2 \beta - 1$ where $\sin \beta \neq 0$.

Try This

Prove that $\dfrac{\sin \alpha \cot \alpha \cos \alpha}{\cos \alpha} = \cos \alpha$.

State any restrictions on the variables.

Prove the identities. State any restrictions on the variables.

⑭ $\dfrac{1 - \sin \theta}{\cos \theta} = \dfrac{\cos \theta}{1 + \sin \theta}$

⑮ $1 - \cos \alpha = \dfrac{\sin^2 \alpha}{1 + \cos \alpha}$

⑯ $\sin^4 \alpha - \cos^4 \alpha = 1 - 2 \cos^2 \alpha$

⑰ $\dfrac{\cos \beta}{1 - \sin \beta} + \dfrac{\cos \beta}{1 + \sin \beta} = \dfrac{2}{\cos \beta}$

 ISBN: 978-1-77149-222-5

Determine whether triangles exist with the given measurements. For those that exist, find the number of possible cases and sketch them.

①
$\angle A = 23°$
$a = 2.5$ cm
$b = 4$ cm

_____ triangle(s)

②
$\angle A = 30°$
$a = 1.8$ cm
$b = 3.6$ cm

_____ triangle(s)

③
$\angle A = 121°$
$a = 6.2$ mm
$b = 8.1$ mm

_____ triangle(s)

④
$\angle A = 21°$
$a = 5.4$ mm
$b = 7.2$ mm

_____ triangle(s)

HINT

Ambiguous Case

When two side lengths and an angle opposite one of the sides are known in a triangle, more than one triangle can exist.

Consider that the measures of $\angle A$, a, and b are known.

$$h = b \sin A$$
— height of triangle

$\angle A$ is acute.

• **Case 1:** $a < h$
no triangles exist

• **Case 2:** $a = h$
one right triangle exists

• **Case 3:** $a = b$ or $a > b$
one triangle exists

• **Case 4:** $h < a < b$
two triangles exist

$\angle A$ is obtuse.

• **Case 1:** $a = b$ or $a < b$
no triangles exist

• **Case 2:** $a > b$
one triangle exists

Find the unknowns using the sine law.

⑤

2.8 cm
3.6 cm
82°
θ

⑥

51°
1.6 m
47°
x

⑦

70° 75°
4.53 m
x

⑧

5.25 cm
120°
2.85 cm
θ

⑨

θ
0.98 m
53°
1.01 m

⑩
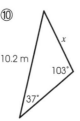
x
10.2 m
103°
37°

HINT

Sine Law

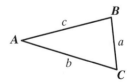

$$\frac{a}{\sin A} = \frac{b}{\sin B} = \frac{c}{\sin C}$$

or

$$\frac{\sin A}{a} = \frac{\sin B}{b} = \frac{\sin C}{c}$$

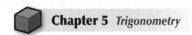

For each given set of measurements, sketch all the possible triangles. Then find the measures of ∠B.

⑪ ∠A = 62°, a = 3.1 m, b = 2.7 m

⑫ ∠A = 134°, a = 5.1 cm, b = 3.6 cm

⑬ ∠A = 32°, a = 3.5 cm, b = 4.1 cm

⑭ ∠A = 81°, a = 0.94 m, b = 0.95 m

Find the unknowns using the cosine law.

⑮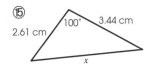

⑯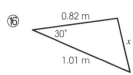

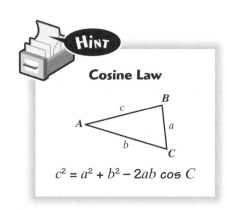

Cosine Law

$c^2 = a^2 + b^2 - 2ab \cos C$

⑰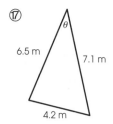

⑱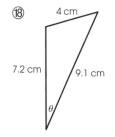

⑲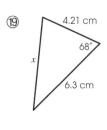

Sketch all the possible triangles for each given set of measurements. Determine the unknowns with the sine law or the cosine law.

⑳ △ *ABC*
$\angle A = 47°$ $b = 60$ cm $c = 20$ cm

Solve for *a*.

㉑ △ *DEF*
$\angle D = 25°$ $\angle E = 75°$ $d = 2$ m

Solve for *e*.

㉒ △ *XYZ*
$\angle X = 141°$ $x = 1.1$ m $y = 0.82$ m

Solve for $\angle Y$.

㉓ △ *PQR*
$\angle P = 45°$ $p = 4.5$ m $q = 6.2$ m

Solve for $\angle Q$.

㉔ △ *LMN*
$\angle M = 52°$ $m = 0.7$ cm $n = 0.8$ cm

Solve for $\angle N$.

㉕ △ *UVW*
$\angle U = 84°$ $v = 28$ m $w = 37$ m

Solve for *u*.

Answer the questions.

㉖ In △*IJK*, $i = 3$ cm and $j = 4$ cm. However, no triangles exist. What can the measure of $\angle I$ be if $\angle I$ is acute?

㉗ In △*DEF*, $\angle D = 31°$ and $e = 1.1$ m. What measure of d will allow two triangles to exist?

Make a sketch to illustrate each scenario. Solve the problem. Show your work.

㉘ Trains A and B left the same station. Train A travelled at a bearing of 317° from the station for 26 km. Train B travelled at a bearing of 225° and was at its destination which was 44.5 km from Train A. How far did Train B travel?

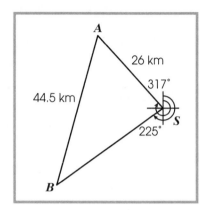

_____

㉙ Tower A is 10 km due west of Tower B. A fire is observed 2.5 km from Tower A at a bearing of 20°. The fire is 9.44 km away from Tower B. What is the bearing of the fire from Tower B?

_____

㉚ Josie and Kenneth are 1.5 km apart on the ground. Josie spots a hot-air balloon at an angle of elevation of 56°. Kenneth spots it too and he is 1.4 km away from it. What is Kenneth's angle of elevation to the balloon? Find all the possible solutions.

_____

㉛ Two ships were 18 km apart and Ship B was at a bearing of 245° from Ship A. Ship A sailed 24 km at a bearing of 39° to reach a dock. Ship B also reached the same dock. How far did Ship B sail?

_____

ISBN: 978-1-77149-222-5

Example

Find the length of BC.

Solution:

To find the length of BC, the length of CD needs to be found first.

$c = \sqrt{7.1^2 - 5^2}$ ← Pythagorean theorem

$c \doteq 5.04$

$d^2 = b^2 + c^2 - 2bc \cos D$ ← cosine law

$d^2 = 5.3^2 + 5.04^2 - 2(5.3)(5.04) \cos 108°$

$d^2 \doteq 70.00$

$d \doteq 8.37$

The length of BC is 8.37 m.

Try This

Find the measure of $\angle YWZ$.

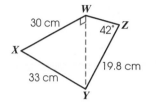

Find the missing measures in the diagrams.

① **measure of $\angle MNO$**

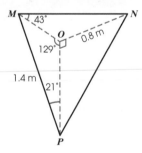

② **length of PR**

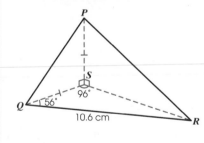

③ **measure of $\angle EDF$**

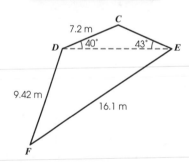

Label the diagram that illustrates each scenario with the correct measurements. Solve the problem. Show your work.

④ Natalie and Rachel are standing 65 m apart and they see the top of a flagpole at angles of elevation of 24° and 36° respectively. The flagpole is 18 m tall. What is the measure of the angle between Natalie, the base of the flagpole, and Rachel?

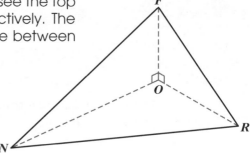

⑤ James parked his car and walked 50 m due east, turned 160° left, and walked 40 m to a building. He then went up 30 m to reach his office. How far is his office from his car?

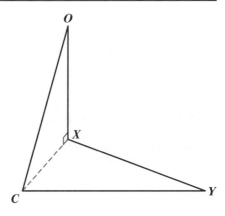

⑥ Two ponds can be seen from a tower. The angles of depression to Pond A and Pond B are 12° and 19° respectively, from a height of 22 m on the tower. The measure of the angle between the lines of sight to the ponds is 78°. Find the distance between the ponds.

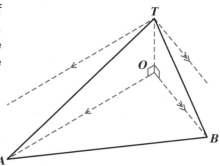

Sketch to illustrate each scenario. Solve the problem. Show your work.

⑦ Agnes and Brian are looking at an art piece hung on a wall at an angle of elevation of 39°
and 55° respectively. The art piece is hung 3.2 m from the ground. The angle between Agnes,
the base of the wall, and Brian is 76°. How far apart are Agnes and Brian?

⑧ Eric and Tony spotted a giraffe across a river. Eric and the giraffe had bearings of 75° and
328° from Tony respectively. Tony saw the top of the giraffe at an angle of elevation of 11.7°.
If Eric and Tony were 35 m apart and the giraffe was 50 m away from Eric, how tall was the
giraffe?

⑨ At an altitude of 315 m, a helicopter located two boats at angles of depression of 29° and
36° of Boat A and Boat B respectively. The helicopter and Boat B had bearings of 32° and
116° from Boat A respectively, and the helicopter had a bearing of 322° from Boat B. How
far apart were the boats?

6 Sinusoidal Functions

Periodic function:

a function that repeats its values in regular intervals

e.g.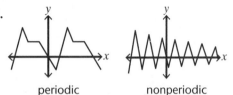

periodic   nonperiodic

Sinusoidal function:

a periodic function that resembles a smooth curve that is symmetrical

e.g.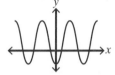

periodic and sinusoidal   periodic but not sinusoidal

6.1 Properties of Periodic Functions

Identify and check the graphs that are periodic. Then answer the question.

①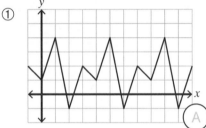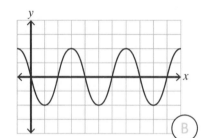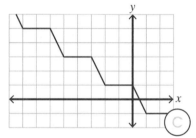

A   B   C

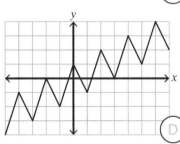 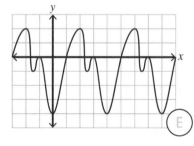 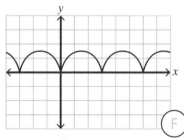

D   E   F

② Which table represents the values of a periodic function? Explain your choice. Then graph the function.

A

x	-5	-4	-3	-2	-1	0	1	2	3	4
y	2	0	-2	4	2	0	-2	4	2	0

B

x	-5	-4	-3	-2	-1	0	1	2	3	4
y	4	3	2	1	0	-1	-2	-3	-4	-5

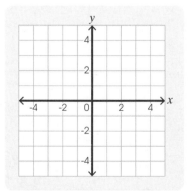

_____

_____

_____

Determine the key features of the periodic graph.

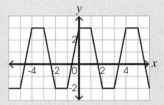

Solution:

period: 4 ◄── The graph repeats its cycle every 4 units on the *x*-axis.

peak: 3 ◄── the maximum *y*-value

trough: -2 ◄── the minimum *y*-value

range: $\{y \in \mathbb{R} \mid 3 \leq y \leq -2\}$ ◄── all possible values of *y*

equation of the axis: $y = \dfrac{3 + (-2)}{2}$

$$y = 0.5$$

amplitude: $\dfrac{3 - (-2)}{2} = 2.5$ ◄── can also be determined using the function's axis

$$3 - 0.5 = 2.5 \text{ or } 0.5 - (-2) = 2.5$$

Try This

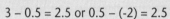

period: _____

peak: _____

trough: _____

range: _____

equation of the axis: _____

amplitude: _____

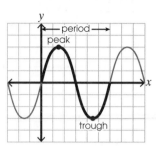

HINT

Key Features of Periodic Functions

- **period:**
  the horizontal distance needed for the graph of a periodic function to complete one cycle

- **peak:**
  the maximum point on a graph

- **trough:**
  the minimum point on a graph

- **range:**
  the set of all *y*-values

- **equation of the axis:**
  the equation of the horizontal line halfway between the maximum and minimum values

  $$y = \frac{\text{max. value} + \text{min. value}}{2}$$

- **amplitude:**
  half the difference between the maximum and minimum values; or the vertical distance from the function's axis to the maximum or minimum value

---

Determine the key features of the periodic graphs.

③

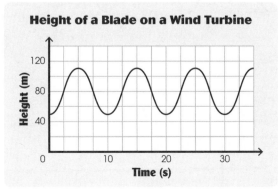

period: _____

peak: _____

trough: _____

amplitude: _____

range:

_____

equation of the axis:

_____

④

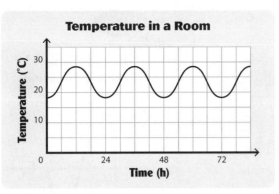

Temperature in a Room

period: _____   range:

peak: _____   _____

trough: _____   equation of the axis:

amplitude: _____   _____

⑤

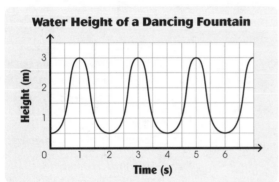

Water Height of a Dancing Fountain

period: _____   range:

peak: _____   _____

trough: _____   equation of the axis:

amplitude: _____   _____

Complete the table. Then match the graphs.

⑥

Graph	A	B	C	D
period	4	4	5	5
peak	3	3	3	3
amplitude	_____	1	_____	2.5
equation of the axis	$y = 0.5$	_____	$y = 2$	_____

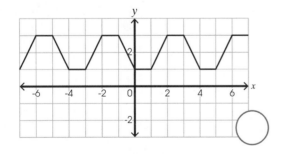

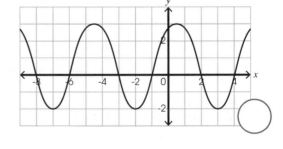

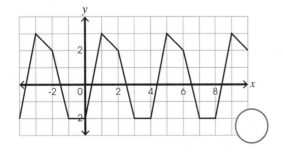

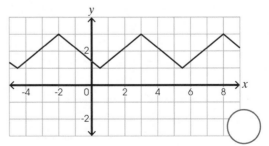

    ISBN: 978-1-77149-222-5

Determine whether each scenario will produce a periodic or a nonperiodic graph. For the periodic graphs, determine the independent and dependent variables.

⑦ May is skipping with a jump rope.

- independent variable: _____
- dependent variable: _____

 **HINT**

An independent variable is a variable whose values are chosen and is usually presented on the *x*-axis.

A dependent variable is a variable whose values are calculated and is usually presented on the *y*-axis.

e.g. Jody is jogging.
- independent variable: time
- dependent variable: distance jogged

⑧ The water level of a bay is changing due to tides.

- independent variable: _____
- dependent variable: _____

⑨ Kobe is swimming and he wants to find out the distance he has swum.

- independent variable: _____
- dependent variable: _____

A table of values is given for each scenario. Plot the points and answer the question.

⑩ Water is pumped into and removed from a tube. The table records the amount of water in the tube at specific times.

A

Time (min)	0	1	2	3	4	5	6	7
Amount (mL)	200	250	250	190	200	250	250	200

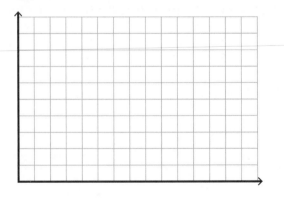

Joshua is on a Ferris wheel. His height above the ground over time is recorded in the table.

B

Time (s)	0	15	30	45	60	75	90
Height (m)	2	8	2	8	2	8	2

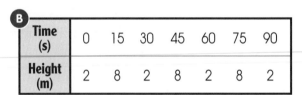

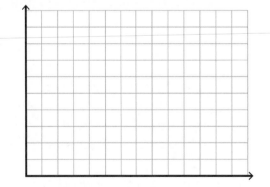

⑪ Which graph is periodic? Find its period, peak, trough, range, equation of the axis, and amplitude.

_____

_____

6.2 Properties of Sinusoidal Functions

Identify whether each graph is periodic, sinusoidal, or neither. Then answer the question.

①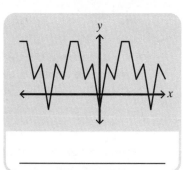

_____

②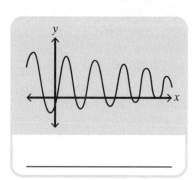

_____

③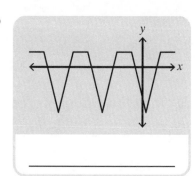

_____

④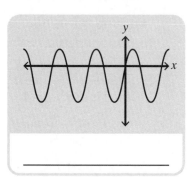

_____

⑤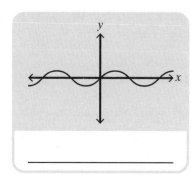

_____

⑥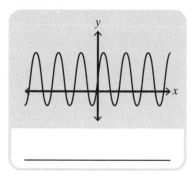

_____

⑦ If a graph is sinusoidal, then it must be periodic. Is it true that if a graph is periodic, then it must be sinusoidal? Explain.

_____

_____

Determine whether each situation could produce a graph that is periodic, sinusoidal, or neither.

⑧ the interest Kathleen earns on an investment over a year   _____

⑨ the height of a spoke on a bicycle tire as the bicycle is ridden   _____

⑩ the note frequencies in hertz of the same set of notes being
played on a piano repeatedly   _____

⑪ the height of a paddle while canoeing   _____

⑫ the total distance that a wheel covers   _____

⑬ the height of a bungee jumper as he bounces up and down   _____

    ISBN: 978-1-77149-222-5

Match the function with each graph where 0° ≤ x ≤ 360°. Then find the key features. You may use a graphing calculator.

⑭

$f(x) = \cos 2x$ $f(x) = \sin (2x) - 1$

$f(x) = \sin x$ $f(x) = \cos (3x) + 1$

A

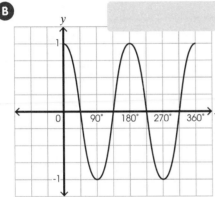

f(x) =

period: _____

amplitude: _____

increasing interval:

_____

decreasing interval:

_____

HINT

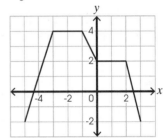

An increasing interval is an interval in which y-values increase as x-values increase. A **decreasing interval** is an interval in which y-values decrease as x-values increase.

e.g.

- **Increasing interval:**
  {x ∈ ℝ | -5 ≤ x ≤ -3}

- **Decreasing interval:**
  {x ∈ ℝ | -1 ≤ x ≤ 0, 2 ≤ x ≤ 3}

B

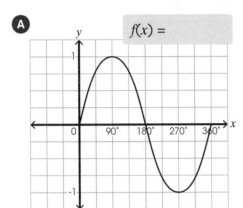

period: _____

amplitude: _____

increasing interval:

_____

decreasing interval:

_____

C

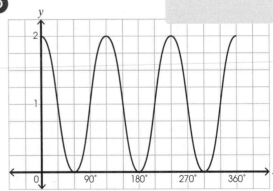

period: _____

amplitude: _____

increasing interval: _____

decreasing interval: _____

D

period: _____

amplitude: _____

increasing interval: _____

decreasing interval: _____

Answer the questions for each scenario using the given graph.

⑮ In a factory, the height of a tooth of a gear above the ground is modelled by $h(t) = 3 \sin(0.5t) + 15$, where t is the time in seconds.

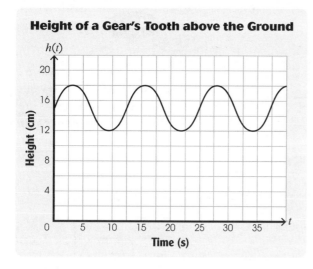

Height of a Gear's Tooth above the Ground

a. Determine the following. What does each represent in this scenario?

• equation of the axis:

_____

• amplitude:

_____

b. What is the rotational speed of the gear in centimetres per second?

_____

_____

⑯ A water turbine is installed in a river. The height of one of the blades relative to the water level is given as $r(t) = 1.5 \cos(4t)$, where t is the time in minutes.

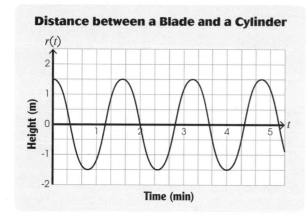

Distance between a Blade and a Cylinder

a. Find the equation of the axis. What does it represent?

_____

b. Can you determine whether the turbine is installed parallelly or perpendicularly to the base of the river? Explain.

_____

_____

⑰ The motion of a pendulum on a clock is observed. Its distance from the centre is modelled by $d(t) = 10 \sin(180t)°$ in centimetres, where t is the time in seconds.

a. Find the period. What does it represent?

_____

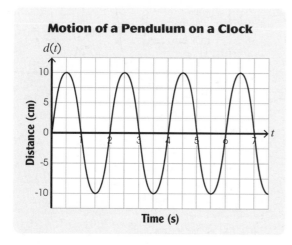

Motion of a Pendulum on a Clock

b. Do you think the clock tells time accurately? Explain.

_____

_____

_____

Plot the points with the given tables of values. Then solve the problems. Show your work.

⑱ Two loads with construction materials are attached to different pulleys. The tables below show the distances the loads move back and forth from their resting positions in metres with respect to time. The motion of Load A is modelled by $d = 3 \sin (45(t - 2)°)$ and the motion of Load B is modelled by $d = 4 \cos (45x)°$, where t is the time in seconds.

Load A

Time (s)	Distance (m)
0	-3
2	0
4	3
6	0
8	-3
10	0
12	3
14	0
16	-3
18	0
20	3
22	0
24	-3
26	0
28	3

Load B

Time (s)	Distance (m)
0	4
2	0
4	-4
6	0
8	4
10	0
12	-4
14	0
16	4
18	0
20	-4
22	0
24	4
26	0
28	-4

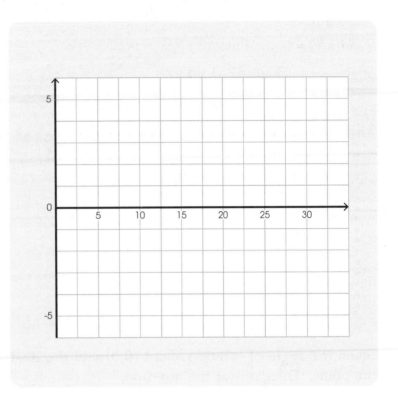

a. Determine each of the following for both loads and describe what it represents.

• period	• amplitude	• equation of the axis

b. Which load will be farther away from its resting position when $t = 40$?

c. Compare the increasing intervals and decreasing intervals of each load. Describe their relationship in this situation.

Example

Determine the coordinates of the point $M(x,y)$ resulting from a rotation of $62°$ centred at $(0,0)$ and starting from $(3,0)$.

Solution:

$M(x,y) = (r \cos \theta, r \sin \theta)$ ⟵ radius: 3
θ: 62°

$\quad\quad\quad = (3 \cos 62°, 3 \sin 62°)$

$\quad\quad\quad \doteq (1.41, 2.65)$

Hint

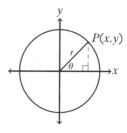

Consider a point $P(x,y)$ on a circle centred at $(0,0)$ with a radius of r and rotated through an angle θ. Its coordinates can be expressed in terms of $\sin \theta$ and $\cos \theta$.

$P(x,y) = P(r \cos \theta, r \sin \theta)$

Try This

Determine the coordinates of the point $A(x,y)$ after a rotation of $48°$ about $(0,0)$ from the point $(4,0)$.

Given the angle of rotation about $(0,0)$ and the starting point, determine the coordinates of the point. Then answer the question.

⑲ a. `75°` `(2,0)`

b. `98°` `(4,0)`

c. `127°` `(3,0)`

⑳ a.

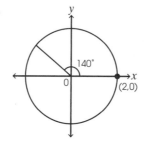

b.

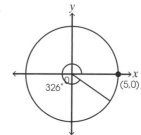

㉑ What are the coordinates of a point resulting from an $86°$ rotation on a circle if the circle has an area of

a. 28.26 square units?   b. 50.24 square units?

ISBN: 978-1-77149-222-5

Match each transformed function with its graph. Describe the transformation applied to $f(x) = \sin x$ or $f(x) = \cos x$ that results in each function for $0° \leq x \leq 360°$. Then check the features that are changed for each function.

① $\quad f(x) = 1.5 \sin x \qquad f(x) = \sin x + 1 \qquad f(x) = \sin (x + 60°)$

$\quad f(x) = \dfrac{1}{2} \cos x \qquad f(x) = \cos x - 1 \qquad f(x) = \cos (x - 90°)$

HINT

Parameters of Sinusoidal Functions

$f(x) = a \sin (k(x - d)) + c$
$f(x) = a \cos (k(x - d)) + c$

The parameters a, k, c, and d affect sinusoidal functions the same way as other functions you have learned previously (i.e. $f(x) = x^2$).

Parameter a
- $|a| > 1$: a vertical stretch by a factor of $|a|$
- $0 < |a| < 1$: a vertical compression by a factor of $|a|$
- $a < 0$: a reflection in the x-axis

Parameter k
- $|k| > 1$: a horizontal compression by a factor of $\left|\dfrac{1}{k}\right|$
- $0 < |k| < 1$: a horizontal stretch by a factor of $\left|\dfrac{1}{k}\right|$
- $k < 0$: a reflection in the y-axis

Parameter c
- $c > 0$: a translation of c units up
- $c < 0$: a translation of $|c|$ units down

Parameter d
- $d > 0$: a translation of d units to the right
- $d < 0$: a translation of $|d|$ units to the left

Sine Functions

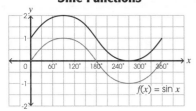

$f(x) = $ _____

_____

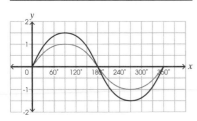

$f(x) = $ _____

_____

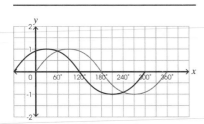

$f(x) = $ _____

_____

Cosine Functions

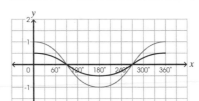

$f(x) = $ _____

_____

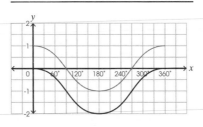

$f(x) = $ _____

_____

$f(x) = $ _____

_____

Function	Range	Max./Min. Value	Period	Amplitude	Equation of the Axis
$f(x) = 1.5 \sin x$					
$f(x) = \sin x + 1$					
$f(x) = \sin (x + 60°)$					
$f(x) = \dfrac{1}{2} \cos x$					
$f(x) = \cos x - 1$					
$f(x) = \cos (x - 90°)$					

ISBN: 978-1-77149-222-5

Determine the transformations of each graph. Then state their features without graphing.

② $f(x) = 3 \sin (x + 45°)$

_____

_____

③ $g(x) = -0.5 \cos (x - 30°) - 5$

_____

_____

④ $h(x) = \dfrac{1}{3} \sin (x - 180°) + 4$

_____

_____

⑤ $k(x) = -2 \cos (4(x + 120°)) + 1$

_____

_____

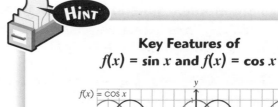

HINT

Key Features of
$f(x) = \sin x$ **and** $f(x) = \cos x$

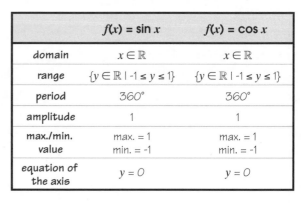

	$f(x) = \sin x$	$f(x) = \cos x$
domain	$x \in \mathbb{R}$	$x \in \mathbb{R}$
range	$\{y \in \mathbb{R} \mid -1 \le y \le 1\}$	$\{y \in \mathbb{R} \mid -1 \le y \le 1\}$
period	360°	360°
amplitude	1	1
max./min. value	max. = 1 min. = -1	max. = 1 min. = -1
equation of the axis	$y = 0$	$y = 0$

	$f(x)$	$g(x)$	$h(x)$	$k(x)$
domain				
range				
period				
amplitude				
max./min. value				
equation of the axis				

Complete the tables of values. Plot the points to graph each function. Then answer the question.

⑥

x	$\sin x$	$\cos (x - 90°)$
0°		
90°		
180°		
270°		
360°		

x	$\cos x$	$\sin (x + 90°)$
0°		
90°		
180°		
270°		
360°		

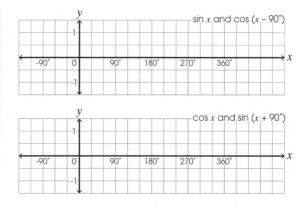

From the graphs, what can you conclude about the relationship between $f(x) = \sin x$ and $f(x) = \cos x$?

_____

   ISBN: 978-1-77149-222-5

Example

Sketch the graph of $f(x) = -\frac{1}{2}\sin(x+30°)+1$.

Solution:

- a vertical compression by a factor of $\frac{1}{2}$
- a reflection in the *x*-axis
- a translation of 30° to the left and 1 unit up

Note:

To graph efficiently, apply all stretches/compressions and reflections before translations.

HINT

Key Points of
$f(x) = \sin x$ and $f(x) = \cos x$

To graph sinusoidal functions, you are not required to find every value of $f(x)$. Simply find the values of the key points.

$f(x) = \sin x$	$f(x) = \cos x$
(0°,0)	(0°,1)
(90°,1)	(90°,0)
(180°,0)	(180°,-1)
(270°,-1)	(270°,0)
(360°,0)	(360°,1)

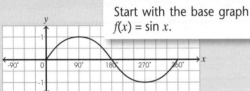

Start with the base graph $f(x) = \sin x$.

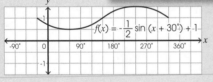

Perform all stretches/compressions and reflections.

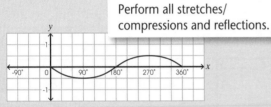

Perform all translations.

$f(x) = -\frac{1}{2}\sin(x+30°)+1$

TRY THIS

Sketch the graph of $f(x) = -\cos(2(x-60°))-1$.

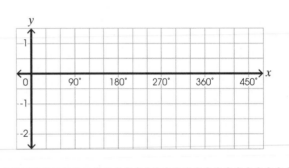

Sketch the graph of each function. Then state its features.

⑦ $f(x) = -2\sin(x-180°)+0.5$

Transformations

_____

_____

_____

Features

- range
- period
- equation of the axis
- amplitude
- max./min. values

_____ _____

_____ _____

_____

⑧ $f(x) = 0.5 \cos (2(x + 120°)) - 1$

Transformations

_____

_____

_____

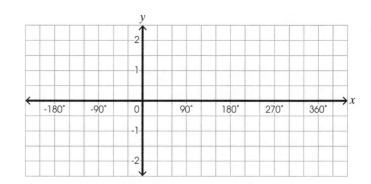

Features

_____ _____ _____
range   period   max./min. values

_____ _____
amplitude   equation of the axis

⑨ $f(x) = \frac{3}{4} \sin (\frac{1}{2}x - 30°) - \frac{1}{2}$

Factor this first.

Transformations

_____

_____

_____

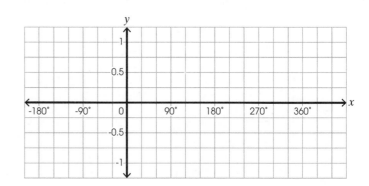

Features

_____ _____ _____
range   period   max./min. values

_____ _____
amplitude   equation of the axis

Determine whether each statement is true or false.

⑩ Consider the sine function $f(x) = a \sin (k(x - d)) + c$.

a. A phase shift will result for $d \neq 0$.   T / F

b. The period of the function is $\frac{360°}{|k|}$.   T / F

c. The equation of the axis is $y = |c|$.   T / F

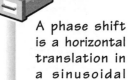

HINT

A phase shift is a horizontal translation in a sinusoidal function.

⑪ The graph of $f(x) = \sin x$ is identical to the graph of $g(x) = \cos x$

a. with a phase shift of 90° to the left on $g(x)$.   T / F

b. with a phase shift of 270° to the left on $g(x)$.   T / F

Example

Determine an equation for the sinusoidal function.

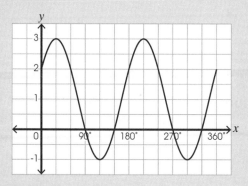

HINT

Each parameter represents one of the key features of a sinusoidal function.

$$f(x) = a \sin (k (x - d)) + c$$
$$f(x) = a \cos (k (x - d)) + c$$

a: amplitude d: phase shift

k: period $= \dfrac{360°}{|k|}$ c: equation of the axis

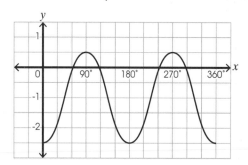

Solution:

amplitude: $\dfrac{3 - (-1)}{2} = 2$

period: $180° = \dfrac{360°}{|k|}$

$k = 2$ ◀——— Since there is no horizontal reflection, $k > 0$.

phase shift: $30°$ ◀———

equation of the axis:

$y = \dfrac{3 + (-1)}{2}$

$y = 1$

This graph is more similar to a cosine curve than a sine curve. The maximum starts at $x = 30°$ while it is at $x = 0°$ for $f(x) = \cos x$. So, there is a phase shift of $30°$ to the right.

$a = 2$
$k = 2$
$d = 30°$ $f(x) = \mathbf{2} \cos (\mathbf{2}(x - \mathbf{30°})) + \mathbf{1}$
$c = 1$

TRY THIS

Determine an equation for the function.

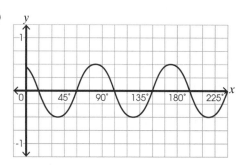

a: k:

_____

d: c:

$f(x) = $ _____

Determine an equation for each sinusoidal function.

①
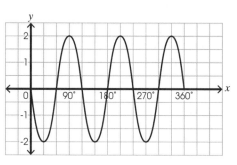

②
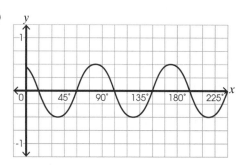

_____   _____

③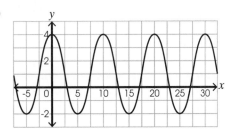

④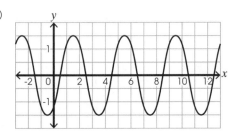

_____

_____

Plot the graph of each sinusoidal function with each table of values. Then represent the function with an equation in two different ways.

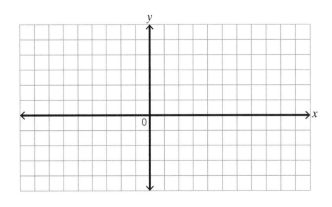

⑤

x	y
-180°	3
-135°	0
-90°	-3
-45°	0
0°	3
45°	0
90°	-3
135°	0
180°	3
225°	0

> **HINT**
>
> A sinusoidal function that is modelled by a sine function can also be modelled by a cosine function, and vice versa, as long as the appropriate phase shift is applied.

_____ _____

⑥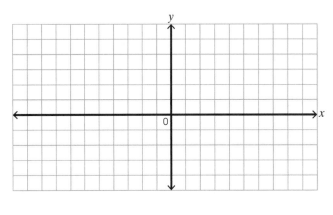

x	y
-10.5	1
-8	5
-5.5	1
-3	-3
-0.5	1
2	5
4.5	1
7	-3
9.5	1

_____

_____

⑦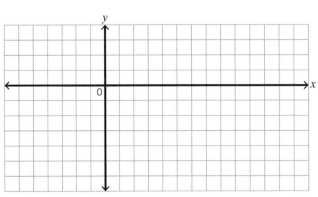

x	y
-2.5	-1.5
-1.25	-0.5
0	-1.5
1.25	-2.5
2.5	-1.5
3.75	-0.5
5	-1.5
6.25	-2.5

_____

_____

ISBN: 978-1-77149-222-5

Determine an equation for each sinusoidal function with the given features.

⑧
- amplitude: 5
- period: 360°
- equation of the axis: $y = 2$
- phase shift: 90° to the left

⑨
- amplitude: 3
- period: 60°
- equation of the axis: $y = -5$
- phase shift: 180° to the right

⑩
- amplitude: 4
- period: 240°
- equation of the axis: $y = -1$
- horizontal translation: 100° to the left

⑪
- a vertical stretch by a factor of 3
- a horizontal compression by a factor of $\frac{1}{2}$
- a translation of 1 unit down

⑫
- a reflection in the x-axis
- a vertical compression by a factor of $\frac{1}{8}$
- a translation of 5 units up and 3 units to the right

⑬
- a reflection in the y-axis
- a horizontal stretch by a factor of 7
- a phase shift of 2.5 units to the right

Match the description of each sinusoidal function with its equation. Then answer the questions.

Equations

⑭
A It has an amplitude of 3 units, a period of 45°, and a minimum at $y = 2$.

B It has an amplitude of 8 units, a period of 270°, and a maximum at $y = 0$.

C It has an amplitude of 8 units, a period of 480°, and a maximum at $y = 0$.

D It has an amplitude of 3 units, a period of 45°, and a minimum at $y = -1$.

○ $f(x) = 8 \sin \left(\frac{4}{3}(x - 30°)\right) - 8$

○ $f(x) = -3 \sin (8x)° + 5$

○ $f(x) = 3 \cos (8x)° + 2$

○ $f(x) = -8 \cos \left(\frac{3}{4}x\right)° - 8$

⑮ Can a sinusoidal function that has an amplitude of 7 units have its maximum at $y = 0$? Explain.

⑯ Write an equation of a sine function that has an amplitude of 4 units, a period of 60°, and a minimum at $y = -4$.

⑰ Write an equation of a cosine function that has an amplitude of 6 units, a period of 120°, and a maximum at $y = -6$.

⑱ Transformations were applied to the graph of $f(x) = \sin x$. After a translation of 2 units down, the new graph has a minimum at $y = -5$. What is its amplitude?

Plot the points for each scenario. Then solve the problem. Show your work.

⑲ An apple hanging on a spring moves up and down after being pressed down. Its height in centimetres from the floor and the amount of time in seconds since it had been pressed are recorded in the table.

Time (s)	Height (cm)
0	5
0.25	20
0.5	35
0.75	19.8
1	5.1
1.25	20
1.5	34
1.75	20.1
2	5.8
2.25	19.9
2.5	32.7
2.75	20
3	6.7
3.25	20.4
3.5	31.9
3.75	19.8
4	8.1

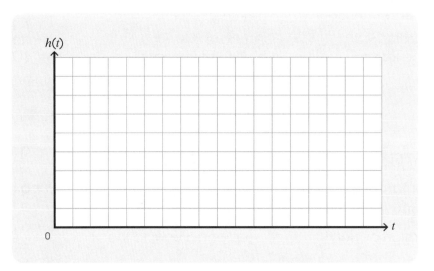

a. Write an equation that models the function.

_____

b. What will the height of the apple be at 6 s?

_____

⑳ The movement of one of the blades of a cruising ship's turbine was observed. Its height relative to the water level in metres and the time the turbine has been running in minutes are recorded in the table.

Time (min)	Height (m)
0	-1.3
0.2	-2
0.4	-0.7
0.6	0.4
0.8	-0.1
1	-1.2
1.2	-2.1
1.4	-0.6
1.6	0.5
1.8	-0.2
2	-1.3
2.2	-1.9

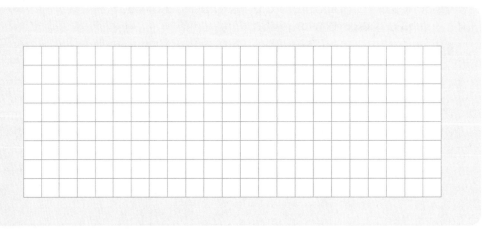

a. Write a sine function that models the graph.

_____

b. What will the height of the blade be at 5 min?

_____

    ISBN: 978-1-77149-222-5

Example

A sinusoidal function has its maximum at 5 when $x = 2$ and its minimum at 1 when $x = 6$. Develop an equation for the graph.

Solution:

1st Plot all the points that can be identified, which are (2,5) and (6,1). For being a sinusoidal function, the next maximum will be at (10,5). Connect the dots to form a curve.

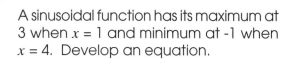

2nd Determine the parameters of the equation.

• amplitude: 2

• period: $8 = \dfrac{360°}{|k|}$; $k = 45°$

• phase shift: 2 units to the right (adopting the cosine curve)

• equation of the axis: $y = \dfrac{5+1}{2}$; $y = 3$

$\begin{array}{ll} a = 2 & k = 45° \\ d = 2 & c = 3 \end{array}$ $f(x) = 2\cos(45(x-2))° + 3$

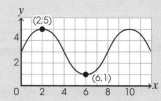

A sinusoidal function has its maximum at 3 when $x = 1$ and minimum at -1 when $x = 4$. Develop an equation.

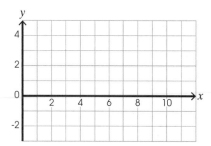

Determine an equation for each sinusoidal function with the given descriptions.

① • maximum at -1 when $x = -3$
  • minimum at -4 when $x = 0$

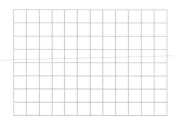

② • maximum at 2 when $x = 1$
  • minimum at -3 when $x = 4$

③ • peak: 10 when $x = -5$
  • trough: -1 when $x = 3$

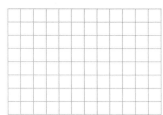

④ • peak: -4 when $x = -10$
  • trough: -8 when $x = -2$

Study each scenario. Determine an equation to model the function. Then answer the questions.

⑤ Two friends, Amy and Benedict, each performed a bungee jump. Their heights above the ground in metres with respect to the time in seconds since their jumps are recorded.

a. Amy's Jump
   • highest at 82 m at 0 s
   • lowest at 40 m at 4.5 s

   _____

b. Benedict's Jump
   • highest at 65 m at 0 s
   • lowest at 38 m at 3.2 s

   _____

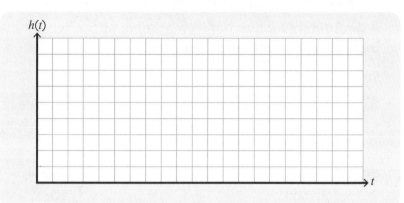

c. There are two options on the bungee jump that differs by the height of the jump. What are the heights? How do you know?

   _____

d. Does an equation that models each sinusoidal function perfectly exist? Explain.

   _____

   _____

⑥ An ecologist studied the populations of two species. He recorded their populations with respect to the time in months since the start of this study. The data resembles a sinusoidal function.

a. Species A Population
   • smallest population of 8000 at 9 months
   • largest population of 17 000 at 16 months

   _____

b. Species B Population
   • largest population of 20 000 at 10 months
   • smallest population of 4000 at 18 months

   _____

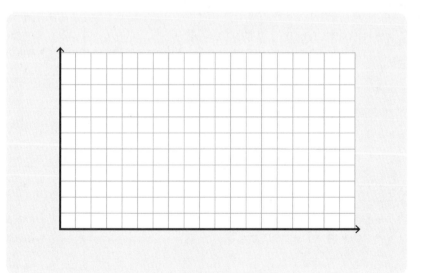

c. Did the species demonstrate a predator-prey interaction? Explain.

   _____

   _____

Study each scenario. Solve the problems. Show your work.

⑦ A performer at a circus show is swinging back and forth on a trapeze. The distance to the front and to the back of his resting position can be modelled by a sinusoidal function. At 2 s, he is 15 m to the front (+15) of his resting position and at 3.5 s, he is 15 m to the back (-15).

a. Find the features of the function and describe what they represent in this scenario.

- amplitude: _____ ; _____

- period: _____ ; _____

- equation of the axis: _____ ; _____

- domain: _____ ; _____

- range: _____ ; _____

b. Determine an equation for the function that describes the performer's location in terms of time. Find his location at 10 s.

_____

⑧ A rolling machine produces aluminum foil by pressing the materials into thin sheets. The roller has a radius of 30 cm. Assume that a scratch mark is at the roller's highest point.

a. Find an equation for the sinusoidal function that represents the height of the scratch in terms of the distance the roller rolls.

_____

b. The roller made 8 revolutions before it stopped due to a power outage. What are the domain and range of the function?

_____

c. What is the height of the scratch when the roller rolls a distance of 1000 cm?

_____

ISBN: 978-1-77149-222-5

7 Discrete Functions

Words TO LEARN

Explicit formula: a formula for any term, depending on the term number

Recursive formula: a formula for the next term, depending on the previous term(s)

Discrete function: a function that has its graph consisting of unconnected, separate parts

Continuous function: a function that has its graph consisting of connected points

Arithmetic sequence: a sequence that has the same difference between consecutive terms

Common difference: a difference between two consecutive terms in an arithmetic sequence

Geometric sequence: a sequence that has the same ratio of consecutive terms

Common ratio: a ratio of any two consecutive terms in a geometric sequence

> **Explicit Formula**
> e.g. $t_n = 2n + 5$
>
> **Recursive Formula**
> e.g. $t_{n+1} = 2 + t_n$

7.1 Discrete Functions and Sequences

Example

Determine whether each function is discrete or continuous. Find its domain and range.

Type: __continuous function__
Domain: __$\{x \in \mathbb{R}\}$__
Range: __$\{y \in \mathbb{R}\}$__

Type: __discrete function__
Domain: __$\{-2, -1, 0, 1, 2, 3\}$__
Range: __$\{-2, -1, 0, 1, 2\}$__

Try This

Type: _____
Domain: _____
Range: _____

Type: _____
Domain: _____
Range: _____

Determine whether each function is discrete or continuous. Find its domain and range.

①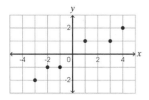

Type: _____

Domain: _____

Range: _____

②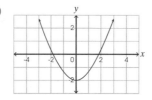

Type: _____

Domain: _____

Range: _____

③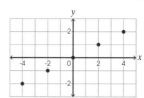

Type: _____

Domain: _____

Range: _____

ISBN: 978-1-77149-222-5

Study each scenario. Complete the table of values and graph the function. Then determine whether the function is discrete or continuous. Explain your answer.

④ The function $y = 25x$ represents the cost, y, in dollars, of x tickets for the admission of a fun fair.

No. of Tickets (x)	1	2	3	4	5
Cost (y)					

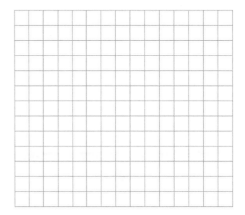

_____

_____

⑤ A bag of chips contains 130 calories. The function $y = 130x$ represents the amount of calorie intake, y, from x bags of chips consumed.

No. of Bags of Chips (x)	1	2	3	4	5
Amount of Calories (y)					

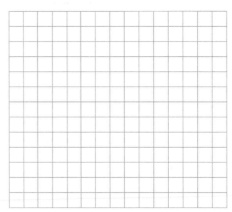

_____

_____

⑥ The function $y = 50 - 8.5x$ represents the amount of money, y, in dollars, that Sue has after buying x storybooks.

No. of Storybooks (x)	1	2	3	4	5
Amount of Money Left (y)					

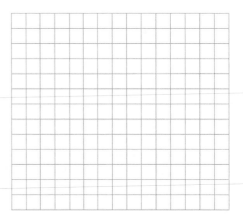

_____

_____

a. What is the domain of the function?

_____

b. What is the range?

_____

c. Is -1 in the domain? Explain.

_____

_____

d. What is the maximum number of books that Sue can buy?

_____

e. What was the initial amount that Sue had?

_____

Find the finite differences to determine whether each sequence is linear or quadratic. Match the explicit formula with the correct sequence. Then determine the 6th term with the formula.

$$f(n) = 3n - 2 \qquad f(n) = 3n^2 - 1 \qquad f(n) = \frac{1}{2}(n^2 + n)$$

$$f(n) = 2n - 3 \qquad f(n) = 10 - 3n \qquad f(n) = n^2 - n$$

⑦ -1, 1, 3, 5, 7

Term No. n	Term t_n	First Difference	Second Difference
1	-1		
2	1	2	
3	3		
4			
5			

sequence: **linear / quadratic**

explicit formula:

_____

the 6th term:

_____

⑧ 2, 11, 26, 47, 74

Term No. n	Term t_n	First Difference	Second Difference

sequence: _____

explicit formula:

_____

the 6th term:

_____

⑨ 1, 3, 6, 10, 15

Term No. n	Term t_n	First Difference	Second Difference

sequence: _____

explicit formula:

_____

the 6th term:

_____

⑩ 7, 4, 1, -2, -5

Term No. n	Term t_n	First Difference	Second Difference

sequence: _____

explicit formula:

_____

the 6th term:

_____

⑪ 0, 2, 6, 12, 20

Term No. n	Term t_n	First Difference	Second Difference

sequence: _____

explicit formula:

_____

the 6th term:

_____

⑫ 1, 4, 7, 10, 13

Term No. n	Term t_n	First Difference	Second Difference

sequence: _____

explicit formula:

_____

the 6th term:

_____

ISBN: 978-1-77149-222-5

For each sequence, make a table of values to find the first difference. Graph the ordered pairs. Then determine the explicit formula in function notation.

⑬   1, 4, 7, 10, 13

Term No. n	Term t_n	

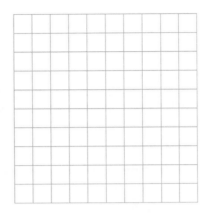

The explicit formula: _____

⑭   0, 3, 8, 15, 24

Term No. n	Term t_n	

The explicit formula: _____

Determine the first three terms for each sequence.

⑮ $t_n = 4n^2 + 1$

⑯ $t_n = 2^n$

⑰ $t_n = 3 - 4n$

⑱ $t_n = \dfrac{n}{n+1}$

⑲ $t_n = 2 - \dfrac{n}{3}$

⑳ $t_n = n^2 - 2n + 6$

7.2 Recursive Procedures

Check if each is a recursive formula.

① (A) $t_n = n - 1$ (B) $t_n = t_{n-1} + 4$

(C) $t_n = t_{n-1} + t_{n-2}$ (D) $t_n = \dfrac{n}{n+1} + 1$

(E) $t_n = 5 - t_{n-1}$ (F) $t_n = 2^n$

(G) $f(n) = \dfrac{n-1}{n} + 1$ (H) $f(n) = \dfrac{f(n-1)}{2}$

(I) $f(n) = n + 2$ (J) $f(n) = f(n-1) + f(n-2) + f(n-3)$

> **HINT**
>
> **Recursive Formula**
>
> a formula that uses the preceding term(s) to determine the next term in a sequence
>
> **e.g.** $t_n = t_{n-1} + 2$
>
> The nth term is related to the $(n-1)$th term.

Example

Determine the first four terms for each sequence.

$$t_1 = 3,\ t_n = t_{n-1} + 1$$

$t_2 = t_1 + 1$	$t_3 = t_2 + 1$	$t_4 = t_3 + 1$
$= \mathbf{3} + 1$	$= \mathbf{4} + 1$	$= \mathbf{5} + 1$
$= 4$	$= 5$	$= 6$

The first four terms are 3, 4, 5, 6.

Try This

$$f(1) = 2,\ f(n) = 10 - f(n-1)$$

$f(2) = 10 - f(\boxed{})$

$\quad = 10 - $

The first four terms are _____ .

Determine the first four terms for each sequence.

② $t_1 = 2,\ t_n = t_{n-1} + 5$

③ $t_1 = \dfrac{1}{2},\ t_n = (t_{n-1})^2$

④ $t_1 = x + 2y,\ t_n = t_{n-1} + 4y$

⑤ $f(1) = -1,\ f(n) = 3f(n-1)$

⑥ $f(1) = 0.5,\ f(n) = 5 - f(n-1)$

⑦ $f(1) = x - y,\ f(n) = f(n-1) + x$

Determine a recursive formula for each sequence.

$$-3, 0, 3, 6, 9...$$

Think Pattern: +3

$t_1 = -3$

$t_2 = 0 = t_1 + 3$

$t_3 = 3 = t_2 + 3$

$t_4 = 6 = t_3 + 3$

The recursive formula is $t_1 = -3$, $t_n = t_{n-1} + 3$.

Try This

$$3, -6, 12, -24, 48...$$

Think Pattern: × -2

$t_1 = \boxed{}$

$t_2 = -6 = t_1 \times \boxed{}$

$t_3 = 12 = $

The recursive formula is

$t_1 = \underline{\hspace{1cm}}$, $t_n = \underline{\hspace{2cm}}$.

Determine a recursive formula for each sequence.

⑧ 15, 17, 19, 21, 23...

⑨ 7, 4, 1, -2, -5...

⑩ -5, -10, -20, -40, -80...

⑪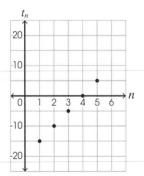

Sequence

-15,

⑫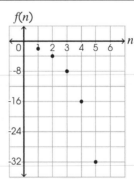

Sequence

⑬ 2, 4, 7, 11, 16...

$t_1 = 2$

$t_2 = 4 = t_1 + \underline{\hspace{1cm}}$

$t_3 = \underline{\hspace{1cm}} = t_2 + \underline{\hspace{1cm}}$

$t_4 = \underline{\hspace{1cm}} = t_3 + \underline{\hspace{1cm}}$

$\therefore t_1 = 2$, $t_n = \underline{\hspace{2cm}}$

⑭ 100, 90, 81, 73, 66...

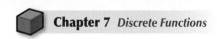

Solve the problems. Show your work.

⑮ Jimmy recorded his jogging distances each day from Monday to Friday last week.

Jogging Distances	
Monday	1.5 km
Tuesday	1.6 km
Wednesday	1.8 km
Thursday	2.1 km
Friday	2.5 km

a. Determine a recursive formula for this sequence.

_____

b. Use the formula to find how far Jimmy jogged on Saturday.

_____

⑯ A new concert hall is built so that the stage can be visible from all seats. The first row has 40 seats, the second has 44, the third has 48, and the next has 52.

a. What is the sequence of the seating layout in the concert hall?

_____

b. Determine a recursive formula for this sequence.

_____

c. Use the formula to find the number of seats in row 8.

_____

⑰ Aisha pays $850 000 for a new house. The value of the house increases by 10% each year.

a. What will the values of the house be each year in the first 5 years?

_____

b. Write a recursive formula to represent the value of the house.

_____

c. Determine the value of the house in the 6th year.

_____

⑱ The production of crude oil at an oil reserve is 2.4 million tonne/year. The production will diminish by 10% each year.

a. What will the production of crude oil be each year in the first 4 years?

_____

b. Write a recursive formula to represent the production of crude oil.

_____

Complete the Pascal's triangle. Then find the answers using Pascal's triangle.

① **Pascal's Triangle**

Horizontal Row Number	Diagonal Row Number	Sum of Each Row (Powers of 2)
$n = 0$	1 $r = 1$	$1 = 2^0$
$n = 1$	1 1 $r = 2$	$2 = 2^1$
$n = 2$	1 2 1 $r = 3$	$4 = 2^2$
$n = 3$	$t_{4,2}$ 1 3 1 $r = 4$	$8 = 2$
$n = 4$	1 4 6 4 1 $r = 5$	$16 =$
$n = 5$	1 5 10 5 1 $r = 6$	
$n = 6$	1 6 20 15 1	

$t_{6,5}$

HINT

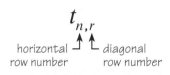

A Term in Pascal's Triangle

$$t_{n,r}$$

horizontal row number ↑ ↑ diagonal row number

Each term is the sum of the two terms immediately above it.

$$t_{n,r} = t_{n-1,r-1} + t_{n-1,r}$$

e.g. $t_{5,3} = t_{4,2} + t_{4,3}$

The first and last terms in each row are always 1.

② The value of each term:

a. $t_{3,2} =$ _____ b. $t_{6,3} =$ _____ c. $t_{4,4} =$ _____ d. $t_{5,4} =$ _____

③ A single term in the form $t_{n,r}$:

a. $t_{5,3} + t_{5,4} =$ _____ b. $t_{2,1} + t_{2,2} =$ _____ c. $t_{4,1} + t_{4,2} =$ _____

④ The sum of two terms in the form $t_{n,r}$:

a. $t_{5,3} =$ _____ b. $t_{3,3} =$ _____ c. $t_{6,4} =$ _____

⑤ The terms in row 7 and row 8 in Pascal's triangle:

$n = 7$ _____

$n = 8$ _____

⑥ The sum of each row in the powers of 2:
  a. row 4   **sum**   b. row 6   **sum**   c. row n **sum**

⑦ The row number that has the sum given:

a. row _____   **sum** 8   b. row _____   **sum** 512   c. row _____   **sum** 128

Expand the powers of the binomials. Complete the Pascal's triangle. Then fill in the blanks.

⑧

Value of n	$(a + b)^n$	Pascal's Triangle
0	$(a + b)^0 = 1$	
1	$(a + b)^1 = \quad a + \quad b$	
2	$(a + b)^2 = \quad a^2 + \quad ab + \quad b^2$	
3	$(a + b)^3 = \quad a^3 + \quad a^2b + \quad ab^2 + \quad b^3$	
4	$(a + b)^4 = \quad a^4 + \quad a^3b + \quad a^2b^2 + \quad ab^3 + \quad b^4$	

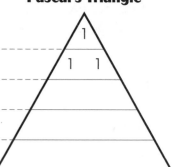

- The coefficients in the expansion of $(a + b)^n$ can be found in row _____ of Pascal's triangle.

- In each expression, the power of a _____ , the power of b _____ ,
  <u>decreases/increases</u>   <u>decreases/increases</u>

  and the degree of each term is always _____ the exponent of the binomial
                                      <u>equal to/different from</u>

  power.

Use Pascal's triangle to expand the power of each binomial.

⑨ $(a + b)^6 = a^6 + \underline{\quad}a^5b + \underline{\quad}a^4b^2 + \underline{\quad}a^3b^3 + \underline{\quad}a^2b^4 + \underline{\quad}ab^5 + b^6$

⑩ $(m - n)^6 = (m)^6(-n)^0 + \underline{\quad}(m)^5(-n)^1 + \underline{\quad}(m)^4(-n)^2 + \underline{\quad}(m)^3(-n)^3 +$

            $\underline{\quad}(m)^2(-n)^4 + \underline{\quad}(m)^1(-n)^5 + \underline{\quad}(m)^0(-n)^6$

        $=$

⑪ $(x + 2y)^7 =$

HINT

Pascal's Triangle

```
              1
            1   1
          1   2   1
        1   3   3   1
      1   4   6   4   1
    1   5  10  10   5   1
  1   6  15  20  15   6   1
1   7  21  35  35  21   7   1
```

⑫ $(a^2 - 2b)^5 =$

⑬ $(\frac{1}{2}x + 2y)^6 =$

Answer the questions.

⑭ The Fibonacci sequence is a series of numbers where a number is found by adding up the two numbers before it. Starting with 1 and 1, this sequence proceeds as shown below.

Fibonacci Sequence

1, 1, 2, 3, 5, 8, 13...

a. Determine a recursive formula for this sequence.

_____

b. Find the next three terms using the recursive formula.

_____

c. Add the numbers in Pascal's triangle diagonally. Describe how the Fibonacci sequence is related to Pascal's triangle.

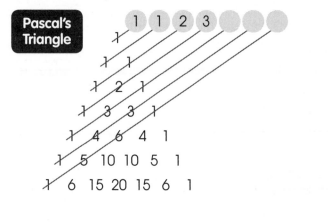

_____

_____

⑮ Describe the meaning of the term $t_{7,4}$ in Pascal's triangle. What is its value? Are there any terms that have the same value as $t_{7,4}$? If so, what are the terms?

_____

⑯ Prove that the expansion of $(-2x + \frac{1}{x})^3$ using the distributive property and the patterns in Pascal's triangle have the same result.

_____

⑰ How many terms are there in each expansion? Is there any constant in the expansion? If so, what is the value of the constant?

a. $(x + \frac{1}{x^2})^6$

b. $(2x^2 - \frac{1}{x})^8$

c. $(x - \frac{1}{2x^2})^4$

7.4 Arithmetic Sequences

Check if it is an arithmetic sequence.

① Ⓐ 3, 5, 7, 9, 11...

Ⓑ 0.5, 0.55, 0.555, 0.5555...

Ⓒ -1, -9, -17, -25...

Ⓓ $\frac{1}{2}$, $\frac{1}{3}$, $\frac{1}{4}$, $\frac{1}{5}$ ...

Ⓔ 1, 1, 2, 3, 5, 8...

Ⓕ -5, -20, -35, -50...

Ⓖ 1, 3, 6, 10, 15...

Ⓗ 0, 4, 0, -4, 0...

Ⓘ $\frac{1}{2}$, 0, $-\frac{1}{2}$, -1, $-1\frac{1}{2}$ ...

Ⓙ 3^5, 3^6, 3^7, 3^8...

> **HINT**
>
> **Arithmetic Sequence**
>
> a sequence where the differences between consecutive terms are constant
>
> e.g. 2, 5, 8, 11, 14, 17...
>
> This sequence has **a difference of 3** between every two consecutive terms. It is an arithmetic sequence.

Example

For each arithmetic sequence, determine the values of the first term, a, and the common difference, d.

$$-12, -17, -22, -27...$$

The first term a: -12

The common difference d: $t_2 - t_1$ ⟵ Choose any two consecutive terms.

$$= -17 - (-12)$$
$$= -5$$

So, a is -12 and d is -5.

Try This

16, 19, 22, 25...

2.5, 2, 1.5, 1...

For each arithmetic sequence, determine the values of the first term, a, and the common difference, d. Then find the next three terms.

② -10, -3, 4, 11...

③ -0.5, -1.5, -2.5, -3.5...

④ $\frac{4}{10}$, $\frac{3}{10}$, $\frac{2}{10}$, $\frac{1}{10}$ ...

The next 3 terms:

_____

The next 3 terms:

_____

The next 3 terms:

_____

⑤ 3, -1, -5, -9...

⑥ $1\frac{1}{8}$, $1\frac{1}{4}$, $1\frac{3}{8}$, $1\frac{1}{2}$ ...

⑦ 6×10^2, 5×10^2, 4×10^2, 3×10^2...

The next 3 terms:

_____

The next 3 terms:

_____

The next 3 terms:

_____

ISBN: 978-1-77149-222-5

Determine the first four terms of each arithmetic sequence with the given first term a and common difference d.

⑧ $a = 2$, $d = 4$

$t_1 = $ _____

$t_2 = $ _____ + _____ = _____

$t_3 = $

$t_4 = $

_____

⑨ $a = 6$, $d = -2$

_____

⑩ $a = \frac{1}{2}$, $d = \frac{1}{4}$

_____

⑪ $a = 1$, $d = -0.5$

_____

⑫ $a = y$, $d = 2$

_____

⑬ $a = 5 - x$, $d = -x$

_____

Determine the first four terms and a recursive formula for each arithmetic sequence.

⑭ $t_2 = 4$, $d = -2$

first four terms

$a = $ _____

$d = $ _____

recursive formula:

_____

⑮ $t_2 = -3$, $a = 1$

first four terms

$a = $ _____

$d = $ _____

recursive formula:

_____

⑯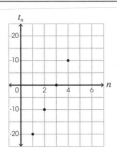

first four terms

$a = $ _____

$d = $ _____

recursive formula:

_____

⑰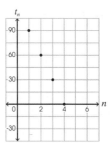

first four terms

$a = $ _____

$d = $ _____

recursive formula:

_____

ISBN: 978-1-77149-222-5

Determine the formula for the general term of each arithmetic sequence. Then find the values of the terms.

HINT

Arithmetic Sequence

$$a, a + d, a + 2d, a + 3d \ldots$$

Term No. (n)	Term (t_n)
1	$t_1 = a$
2	$t_2 = a + d = a + (2-1)d$
3	$t_3 = a + 2d = a + (3-1)d$
4	$t_4 = a + 3d = a + (4-1)d$
n	$t_n = a + (n-1)d$

Formula for General Terms:
$$t_n = a + (n-1)d$$

⑱ $a = 3, d = -2$

t_n = _____

t_{10} = _____

t_{15} = _____

t_{100} = _____

⑲ $a = -5, d = \dfrac{1}{2}$

t_n = _____

t_8 = _____

t_{20} = _____

t_{50} = _____

⑳ $a = -0.5, d = -0.25$

t_n = _____

t_8 = _____

t_{20} = _____

㉑ $a = 0, d = 12.5$

t_n = _____

t_{10} = _____

t_{50} = _____

㉒ $a = -7, d = x$

t_n = _____

t_5 = _____

t_{10} = _____

㉓ $a = x + y, d = -y$

t_n = _____

t_7 = _____

t_{12} = _____

Determine the formula for the general term of each arithmetic sequence. Then determine the term number of the term in bold.

㉔ 2, 4, 6, 8… , **60**…

㉕ 40, 50, 60… , **170**…

㉖ $\dfrac{1}{2}, \dfrac{3}{2}, \dfrac{5}{2} \ldots , \dfrac{\mathbf{19}}{\mathbf{2}} \ldots$

the _____ th term: 60

_____

_____

Determine the first term, a, common difference, d, and the formula for the general term of each arithmetic sequence.

㉗ $t_{15} = 0$ and $t_{31} = 8$

㉘ $t_7 = 21.5$ and $t_{18} = 65.5$

㉙ $t_8 = x + 6y$ and $t_{21} = x + 19y$

$a =$ _____ $d =$ _____

$t_n =$ _____

$a =$ _____ $d =$ _____

$t_n =$ _____

$a =$ _____ $d =$ _____

$t_n =$ _____

ISBN: 978-1-77149-222-5

Solve the problems. Show your work.

㉚ How many terms are there in each arithmetic sequence?

   a. 10, 20, 30..., 200   _____

   b. -25, -10, 5..., 200   _____

   c. -33, -32.5, -32..., 200   _____

   d. 608, 600, 592..., 200   _____

㉛ An arithmetic sequence has an 11th term of -360 and a 20th term of -576. Determine its first term, a, common difference, d, formula for the nth term, and a recursive formula.

_____

㉜ To rent a chainsaw at Simon's hardware store, it costs $30 for the first hour and $2 for each successive hour.

   a. Show the renting cost as an arithmetic sequence for the first four hours.

_____

   b. Write a formula for the general term. Then find the cost of renting the chainsaw for 3 days.

_____

㉝ Billy is stacking alphabetical blocks in the pattern shown. The number of blocks in each stack represents a term in an arithmetic sequence. In which stack will Billy place the letter "L" at the top of the stack?

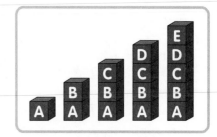

_____

㉞ The starting salary of a teacher is $58 000 a year. The salary goes up by $3800 each year.

   a. How much does a teacher earn in Year 5?

_____

   b. How long will it take for a teacher to earn $84 600 a year?

_____

ISBN: 978-1-77149-222-5

7.5 Geometric Sequences

Determine whether each sequence is arithmetic, geometric, or neither. Justify your answer.

Geometric Sequence

a sequence where the ratio of consecutive terms is a constant

e.g. 2, 6, 18, 54...

$$\frac{6}{2} = 3 \quad \frac{18}{6} = 3 \quad \frac{54}{18} = 3$$

This sequence has a common ratio of 3. So, it is a geometric sequence.

① 2, 4, 8, 16...

_____

② 1, 5, 9, 13...

_____

③ 1, 2, 4, 16...

_____

④ -3, -9, -27, -81...

_____

⑤ $\frac{1}{2}, \frac{5}{2}, \frac{25}{2}, \frac{125}{2} ...$

_____

⑥ $\frac{5}{8}, \frac{7}{8}, \frac{9}{8}, \frac{11}{8} ...$

_____

Determine the common ratio and the next two terms of each geometric sequence.

Geometric Sequence

the terms obtained by multiplying the first term, a, and each subsequent term by a common ratio*, r

$$a, ar, ar^2, ar^3...$$

*common ratio:
divide each term by the previous term

⑦ 12, -24, 48, -96 ...

common ratio: _____   next 2 terms: _____

⑧ 100, 20, 4, 0.8 ...

common ratio: _____   next 2 terms: _____

⑨ $\frac{1}{2}, \frac{1}{6}, \frac{1}{18}, \frac{1}{54} ...$

common ratio: _____   next 2 terms: _____

⑩ $\frac{1}{4}, -\frac{1}{4}, \frac{1}{4}, -\frac{1}{4} ...$

common ratio: _____

next 2 terms: _____

⑪ $4a, 8a^2, 16a^3, 32a^4 ...$

common ratio: _____

next 2 terms: _____

⑫ $\frac{\sqrt{y}}{2}, \frac{y}{4}, \frac{y^{\frac{3}{2}}}{8}, \frac{y^2}{16} ...$

common ratio: _____

next 2 terms: _____

⑬ $(x + y)^4, (x + y)^3, (x + y)^2, (x + y)^1 ...$

common ratio: _____

next 2 terms: _____

ISBN: 978-1-77149-222-5

Determine the formula for the general term of each geometric sequence.

$$a, ar, ar^2, ar^3... \quad \text{(common ratio: } r\text{)}$$

Term No. (n)	Term (t_n)
1	$t_1 = a$
2	$t_2 = ar = ar^{2-1}$
3	$t_3 = ar^2 = ar^{3-1}$
4	$t_4 = ar^3 = ar^{4-1}$
n	$t_n = ar^{n-1}$

The formula for the general term is $t_n = ar^{n-1}$.

Try This

324, -108, 36, -12...

$a =$ _____ $r =$ ———— = ————

$t_n = ar^{n-1}$

$= \left(\right)^{n-1}$

———————————————

$t_5 = \left(\right)^{5-1}$

$=$

$t_6 = \left(\right)^{6-1}$

$=$

Determine the formula for the general term of each geometric sequence. Then determine the next two terms.

⑭ 6, 12, 24, 48...

$a =$ _____ $r =$ _____

general term: $t_n =$ _____

next 2 terms: _____

⑮ $\dfrac{1}{3}$, $\dfrac{1}{6}$, $\dfrac{1}{12}$, $\dfrac{1}{24}$ ...

$a =$ _____ $r =$ _____

general term: _____

next 2 terms: _____

⑯ 0.25, 2.5, 25, 250...

$a =$ _____ $r =$ _____

general term: _____

next 2 terms: _____

⑰ $\dfrac{2x}{y}$, $\dfrac{-4x}{y}$, $\dfrac{8x}{y}$, $\dfrac{-16x}{y}$ ...

$a =$ _____ $r =$ _____

general term: _____

next 2 terms: _____

⑱ $\dfrac{m}{u^2}$, $\dfrac{m}{u}$, m, mu...

$a =$ _____ $r =$ _____

general term: _____

next 2 terms: _____

⑲ $0.5a$, $a^{\frac{3}{2}}$, $2a^2$, $4a^{\frac{5}{2}}$ ...

$a =$ _____ $r =$ _____

general term: _____

next 2 terms: _____

Find the first three terms for each geometric sequence.

⑳ $f(n) = -2(3)^{n-1}$

㉑ $t_n = 24\left(\dfrac{1}{4}\right)^{n-1}$

㉒ $a = \dfrac{1}{3}$ and $r = -3$

general term: _____

Determine the number of terms in each geometric sequence.

㉓ 5, 10, 20, 40 ..., **20 480**

$a =$ _____ $r =$ _____ $t_n =$ _____

$t_n = ar^{n-1}$

[ ] = [ ] ([ ])$^{n-1}$ ← Solve for n.

[ ] = [ ]$^{n-1}$ ← Write 4096 as a power of 2.

There are _____ terms.

㉔ 16, -8, 4, -2 ..., $\dfrac{1}{4}$

There are _____ terms.

㉕ 5, 5$\sqrt{5}$, 25, 25$\sqrt{5}$ ..., **3125**

There are _____ terms.

㉖ 0.1, 100, 100 000 ..., $\mathbf{10^{11}}$

There are _____ terms.

㉗ $\dfrac{3}{16}$, $\dfrac{3}{4}$, 3, 12 ..., **768**

There are _____ terms.

㉘ $\dfrac{m^2}{n}$, $\dfrac{2m}{n}$, $\dfrac{4}{n}$, $\dfrac{8}{mn}$ ..., $\mathbf{\dfrac{512}{m^7 n}}$

There are _____ terms.

Determine the first term, a, and the common ratio, r, for each geometric sequence.

㉙ $t_5 = 80$ and $t_{12} = -10\ 240$

㉚ $t_4 = \dfrac{27}{2}$ and $t_{10} = \dfrac{1}{54}$

㉛ $t_3 = 9$ and $t_8 = \dfrac{2187}{32}$

Solve the problems. Show your work.

32. The graphs of the sequences are shown below. Identify each sequence as arithmetic or geometric. Explain your reasoning. Determine the formula for the general term of each sequence.

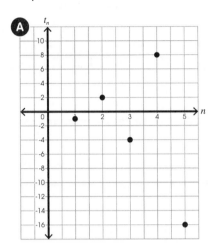 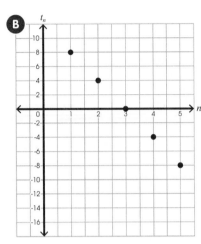 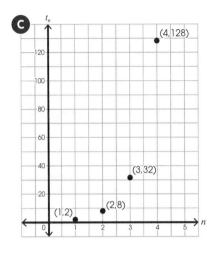

A _____

B _____

C _____

33. *E. coli* is a species of bacteria that doubles in number every 20 minutes. If there are 110 bacteria in a colony,

a. how many will there be after 3 hours?

b. how long will it take to have 3520 bacteria?

34. A study is being done on the number of people who vote in elections of their city. Elections take place every four years. In the year 2010, 3500 people voted. This number decreased by 2% in each subsequent election. Predict the number of votes for the next five elections.

ISBN: 978-1-77149-222-5

7.6 Arithmetic Series

Example

Determine the sum of the first 15 terms for each arithmetic series.

$$a = 4, d = -2, t_{15} = -24$$

$$S_n = \frac{n}{2}(a + t_n)$$

$$S_{15} = \frac{15}{2}(4 + (-24)) = -150$$

or

$$S_n = \frac{n}{2}(2a + (n - 1)d)$$

$$S_{15} = \frac{15}{2}(2(4) + (15 - 1)(-2)) = -150$$

Both formulas give the same answer -150.

The sum of the first 15 terms is -150.

Formulas for Finding the Sum of an Arithmetic Series

$$S_n = \frac{n}{2}(a + t_n)$$ — Substitute $t_n = a + (n - 1)d$

$$S_n = \frac{n}{2}(2a + (n - 1)d)$$

TRY This

$$a = -8, d = 5, t_{15} = 62$$

$$S_n = \frac{n}{2}(a + t_n)$$ $$S_n = \frac{n}{2}(2a + (n - 1)d)$$

$$=$$ $$=$$

The sum of the first 15 terms is _____ .

Determine the sum of each arithmetic series by using its first and last terms. Write the formula to be used in the box.

① Formula: $S_n =$

a. $a = 12, t_9 = 16$

b. $a = -2\sqrt{2}, t_{10} = 7\sqrt{2}$

c. $a = 10^2, t_{19} = 28$

_____

_____

_____

d. $a = -2x, t_{16} = 13x$

e. $a = -7, t_{12} = 11y - 7$

f. $a = x + y, t_8 = x - 5y$

_____

_____

_____

Determine the sum of each arithmetic series by using its first term, common difference, and the given term number. Write the formula to be used in the box.

② Formula: $S_n =$

a. $a = -2, d = \frac{3}{2}, n = 9$

b. $a = \frac{1}{2}, d = -\frac{5}{2}, n = 45$

c. $a = -8, d = -6, n = 20$

_____

_____

_____

d. $a = 3x, d = -x, n = 10$

e. $a = x - y, d = y, n = 32$

f. $a = 1 - m, d = 2m, n = 16$

_____

_____

_____

   ISBN: 978-1-77149-222-5

Determine the sum of the first 12 terms for each series.

③ $a = 3$, $d = -2$

④ $a = -2$, $d = y$

⑤ $a = \sqrt{5}$, $d = -\sqrt{5}$

⑥ $a = \frac{2}{9}$, $d = \frac{-5}{9}$

⑦ $a = 2x^2$, $d = -x^2$

⑧ $a = -x + 5$, $d = x + 1$

⑨ $a = 3 - x$, $d = x$

Determine the first term, a, and the common difference, d, of each arithmetic sequence. Then find the sum of the first 20 terms.

⑩ $\frac{1}{2}$, $\frac{3}{4}$, 1, $\frac{5}{4}$ ...

$a =$ _____ $d =$ _____

$S_{20} =$

⑪ 3, -2, -7, -12...

$a =$ _____ $d =$ _____

$S_{20} =$

⑫ $\sqrt{2}x$, 0, $-\sqrt{2}x$, $-2\sqrt{2}x$...

$a =$ _____ $d =$ _____

$S_{20} =$

⑬ $\frac{5}{9}$, $\frac{11}{9}$, $\frac{17}{9}$, $\frac{23}{9}$ ...

$a =$ _____ $d =$ _____

$S_{20} =$

⑭ $x + y$, $2x$, $3x - y$, $4x - 2y$...

$a =$ _____ $d =$ _____

$S_{20} =$

⑮ $\frac{-3}{y}$, $\frac{-5}{y}$, $\frac{-7}{y}$, $\frac{-9}{y}$ ...

$a =$ _____ $d =$ _____

$S_{20} =$

Determine the number of terms in each arithmetic series. Then find the sum of the series.

⑯ $\frac{1}{5} + \frac{3}{5} + 1 + ... + \frac{57}{5}$

⑰ $2\sqrt{3} + 5\sqrt{3} + 8\sqrt{3} + ... + 83\sqrt{3}$

⑱ $x - 3x - 7x - ... - 107x$

⑲ $(5a - 3b) + (4a - 2b) + (3a - b) + ... + (-5a + 7b)$

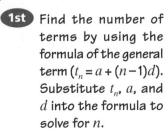

HINT

1st Find the number of terms by using the formula of the general term ($t_n = a + (n-1)d$). Substitute t_n, a, and d into the formula to solve for n.

2nd Find the sum of the series by using the formula below.

$$S_n = \frac{n}{2}(a + t_n)$$

ISBN: 978-1-77149-222-5

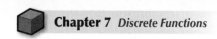

Solve the problems. Show your work.

⑳ What is the value of x so that the following expressions form the first three terms of an arithmetic sequence? Determine the sum of the first 10 terms of the sequence.

$2x + 4$, $4x + 1$, $40 - x$ ...

㉑ The 7th and 10th terms of an arithmetic series are $5x$ and $\frac{37}{5}x$ respectively. What is the sum of the first 20 terms of the arithmetic series?

㉒ A display of paint cans in a store is in the shape of a triangle. There are 3 paint cans in the top row and 15 cans in the bottom row. Each row from the top has 1 fewer can than the row underneath. How many cans are there in total?

㉓ Kevin has $2.25 in his piggy bank on May 1. He adds $2.75 on May 2, $3.25 on May 3, and so on until the last day of May.

a. How much will Kevin have on May 20?

b. What will Kevin's total savings be for the month of May?

㉔ There are 18 rows of seats in a concert hall – 68 seats in the 1st row, 72 seats in the 2nd row, 76 seats in the 3rd row, and so on.

a. How many seats are there in the 15th row?

b. If the price of a ticket is $85, what will the total sales be for a concert with all seats filled?

7.7 Geometric Series

Fill in the blanks to derive a formula for the sum, S_n, of the first n terms of a geometric series. Then find the sum of each geometric series by using the formula.

①

A Formula for the Sum (S_n) of n Terms of a Geometric Series:

$$S_n = a + ar + \boxed{} + ... + ar^{n-1} \longleftarrow \text{Write the series.}$$

$$\boxed{} S_n = ar + ar^2 + ... + ar^{n-1} + ar^n \longleftarrow \text{Multiply both sides by } r \text{ and align like terms.}$$

Subtract the first expression from the second one.

$$rS_n - \boxed{} = ar^n - \boxed{}$$

$$S_n\left(\boxed{} - \boxed{}\right) = a\left(\boxed{} - \boxed{}\right)$$

$$S_n = \frac{a\left(\boxed{} - \boxed{}\right)}{\boxed{} - \boxed{}}, r \neq 1$$

HINT

When the terms of a geometric sequence are added, the resulting expression is called a geometric series.

---

② $6 + 18 + 54 + 162 + ...$

$a =$ _____ | $S_6 =$ | $S_{10} =$

$r =$ _____ |

③ $12 - 6 + 3 - 1.5 + ...$

$a =$ _____ | $S_8 =$ | $S_{20} =$

$r =$ _____ |

---

④ $0.1 + 1 + 10 + 100 + ...$

$a =$ _____ | $S_7 =$ | $S_{10} =$

$r =$ _____ |

⑤ $5 - 5 + 5 - 5 + ...$

$a =$ _____ | $S_{18} =$ | $S_{27} =$

$r =$ _____ |

---

⑥ $\sqrt{3}\,x + 3x + 3\sqrt{3}\,x + 9x + ...$

$a =$ _____ | $S_8 =$ | $S_{11} =$

$r =$ _____ |

⑦ $2 - 2x + 2x^2 - 2x^3 + ...$

$a =$ _____ | $S_{15} =$ | $S_{30} =$

$r =$ _____ |

---

⑧ $\dfrac{1}{3x} - \dfrac{1}{2x} + \dfrac{3}{4x} - \dfrac{9}{8x} + ...$

$a =$ _____ | $S_6 =$ | $S_{11} =$

$r =$ _____ |

⑨ $128 + \dfrac{64}{x} + \dfrac{32}{x^2} + \dfrac{16}{x^3} + ...$

$a =$ _____ | $S_5 =$ | $S_8 =$

$r =$ _____ |

Example

Find the number of terms in each geometric series. Then determine the sum of the series.

$$\overset{a}{\boxed{1300}} + 130 + 13 + ... + \overset{r_n}{\boxed{0.00013}}$$

$$a = 1300 \qquad r = \frac{130}{1300} = 0.1$$

the nth term $\longrightarrow r_n = ar^{n-1}$

$$0.00013 = (1300)(0.1)^{n-1}$$
$$0.0000001 = (0.1)^{n-1}$$
$$(0.1)^7 = (0.1)^{n-1}$$
$$n - 1 = 7$$
$$n = 8$$

$$\therefore S_8 = \frac{1300\,((0.1)^8 - 1)}{0.1 - 1} \doteq 1444.44$$

$$\overset{a}{\boxed{81}} + 27 + 9 + ... + \overset{r_n}{\boxed{\dfrac{1}{243}}}$$

$$a = \underline{\qquad} \qquad r = \underline{\qquad}$$

$$r_n = ar^{n-1}$$
$$\boxed{} = \boxed{} \left(\boxed{}\right)^{n-1}$$

Determine the sum of each geometric series.

⑩ $10 + 5 + \dfrac{5}{2} + ... + \dfrac{5}{128}$

⑪ $4 + 16 + 64 + ... + 65\,536$

⑫ $-59\,049 + 19\,683 - 6561 + ... + 3$

⑬ $1 - \dfrac{3}{4} + \dfrac{9}{16} - ... + \dfrac{729}{4096}$

⑭ $-2 + \dfrac{1}{2} - \dfrac{1}{8} + ... - \dfrac{1}{32\,768}$

⑮ $3 + 3a + 3a^2 + ... + 3a^x$

ISBN: 978-1-77149-222-5

Solve the problems. Show your work.

⑯   If the sum of the geometric series below is 7812, what is the value of n?

$2 \cdot 1 + 2 \cdot 5 + 2 \cdot 5^2 + 2 \cdot 5^3 + ... + 2 \cdot 5^n$

⑰   The first three terms of a geometric sequence are $(x + 1)$, $(7x - 2)$, and $(50 - x)$. What is the sum of the first five terms of this geometric series if they are all positive?

⑱   The 10th and 15th terms of a geometric sequence are $\frac{3}{512}$ and $\frac{3}{16\,384}$ respectively. What is the sum of the first ten terms of the series?

⑲   Ted is creating a design with triangles. He starts his design with an equilateral triangle. Then he cuts it to make four small equilateral triangles. Then he keeps cutting each small equilateral triangle to create smaller equilateral triangles.

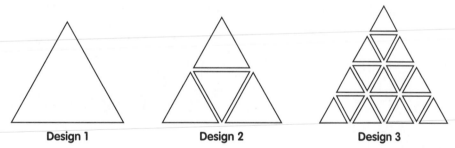

Design 1   Design 2   Design 3

a. How many small equilateral triangles will there be in Design 5?

b. How many equilateral triangles will there be in total in the first 6 designs?

8 *Financial Applications*

Words TO LEARN

Simple Interest	**Compound Interest**
interest calculated on the original principal	interest calculated at regular compounding periods and added to the principal for the following compounding period

Simple Interest:

interest ↴   ↴ principal
$$I = Prt \longleftarrow \text{time}$$
interest rate ↗

Compound Interest:

amount → $A = P(1 + i)^n$ ← compounding period
principal ↗   interest rate ↗

Present Value	**Annuity**
the principal invested/borrowed today which results in a given future amount	a sum of money paid as a series of regular payments

Present Value:

present value ↴   ↴ future value
$$PV = \frac{FV}{(1 + i)^n} \longleftarrow \text{compounding period}$$
interest rate ↗

Annuity:

regular payment   compounding period
total amount ↴   ↴   ↴
$$A = \frac{R((1 + i)^n - 1)}{i} \longleftarrow \text{interest rate}$$

8.1 Simple Interest

Example

Determine how much interest is earned for each situation.

• $1500 is invested at 4% per year simple interest for 3 years

Formula: $I = Prt$ ←

> r – annual interest rate
> t – time in years

$= 1500(0.04)(3)$
$= 180$

The interest earned is $180.

Try This

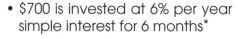

• $700 is invested at 6% per year simple interest for 6 months*

*Represent 6 months in terms of years.

Formula: $I = $ _____

$= $

The interest earned is _____ .

Mr. Green is going to put $8000 into an investment account. Determine the simple interest for each investment. Then check the one that gives him the highest interest.

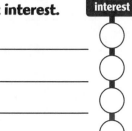

highest interest

① at 3.5% annual simple interest for 6 years   _____

② at 4% annual simple interest for 5 years   _____

③ at 8% annual simple interest for 5 months   _____

④ at 2% annual simple interest for 17 weeks   _____

ISBN: 978-1-77149-222-5

Complete the table.

⑤

	Principal (P)	Interest Rate (r)	Time (t)	Interest (I)	Total Amount (A)
a.	$15 000	2%	6 years		
b.	$2500		5 years	$500	
c.	$8000	2.5%		$50	
d.		3%		$1012.50	$8512.50
e.	$60 000		2.5 years		$66 750
f.		3.8%	8 months	$30.40	

Formula for Finding Interest

$$I = Prt$$

The total amount is the sum of the principal and the interest.

$$A = P + I$$
$$= P + Prt$$
$$= P(1 + rt)$$

The table shows the total amount of an investment earning simple interest over several years. Complete the table. Then answer the questions.

⑥

The Total Amount of an Investment

Time (years)	Amount ($)	First Difference
1	$1266	
2	$1332	
3	$1398	
4	$1464	
5	$1530	
6	$1596	

a. What do the values of the first differences represent?

_____

b. What is the initial principal of this investment?

_____

c. What is the interest rate?

_____

d. Graph to show how the amount is related to time.

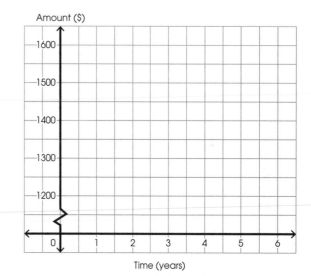

Amount ($)

Time (years)

e. What is the slope of the line? What does it represent?

_____

f. Write an equation to relate the amount of the investment to time.

_____

ISBN: 978-1-77149-222-5

Solve the problems. Show your work.

⑦ Corinne borrowed $14 000 from a bank to buy a car at 8% simple interest per year. If she paid $7840 in interest, how long did it take her to pay back the loan?

_____

⑧ How long did it take Samuel to pay back a loan of $2400 if the annual simple interest rate was 5.5% and he paid $495?

_____

⑨ How much interest is earned if $1800 is invested for 7 years at a rate of 3.2% simple interest per year?

_____

⑩ Refer to Question 9. What must the interest rate be

a. to earn the same amount of interest in 5 years?

_____

b. to earn twice the amount of interest in two years and 6 months?

_____

⑪ To save for a computer, Harry put $600 in a savings bond that earns at an annual rate of 3.8% simple interest.

a. Represent the above in an equation using the format $A = P + I$.

_____

b. How much money will Harry have after 3 months?

_____

c. How long will it take Harry to have $670?

_____

⑫ Kiko wants to borrow $6200 to buy a car. He has two options:

Ⓐ Borrow $6200 at an annual rate of 10% simple interest.

Ⓑ Pay an administration fee of $300 and get an annual rate of 8.9% simple interest.

Which is a better option if it will take Kiko 5 years to repay the loan?

_____

   ISBN: 978-1-77149-222-5

Fill in the missing information to complete the table. Then write the compound interest formula.

①

Compounding Period	Principal for the Period	Amount Calculation	Amount at the End of the Period
1	P	$A = P(1 + i)$	$P(1 + i)$
2	$P(1 + i)$	$A = P(1 + i)(1 + i) = P(1 + i)^2$	$P(1 + i)^2$
3	$P(1 + i)^2$	$A =$	
4			
⋮	⋮	⋮	⋮
n	$P(1 + i)^{n-1}$	$A = P(1 + i)^{n-1}(1 + i) =$	

the new principal for the second compounding period (i – interest rate)

the new principal for the third compounding period

Compound Interest Formula

$$A = \boxed{} (\boxed{} + \boxed{})^{\boxed{}}$$

↑ amount   └ principal

i – the interest rate per compounding period

n – number of compounding periods

Determine the amount after the specified year. Then find the interest.

② Darren invests $2000 at an interest rate of 2.5% per year compounded annually for 6 years.

Amount | **Interest**

③ Sam borrows $5000 at 3.25% interest per year compounded annually for 3 years.

Amount | **Interest**

④ Eric invests $600 and earns 6% interest per year compounded annually for 5 years.

Amount | **Interest**

⑤ Charlie borrows $3000 at an interest rate of 1.8% per year compounded annually for 2 years.

Amount | **Interest**

For each compounding condition, determine the interest rate per compounding period, expressed as a decimal and the number of compounding periods.

⑥   Interest Rate: 5% per year   Time: 3 years

Frequency of Compounding	No. of Times per Year that Interest is Compounded	Interest Rate per Compounding Period	Total no. of Compounding Periods
semi-annually	2 (every 6 months)	$\dfrac{0.05}{2} =$ _____	$2 \times 3 =$ _____
quarterly	4 (every 3 months)	$\dfrac{0.05}{} =$	$ \times 3 =$ _____
monthly	12 (every month)		
bi-weekly	____ (every 2 weeks)		
daily	____ (every day)		

HINT

When the annual interest rate is not compounded annually, remember to determine the following before applying the formula $A = P(1 + i)^n$ to find the amount.

❶ the interest rate per compounding period

❷ the total no. of compounding periods

Solve the problems.

⑦   Find the amount and the interest of each scenario.

a. $600 at 3% interest per year compounded monthly for 3 years

$$i = \frac{}{12} = \text{\_\_\_\_\_} \qquad n = \times 3 = \text{\_\_\_\_\_}$$

b. $5000 at 2.6% interest per year compounded quarterly for 1.5 years

c. $1200 at 4% interest per year compounded bi-weekly for 6 months

d. $2800 at 3.2% interest per year compounded daily for 30 days

⑧   Ted invests $8000 in an account that earns 3.25% interest per year compounded semi-annually for 30 months. What are the amount and interest?

Solve the problems. Show your work.

⑨ Zoe has $4800 in her bank account which earns 1.3% interest per year compounded daily. How much interest will she earn

    a. in 45 days?

_____

    b. in January and February?

_____

⑩ Lucy borrows $800 at 11% interest per year for 5 years. Determine the interest charged for each scenario. Which scenario is the best for Lucy? Which one is the worst?

  A simple interest

  B compounded annually

  C compounded quarterly

  D compounded monthly

⑪ Sidra borrowed $550 at an interest rate that was compounded semi-annually for 6 years. After 6 years, she repaid $842. What was the annual interest rate charged?

_____

⑫ Kayla has $3200 to invest. At KM Bank, she can invest and earn 4% interest compounded semi-annually for 5 years. At Direct Bank, she can also invest for 5 years, but earns 3.8% interest per year compounded monthly instead. Which bank should Kayla invest in?

_____

8.3 Present Value

Complete the missing information to show how to derive the present value formula from the compound interest formula.

①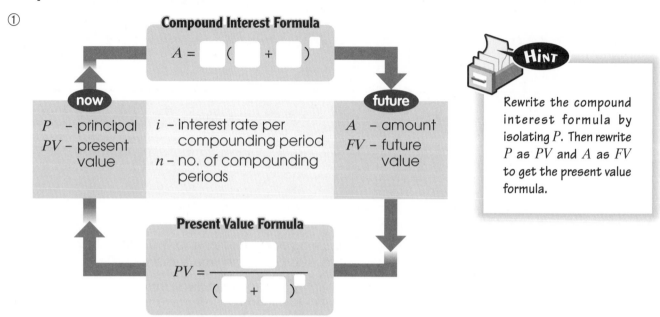

Compound Interest Formula

$$A = \boxed{} (\boxed{} + \boxed{})^{\boxed{}}$$

now

| P – principal | i – interest rate per compounding period | A – amount |
| PV – present value | n – no. of compounding periods | FV – future value |

future

HINT

Rewrite the compound interest formula by isolating P. Then rewrite P as PV and A as FV to get the present value formula.

Present Value Formula

$$PV = \frac{\boxed{}}{(\boxed{} + \boxed{})^{\boxed{}}}$$

Solve the problems.

② The future value of a fund is $10 000. The term is 6 years at 5% interest per year compounded annually. What is the present value of the fund?

③ Angela deposits $2000 into her bank account today. After 10 years, she is expected to have $4317.85 in her bank account. What is the interest rate if it is compounded annually?

④ An investment will be worth $900 in 4 years. If the investment starts today at an interest rate of 6% compounded annually, what is the invested amount?

⑤ The future value of an investment doubles its present value in 15 years. What is the interest rate per year compounded annually?

⑥ A packet of sugar cost $1.69 in 2008. What was the price of a similar packet of sugar in 1988, assuming an average inflation rate of 2.5% per year compounded annually?

⑦ Refer to Question 6. What was the price difference of a packet of sugar in 1998 and 2008?

ISBN: 978-1-77149-222-5

Check the correct equation to solve each problem. Then explain your choice and find the answer.

HINT

$$PV = \frac{FV}{(1 + i)^n}$$

PV – present value
FV – future value
i – interest rate per compounding period
n – no. of compounding periods

⑧ An investment can earn 4% annual interest compounded monthly. What amount must Mr. Smith invest now in order to get $10 000 after $3\frac{1}{2}$ years?

(A) $PV = \dfrac{10\,000}{(1 + 0.0033)^{42}}$

(B) $PV = \dfrac{10\,000}{(1 + 0.04)^{3.5}}$

_____

⑨ In 6 years, a loan at an interest rate of 5% per year compounded quarterly will grow to $8353.58. How much money was borrowed? What is the interest charged on this loan?

(A) $PV = \dfrac{8353.58}{(1 + 0.025)^{12}}$

(B) $PV = \dfrac{8353.58}{(1 + 0.0125)^{24}}$

_____

⑩ Shayon borrows $600 from his parents to buy a laptop. He agrees to pay back the money in 2 years with interest for a total amount of $695. If the interest is compounded monthly, what is the annual interest rate?

(A) $600 = \dfrac{695}{\left(1 + \dfrac{r}{12}\right)^{24}}$

(B) $695 = \dfrac{600}{\left(1 + \dfrac{r}{12}\right)^{24}}$

_____

⑪ Hannah received a university scholarship, which she invested to earn 7.2% annual interest compounded semi-annually. After 4 years, she had $1592.43, how much was the scholarship? How much interest did Hannah earn?

(A) $PV = \dfrac{1592.43}{\left(1 + \dfrac{0.072}{2}\right)^{4}}$

(B) $1592.43 = \dfrac{FV}{\left(1 + \dfrac{0.072}{2}\right)^{8}}$

(C) $PV = \dfrac{1592.43}{\left(1 + \dfrac{0.072}{2}\right)^{8}}$

_____

ISBN: 978-1-77149-222-5   **COMPLETE MATHSMART (GRADE 11)**

Solve the problems. Show your work.

⑫ After 12 years, an investment earning 5.1% annual interest compounded monthly will have a value of $26 924.20. What is the present value of the investment?

_____

⑬ On average, it costs $2.69 to buy a litre of milk in 2017. Assume that the inflation rate is 2% per year compounded annually,

a. how much did the milk cost in 2000?

_____

b. how much will the milk cost in 2025?

_____

⑭ The value of an investment after 3 years will be $3600. What is the present value if each of the following compounding conditions is in place for an annual interest rate of 4%?

a. compounded annually	b. compounded quarterly
c. compounded bi-weekly	d. compounded daily

⑮ Shirley and Steve are saving for a car. They would like to have $8000 in 3 years. They are considering two investment plans. Which plan should they choose? Explain.

Plan A: annual interest 5.8% compounded quarterly

Plan B: annual interest 5.5% compounded monthly

_____

⑯ Sam borrowed money from the bank at an annual interest rate of 6.8% compounded quarterly. Two years later, he paid back $4000 for both the principal and the interest. After another year, he paid another $4000. After another 3 years, he paid the remaining balance of $3000. How much did Sam borrow originally?

_____

Determine the amount of annuity shown in the timeline. Then derive a formula for the amount of annuity.

① Katie deposits $400 at the end of every year in an account that earns 6% interest per year compounded annually for 5 years. What is the amount of annuity?

Compounding Period (in years)

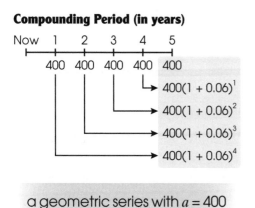

a geometric series with $a = 400$
and $r = 1 + 0.06$

$A = 400 + 400(1 + 0.06) + 400(1 + 0.06)^2 +$ _____

$$= \frac{400((\quad)^{\quad} - \quad)}{(\quad) - 1}$$ ← $\dfrac{a(r^n - 1)}{r - 1}$

$$= \frac{400((\quad)^{\quad} - \quad)}{\quad}$$

$\doteq$

The amount of annuity is _____ .

② A regular payment R in dollars is deposited into an account at the end of each compounding period for n periods. The account pays an interest rate i per compounding period.

Compounding Period

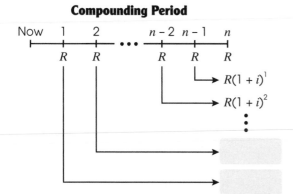

$A = R +$ _____

$$= \frac{R((\quad)^{\quad} - 1)}{(\quad) - 1}$$ ← $\dfrac{a(r^n - 1)}{r - 1}$

$=$

This equation can also be written in terms of
future value as $FV = \dfrac{R((1 + i)^n - 1)}{i}$.

Calculate the amount of annuity shown in the timeline by using the formula.

③ **Compounding Period**

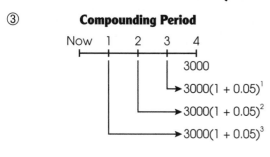

④ **Compounding Period**

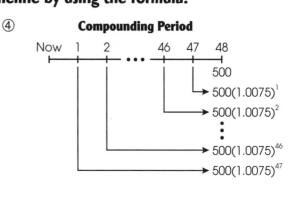

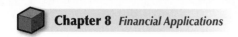

Draw a timeline to represent the annuity in each problem. Then solve the problem.

⑤ To save money to buy a puppy, Collin puts $150 into an account that earns 5.2% interest per year compounded annually at the end of every year for 4 years.

Compounding Period

Now

a. What is the amount of annuity?

_____

b. How much interest will be earned?

_____

⑥ Cassidy puts $15 into an account at the end of each week for 2 years. Her account earns 6.5% interest per year compounded weekly.

Compounding Period

Now

a. What is the amount of annuity?

_____

b. How much interest will be earned?

_____

⑦ How much money must be invested each year for 7 years to reach an amount of $12 000 if the interest rate is 5.75% per year compounded annually?

Compounding Period

Now

_____

⑧ Sara wants to have $16 000 available in 2 years to renovate her apartment. If her account earns 7.8% interest per year compounded monthly, how much should she invest each month?

_____

   ISBN: 978-1-77149-222-5

Solve the problems. Show your work.

⑨ Mrs. Remoto saves $350 at the end of each month in a fund that gives her an annual interest of 9% compounded monthly for 4 years. Will Mrs. Remoto have enough money to buy a car that costs $20 000 after 4 years?

_____

⑩ Sally and Sanjit want to save up $275 000 for their retirement. The annual interest rate of the investment is 3.25% compounded monthly. If they save $1200 a month for 5 years,

a. what will the amount of the annuity be?

_____

b. how much interest will be earned?

_____

c. for how many more months will they have to save?

_____

⑪ A bank offers Karen the following options for investments. Which option should Karen choose? Explain your answer.

Option A $6000 is invested at 4% per year simple interest for 5 years.

Option B $6000 is invested at 3.8% per year compounded monthly for 5 years.

Option C $100 is invested monthly at 7% interest per year compounded monthly for 5 years.

_____

⑫ Faisal wants to have $50 000 in his account before he retires. He plans to invest for the next 45 years into an account each week that has an annual interest rate of 4.8% compounded weekly. How much should he deposit weekly?

_____

8.5 Present Value of an Annuity

ISBN: 978-1-77149-222-5

Example

Sahara decides to take 1 year off from work to study. During this time, she would like to have $800 per month to support her living. What amount should she deposit into her account now if the interest in the account is earned at a rate of 4% per year compounded monthly?

$$i = \frac{0.04}{12} = 0.003, n = 12$$

Time (months)

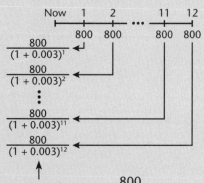

geometric series: $a = \dfrac{800}{1 + 0.003}$, $r = \dfrac{1}{1 + 0.003}$

$$PV = \frac{800(1 - (1 + 0.003)^{-12})}{0.003} \doteq 9415.39$$

∴ Sahara should deposit $9415.39 into her account now.

HINT

Present Value of an Annuity

Time (*n* periods)

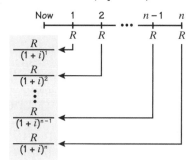

$$PV = \frac{R}{(1 + i)^1} + \frac{R}{(1 + i)^2} + ... + \frac{R}{(1 + i)^n}$$

geometric series:

$$a = \frac{R}{1 + i} , r = \frac{1}{1 + i}$$

$$\therefore PV = \frac{\dfrac{R}{1 + i}\left(\left(\dfrac{1}{1 + i}\right)^n - 1\right)}{\dfrac{1}{1 + i} - 1}$$

$$S_n = \frac{a(r^n - 1)}{r - 1}$$

$$PV = \frac{R((1 + i)^{-n} - 1)}{1 - (1 + i)}$$

$$PV = \frac{R(1 - (1 + i)^{-n})}{i}$$

TRY THIS

If Sahara decides to take 2 years off instead, what amount should she deposit now?

$$i = \frac{0.04}{12}$$

$$= \underline{\qquad}$$

$$n = \underline{\qquad} \times 2$$

$$= \underline{\qquad}$$

Time (months)

Now 1 2   23 24

800 800 ... 800 800

$$\frac{800}{(1 + 0.003)^1}$$
$$\frac{800}{(1 + 0.003)^2}$$
$$\vdots$$
$$\frac{800}{(1 + 0.003)^{23}}$$
$$\frac{800}{(1 + 0.003)^{24}}$$

$R = \underline{\qquad}$ $i = \underline{\qquad}$ $n = \underline{\qquad}$

$$PV = \frac{R\,(1 - (1 + \boxed{}\,i\,)^{-n})}{i}$$

$$= \frac{(1 - (1 + \boxed{})^{-})}{\boxed{}}$$

$$\doteq \underline{\qquad}$$

∴ Sahara should deposit _____ into her account now.

ISBN: 978-1-77149-222-5

Use the timelines to calculate the present value of the annuity. Then answer the questions.

① **A**

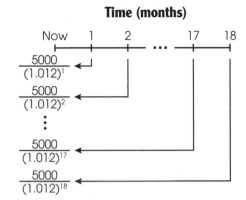

B

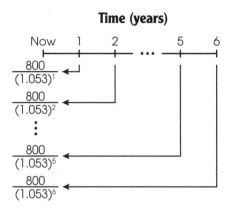

C

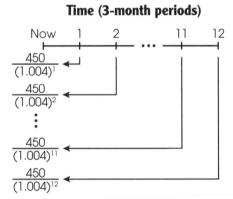

D

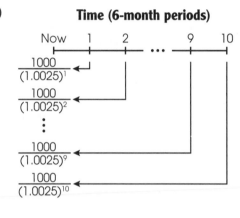

A $PV =$

_____

B

_____

C

_____

D

_____

HINT

Present Value of an Annuity

$$PV = \frac{R(1 - (1 + i)^{-n})}{i}$$

PV – present value

R – regular withdrawal

i – interest rate per compounding period

n – no. of compounding periods

② If the interest rate in **B** is compounded monthly and the regular withdrawal is $66.67, what will the new interest rate per compounding period be? What will the new present value of the annuity be?

_____

ISBN: 978-1-77149-222-5

Determine the present value of each annuity.

③ payment: $4000/year

interest rate per year: 6.2%

compounding period: annually

time: 6 years

$PV =$

④ payment: $850/2 weeks

interest rate per year: 9.3%

compounding period: bi-weekly

time: 5 years

⑤ payment: $225/3 months

interest rate per year: 4.8%

compounding period: quarterly

time: 4 years

⑥ monthly withdrawal: $700

interest rate per year: 2.8%

compounding period: monthly

time: 2.5 years

⑦ annual withdrawal: $1500

interest rate per year: 3.5%

compounding period: annually

time: 36 months

⑧ withdrawal: $400/3 months

interest rate per year: 5%

compounding period: quarterly

time: 18 months

Solve the problems. Show your work.

⑨ An annuity has an initial balance of $7500 in an account that earns 6.2% interest per year compounded annually. What amount can be withdrawn at the end of each year of the 8 years of this annuity?

⑩ How much should Dawson deposit into his account today if he wants to withdraw $18 000 at the end of each year for the next 25 years? The interest rate of this account is 7.2% per year compounded annually.

ISBN: 978-1-77149-222-5

⑪ Ernest won $1 000 000 in a lottery. He wants to quit his job and live on $5500 a month.

a. Ernest's savings account earns 3.75% interest per year compounded monthly. Can Ernest afford to live off his lottery winnings for 40 years?

_____

b. If not, how much money can Ernest withdraw at most per month for 40 years from the savings account?

_____

⑫ Farah has $7500 to invest in an annuity from which she wants to withdraw money for 4 years. There are two options:

Option 1 7% interest rate per year compounded quarterly; withdrawals made quarterly

Option 2 6.75% interest rate per year compounded monthly; withdrawals made monthly

a. Determine the regular withdrawal for each option.

b. Determine the total interest earned for each option.

c. If you were Farah, which option would you choose? Explain your choice.

_____

_____

⑬ As a settlement in an automobile lawsuit, the insurance company has offered Kelsey two options. Which option should she accept?

Option 1 Receive $30 000 each year for the next 25 years. (The money can be invested at 9% annual interest compounded annually.)

Option 2 Receive a one-payment settlement of $300 000 now.

_____

ISBN: 978-1-77149-222-5

Complete MathSmart 11
Cumulative Review

In this review, the questions are classified into the four categories below.

- **K** Knowledge and Understanding
- **A** Application
- **C** Communication
- **T** Thinking

The icons beside the question numbers indicate in which categories the questions belong.

ISBN: 978-1-77149-222-5

Circle the correct answers.

① Which of the following helps determine if a relation is a function?

K A. the determinant

B. the first differences

C. the vertical test

D. the horizontal test

② What is the range of the function $f(x) = x^2 + 9$?

K A. $\{y \in \mathbb{R} \mid y \geq 9\}$

B. $\{y \in \mathbb{R} \mid y > 0\}$

C. $\{y \in \mathbb{R} \mid y \leq 9\}$

D. $\{y \in \mathbb{R} \mid y \geq -9\}$

③ What is the vertex of $y = -3x^2 + 6x - 2$?

K A. (1,1)

B. (-1,-1)

C. (1,-2)

D. (-1,-2)

④ What transformations have been applied to transform the parent function $f(x) = x^2$ into

K $h(x) = (x + 5)^2 - 4$?

A. translation of 4 units to the left and 5 units down

B. translation of 4 units to the right and 5 units down

C. translation of 5 units to the right and 4 units down

D. translation of 5 units to the left and 4 units down

⑤ State the restrictions for the expression $\dfrac{(x + 3)(x - 1)}{x(x - 8)(x + 6)}$.

K A. $x \neq -3, 1$

B. $x \neq -6, 0, 8$

C. $x \neq -8, -6, 0$

D. $x \neq -3, 0, 1$

⑥ The period of a periodic graph is

  A. the same as the domain.

  B. the same as the range.

  C. the length of one cycle.

  D. the distance from the maximum to the minimum values of the relation.

⑦ If the domain of a graph is $\{\theta \in \mathbb{R} \mid 0 < \theta < 2\pi\}$, which of the following is a solution to $\sin \theta = -1$?

  A. 0

  B. -1.57

  C. π

  D. $\dfrac{3\pi}{2}$

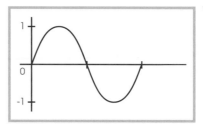

⑧ Which of the following describes exponential functions?

  A. The first differences are constant.

  B. The first differences are equal to 0.

  C. The second differences are constant.

  D. The ratio of first differences is constant.

⑨ What is the exact value of $\sin \left(\dfrac{7\pi}{6}\right)$?

  A. $\dfrac{1}{2}$

  B. $-\dfrac{\sqrt{3}}{2}$

  C. $-\dfrac{1}{2}$

  D. $-\dfrac{2}{\sqrt{3}}$

⑩ What is the value of $16^{-\frac{1}{2}}$?

  A. $\dfrac{1}{4}$

  B. $-\dfrac{1}{4}$

  C. 4

  D. 8

ISBN: 978-1-77149-222-5

⑪
K
In $\triangle ABC$, $\angle A = 30°$, $\angle C = 60°$, and $b = 14$ cm. Which of the following should be used to find a?

A. the Pythagorean theorem

B. the primary trigonometric ratios

C. the cosine law

D. none of the above

⑫
K
What is the formula for the general term of an arithmetic sequence with $a = 6$ and $d = 3$?

A. $t_n = 3 + (n - 1)6$

B. $t_n = 6 + (n - 1)3$

C. $t_n = 6(3^{n-1})$

D. $t_n = 3(6^{n-1})$

⑬
K
For a particular sequence, $t_1 = 2$ and $t_n = 3t_{n-1} + 1$. What is the value of t_5?

A. 22

B. 67

C. 202

D. 607

⑭
K
$1000 is invested at 3% per year compounded semi-annually for 4 years. What is the total number of compounding periods?

A. 4

B. 6

C. 8

D. 16

⑮
K
What is the amplitude of the function $y = -2 \sin (x + 30°) + 1$?

A. 1

B. -30°

C. 360°

D. 2

ISBN: 978-1-77149-222-5

⑯ Which is the correct equation when the graph of $y = 2^x$ is translated 3 units up and 4 units left?

K

A. $y = 2^{x-4} + 3$

B. $y = 2^{x+4} - 3$

C. $y = 2^{x+4} + 3$

D. $y = 2^{x-4} - 3$

⑰ Which of the following correctly describes the relationship of the terms in Pascal's triangle if n is the horizontal row number and r is the diagonal row number for n, $r \in \mathbb{N}$ and $r \le n$?

K

A. $t_{n,r} = t_{n-1, r-1} + t_{n-1, r}$

B. $t_{n,r} = t_{n-1, r+1} + t_{n-1, r+1}$

C. $t_{n,r} = t_{n+1, r-1} + t_{n+1, r-1}$

D. $t_{n,r} = t_{n-1, r-1} + t_{n-1, r-2}$

⑱ "3, m, 12, n ..." is a geometric sequence.

K

a. What are the values of m and n?

A. $m = 2$, $n = 14$

B. $m = 6$, $n = 15$

C. $m = 9$, $n = 36$

D. $m = 6$, $n = 24$

b. What is the sum of the first 6 terms of this sequence?

A. 94.5

B. 189

C. 728

D. 48

⑲ What is the present value of the annuity shown?

K

A. $3137.72

B. $1903.86

C. $1847.69

D. $2164.86

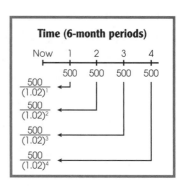

For each statement, circle T for true and F for false.

⑳ K The inverse of the function $f(x) = 2x^2 + 16x + 29$ is $f^{-1}(x) = \pm\sqrt{\dfrac{x+3}{2}} - 4$. **T / F**

㉑ T If $f(x)$ is a function, its inverse must be a function. **T / F**

㉒ T The cosine law is used to solve oblique triangles when two sides and a contained angle or three sides and no angles are given. **T / F**

㉓ K The exponential function $f(x) = -2 \times 3^x$ has a y-intercept of -2. **T / F**

㉔ T "SSA" is a case that would indicate the ambiguous case of the sine law. **T / F**

㉕ K The value of $\sin\theta$ is positive only if θ is greater than 0. **T / F**

㉖ K The graph $g(x) = f(x - d)$ is a horizontal translation of the graph $f(x)$ by d units. **T / F**

Determine whether the given linear and quadratic functions intersect. If they do, determine how many points of intersection there are.

㉗ K $y = 2x^2 - x + 5$ and $y = x + 1$

㉘ K $y = -x^2 + 3x + 8$ and $y = 2x - 1$

㉙ K $y = -x^2 - 3x + 10$ and $y = x + 5$

㉚ K $x^2 - 5x + 8 = y$ and $y + x + 4 = 0$

㉛ K $y = x^2 + kx + 25$ and $y - kx = 0$

㉜ K $y = -a^2x^2 - 3ax + 3$ and $ax + y - 4 = 0$

State the domain and range of each relation.

③③ a.

x	$f(x)$
-4	9
-3	6
-2	3
-1	0

b.

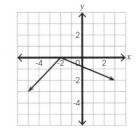

c.

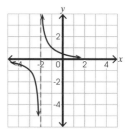

D: _____

D: _____

D: _____

R: _____

R: _____

R: _____

Determine the value(s) of k for each situation.

③④ The quadratic equation $0 = x^2 + kx + 16$ will have

T

a. no roots. | b. one root. | c. two distinct real roots.

③⑤ The quadratic equation $x^2 + 10 = -kx$ can be solved by factoring.

T

Simplify and state the restrictions.

③⑥ $\dfrac{x + 12}{x^2 - 25} \div \dfrac{x^2 + 13x + 12}{x - 5}$

K

③⑦ $\dfrac{x^2 - x - 6}{x^2 + 3x - 18} - \dfrac{x + 17}{x^2 + 7x + 6}$

K

Solve the problems.

(38) For the function $f(x) = 2(x + 1)^2 - 3$,

K a. determine $f^{-1}(x)$.

_____

b. state the domain of the function $f(x)$ so that the inverse is a function.

_____

(39) An orchard owner has estimated that 15 apple trees planted in an enclosed area will yield an average of 250 apples each. For every new tree planted, each tree will yield 10 fewer apples. Determine how many trees should be planted to obtain the maximum yield of apples. Then find the maximum number of apples.

A

_____

(40) Prove each identity.

K

a. $\tan \theta + \dfrac{1}{\tan \theta} = \dfrac{1}{\sin \theta \cos \theta}$

b. $\csc \theta \left(\dfrac{1}{\cot \theta} + \dfrac{1}{\sec \theta}\right) = \sec \theta + \cot \theta$

c. $\dfrac{\sin \theta \tan \theta}{1 - \cos \theta} = 1 + \sec \theta$

d. $\dfrac{1 + \sin \theta}{\cos \theta} + \dfrac{\cos \theta}{1 + \sin \theta} = 2 \sec \theta$

ISBN: 978-1-77149-222-5

④ **A** Andrea had $312 in her piggy bank. At the end of the week, she deposited $5. Each subsequent week, she deposits $3 more than she deposited the previous week. How much money will there be in the piggy bank at the end of 10 weeks?

_____

⑫ **A** **C** Amy decided on her 25th birthday to begin saving for her retirement and asked her bank advisor for options. Below are the options for her.

Option A: At the end of each year, Amy deposits $2200 into an investment that pays 9% interest per year compounded annually.

Option B: At the end of each month, Amy deposits $190 into an investment that pays 8% interest per year compounded monthly.

a. Determine the amount of money Amy will have when she turns 50 years old. Which option should Amy choose? Explain your answer.

_____

b. Assume that Amy chose the option that you suggested in Part a. If Amy is 50 years old and decides to leave the investment in the account until she turns 65, how much will she have saved by the time she is 65 years old?

_____

⑬ **A** **T** A sweepstake is giving away $1 000 000. The first ticket drawn wins $10, the second $30, the third $90, and so on.

a. The winning prizes follow a sequence. Is this sequence arithmetic or geometric? Write a formula to determine the winning amount for each draw.

_____

b. How many tickets can be drawn in this sweepstake?

_____

c. How much money is left after all the prizes are awarded?

_____

㊹ Determine the features of each function. Sketch two cycles of the graph of each function
Ⓚ with an appropriate scale on each axis. Then state the domain and range of each function.

a. $y = 3 \sin\left(\frac{1}{2}(x + 45°)\right) - 1$

amplitude: _____

period: _____

phase shift: _____

vertical shift: _____

b. $y = -2 \cos(4(x - 30°)) + 2$

amplitude: _____

period: _____

phase shift: _____

vertical shift: _____

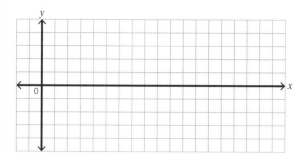

㊺ Erin works in a clothing store. She earns $300 a week plus 7% commission from her sales.
Ⓐ a. Write a function to represent Erin's earnings.

_____

b. If Erin targets to earn $1000 next week, how much sales does she need to make?

_____

㊻ Tim rides his bike 4 km north of his school to a river. He then makes a 145° turn and rides
Ⓐ 7.2 km along a bike lane to a library. Draw a diagram to illustrate the scenario. How far is
the school from the library? What is the bearing of the library from the school?

_____

ISBN: 978-1-77149-222-5

47 **K C**

Write the first six rows of Pascal's triangle. Describe how you would use Pascal's triangle to expand $(a + b)^6$. Then expand each power of a binomial.

Row	Pascal's Triangle
0	1
1	1 1
2	
3	
4	
5	
6	

Expansion of $(a + b)^6$

_____

_____

_____

_____

_____

a. $(a + 2b)^5 =$

_____

b. $(\frac{1}{2}x - \frac{1}{x})^6 =$

_____

48 **A T**

In a theatre, seats are arranged so that the first row has 150 seats, the second row has 147 seats, the third row has 144 seats... and the last row has 30 seats. Determine whether the seat arrangement is an arithmetic or a geometric series. Then find how many seats there are in total.

_____

49 **A T**

Helga wants to have $2000 in her account in 3 years. Which bank should she choose? Explain your answer. How much should she invest today?

• KC Bank: interest rate 8% per year compounded quarterly
• Bank of Branford: interest rate 7.5% per year compounded monthly

⑤⓪ The coordinates of a point on the terminal arm of an angle θ are shown. Determine the
K exact primary trigonometric ratios for θ. Then determine the primary trigonometric ratios
T for another angle between 0° and 360° that has the same sine value.

a.

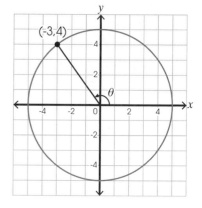

_____

b.

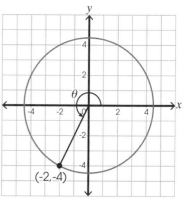

_____

⑤① When Sam boarded a Ferris wheel, his feet were 1 m off the ground. At the highest point of
A the ride, his feet were 99 m above the ground. It takes 30 seconds for the ride to complete
one full revolution.

a. Use a sinusoidal function to model the height of
Sam's feet above the ground as a function of
time. Graph the function over two cycles.

_____

b. At what two times within the first cycle were Sam's feet exactly 90 m off the ground?

_____

ISBN: 978-1-77149-222-5

(52) A T Since January 2015, the population of Vistaville has grown according to a mathematical model.

a. Check the function that best represents the population growth of Vistaville, where x is the number of years since January 2015. Explain your choice.

(A) $f(x) = 52\,500(1.021)^x$

(B) $f(x) = 52\,500(0.96)^x$

b. Explain what the two numbers in the function that you selected mean.

c. What will the population in 2045 be if the change continues at the same rate?

d. Use this model to predict when the population of Vistaville will reach 120 000.

(53) A To measure the height of a cliff, surveyors John and Eric make the measurements shown in the picture. Find the height of the cliff.

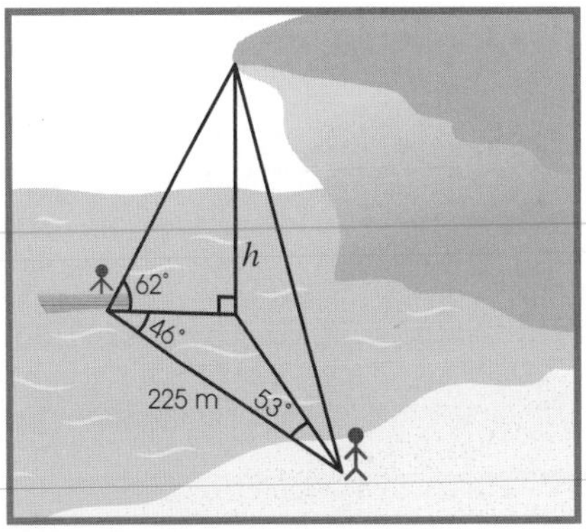

*not to scale

(54) A Julie is offered a $20 000 scholarship by a university. She deposits the money into an account that earns 6% interest per year compounded quarterly. What quarterly withdrawals can Julie make during her 4 years at university?

ISBN: 978-1-77149-222-5

Quadratic Functions

Algebraic Expressions

Consider any polynomials a, b, and c.

$ab = ba$ ← commutative

$(ab)c = a(bc)$ ← associative

$a(b + c) = ab + ac$ ← distributive

e.g. $2(x + 1)x$

$= 2x(x + 1)$ ← commutative

$= 2x^2 + 2x$ ← distributive

Characteristics of Functions

domain: the set of all values of the independent variable of a relation

range: the set of all values of the dependent variable of a relation

x-**intercept:** the point at which the x-axis and a graph meet

y-**intercept:** the point at which the y-axis and a graph meet

maximum/minimum value: the y-value of the vertex

e.g.

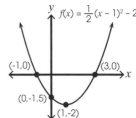

Domain: $\{x \in \mathbb{R}\}$
Range: $\{y \in \mathbb{R} \mid y \geq -2\}$
x-intercepts: (-1,0) and (3,0)
y-intercept: (0,-1.5)
minimum value: (1,-2)

Solving Quadratic Equations

- **by factoring**

  $a^2 + 2ab + b^2 = (a + b)^2$
  $a^2 - 2ab + b^2 = (a - b)^2$
  $a^2 - b^2 = (a + b)(a - b)$

  e.g. $2x^2 + 2x - 12 = 0$
  $2(x^2 + x - 6) = 0$
  $2(x - 2)(x + 3) = 0$
  $x - 2 = 0$ or $x + 3 = 0$
  $x = 2$ $x = -3$
  So, x is 2 or -3.

- **using the quadratic formula**

  $$x = \frac{-b \pm \sqrt{b^2 - 4ac}}{2a}$$

  Discriminant
  $b^2 - 4ac > 0$: 2 real roots
  $b^2 - 4ac = 0$: 1 real root
  $b^2 - 4ac < 0$: no real roots

  e.g. $x^2 + 6x + 4 = 0$

  $a = 1$, $b = 6$, $c = 4$

  $$x = \frac{-6 \pm \sqrt{6^2 - 4(1)(4)}}{2(1)}$$

  $x \doteq -0.76$ or -5.24

  So, x is -0.76 or -5.24.

Tangent Line

A tangent line touches a curve at one point and has the same slope as the curve at that point.

Finding the equation of a tangent line

1st Equate the equations of the function and the tangent line.

2nd Determine the equation of the tangent line.

e.g. function: $y = x^2 - x + 6$
slope of tangent line: 2
    $x^2 - x + 6 = 2x + b$
$x^2 - 3x + 6 - b = 0$
    $(-3)^2 - 4(1)(6 - b) = 0$ ← $b^2 - 4ac = 0$
            $b = 3.75$

The tangent line is $y = 2x + 3.75$.

ISBN: 978-1-77149-222-5

Transformations of Functions

When performing transformations, consider the parameters a and k together before c and d together for efficiency.

$$f(x) \longrightarrow f(kx) \longrightarrow af(kx) \longrightarrow af(k(x-d)) + c$$

$y = f(kx)$
- $0 < |k| < 1$
  horizontal stretch by a scale factor of $\left|\dfrac{1}{k}\right|$
- $|k| > 1$
  horizontal compression by a scale factor of $\left|\dfrac{1}{k}\right|$
- $k < 0$
  reflection in the y-axis

$y = af(x)$
- $|a| > 1$
  vertical stretch by a scale factor of $|a|$
- $0 < |a| < 1$
  vertical compression by a scale factor of $|a|$
- $a < 0$
  reflection in the x-axis

$y = f(x - d)$
- $d > 0$
  horizontal translation to the right
- $d < 0$
  horizontal translation to the left

$y = f(x) + c$
- $c > 0$
  vertical translation up
- $c < 0$
  vertical translation down

Exponential Functions

- **Laws of Exponents**

$$a^{-n} = \frac{1}{a^n}$$

$$\left(\frac{a}{b}\right)^{-n} = \left(\frac{b}{a}\right)^n$$

$$a^{\frac{1}{n}} = \sqrt[n]{a}$$

$$a^{\frac{m}{n}} = (\sqrt[n]{a})^m = (\sqrt[n]{a^m})$$

$$a^m \times a^n = a^{m+n}$$

$$a^m \div a^n = a^{m-n}$$

$$(a^m)^n = a^{mn}$$

- **Exponential Growth and Exponential Decay**

For any exponential function, $f(x)$ can never be 0 for any value of x. Therefore, it must have a horizontal asymptote.

$$f(x) = \left(\frac{1}{2}\right)^x - 5$$
(exponential decay)

$$f(x) = 2^x - 5$$
(exponential growth)

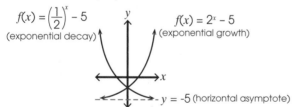

$y = -5$ (horizontal asymptote)

final value · · · initial value

$$f(x) = a\,b^x \longleftarrow \text{no. of periods}$$

- $b > 1$: exponential growth
  $b = 1 + \text{growth rate}$

- $0 < b < 1$: exponential decay
  $b = 1 - \text{decay rate}$

- **Transformations of Exponential Functions**

The parameters a, k, c, and d affect the graphs of exponential functions $f(x) = ab^{k(x-d)} + c$ the same way they affect the graphs of $f(x) = af(k(x - d)) + c$.

e.g. $f(x) = -\dfrac{1}{4}(3^{2(x+1)}) - 2$

- a reflection in the x-axis
- a vertical compression by a factor of $\dfrac{1}{4}$
- a horizontal compression by a factor of $\dfrac{1}{2}$
- a horizontal translation of 1 unit to the left
- a vertical translation of 2 units down

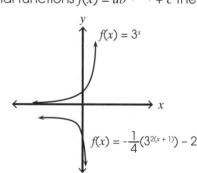

   ISBN: 978-1-77149-222-5

Handy Reference

Trigonometric Functions

Trigonometry

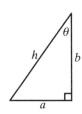

Trigonometric Ratios

$$\sin \theta = \frac{a}{h}$$

$$\cos \theta = \frac{b}{h}$$

$$\tan \theta = \frac{a}{b}$$

Reciprocal of Trigonometric Ratios

$$\csc \theta = \frac{1}{\sin \theta} = \frac{h}{a}$$

$$\sec \theta = \frac{1}{\cos \theta} = \frac{h}{b}$$

$$\cot \theta = \frac{1}{\tan \theta} = \frac{b}{a}$$

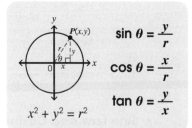

$$\sin \theta = \frac{y}{r}$$

$$\cos \theta = \frac{x}{r}$$

$$\tan \theta = \frac{y}{x}$$

$$x^2 + y^2 = r^2$$

- **Special Angles**

  They are angles with measures of 30°, 45°, and 60°. They give exact values of primary trigonometric ratios.

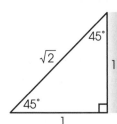

$$\sin 45° = \frac{1}{\sqrt{2}}$$

$$\cos 45° = \frac{1}{\sqrt{2}}$$

$$\tan 45° = 1$$

$$\sin 30° = \frac{1}{2} \qquad \sin 60° = \frac{\sqrt{3}}{2}$$

$$\cos 30° = \frac{\sqrt{3}}{2} \qquad \cos 60° = \frac{1}{2}$$

$$\tan 30° = \frac{1}{\sqrt{3}} \qquad \tan 60° = \sqrt{3}$$

- **Angles in the Cartesian Plane**

  - **initial arm:**
    lies on the positive x-axis and is fixed

  - **terminal arm:**
    rotates from the initial arm

  - **principal angle (θ):**
    the angle measured counterclockwise from the initial arm to the terminal arm

  - **related acute angles (β):**
    the acute angle between the terminal arm and the x-axis

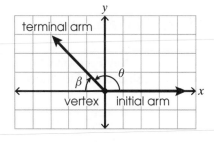

$\sin (180° - \theta) = \sin \theta$ $\cos (180° - \theta) = -\cos \theta$ $\tan (180° - \theta) = -\tan \theta$
$\sin (180° + \theta) = -\sin \theta$ $\cos (180° + \theta) = -\cos \theta$ $\tan (180° + \theta) = \tan \theta$
$\sin (360° - \theta) = -\sin \theta$ $\cos (360° - \theta) = \cos \theta$ $\tan (360° - \theta) = -\tan \theta$

The CAST rule can help you remember which trigonometric ratios are positive in each quadrant.

S only sine is positive	**A** all ratios are positive
T only tangent is positive	**C** only cosine is positive

e.g. $\sin \theta = 0.9563$

- quadrant I:
  $\theta = \sin^{-1} 0.9563$
  $\theta \doteq 73°$

- quadrant II:
  $\theta = 180° - 73°$
  $\theta = 107°$

θ can be either 73° or 107°.

Handy Reference

- ## Trigonometric Identities

Reciprocal Identities

$$\csc \theta = \frac{1}{\sin \theta}$$

$$\sec \theta = \frac{1}{\cos \theta}$$

$$\cot \theta = \frac{1}{\tan \theta}$$

Quotient Identities

$$\tan \theta = \frac{\sin \theta}{\cos \theta}$$

$$\cot \theta = \frac{\cos \theta}{\sin \theta}$$

Pythagorean Identities

$$\sin^2 \theta + \cos^2 \theta = 1$$

$$1 + \tan^2 \theta = \sec^2 \theta$$

$$1 + \cot^2 \theta = \csc^2 \theta$$

- ## Sine Law and Cosine Law

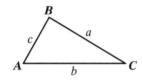

Sine Law

$$\frac{a}{\sin A} = \frac{b}{\sin B} = \frac{c}{\sin C}$$

Cosine Law

$$c^2 = a^2 + b^2 - 2ab \cos C$$

Ambiguous Case

Consider that the measures of $\angle A$, a, and b are known.

$$h = b \sin A$$

$\angle A$ is acute.

- Case 1: $a < h$
  no triangles exist
- Case 2: $a = h$
  one right triangle exists
- Case 3: $a = b$ or $a > b$
  one triangle exists
- Case 4: $h < a < b$
  two triangles exist

$\angle A$ is obtuse.

- Case 1: $a = b$ or $a < b$
  no triangles exist
- Case 2: $a > b$
  one triangle exists

Sinusoidal Functions

Key Features of Sinusoidal Functions

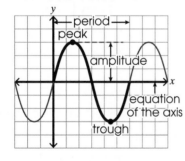

- **period**: the horizontal distance for a graph to complete one cycle
- **peak**: the maximum point of a graph
- **trough**: the minimum point of a graph
- **equation of the axis**: the equation of the horizontal line halfway between the maximum and minimum values

$$y = \frac{\text{max. value} + \text{min. value}}{2}$$

- **amplitude**: half the difference between the maximum and minimum values, or the vertical distance from the function's axis to the maximum or minimum value

e.g.

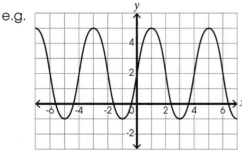

period: 4

peak: 5

trough: -1

equation of the axis: $y = 2$

amplitude: 3

domain: $\{x \in \mathbb{R}\}$

range: $\{y \in \mathbb{R} \mid -1 \le y \le 5\}$

ISBN: 978-1-77149-222-5

- ## Transformations of Sinusoidal Functions

$$f(x) = a \sin (k (x - d)) + c$$
$$f(x) = a \cos (k (x - d)) + c$$

a: amplitude

d: phase shift

k: period $= \dfrac{360°}{|k|}$

c: equation of the axis

The parameters a, k, c, and d affect sinusoidal functions the same way they affect other functions you learned previously.

When doing transformations, you are not required to find all the values of $f(x)$; finding the values of the key points is sufficient.

Key Points

$f(x) = \sin x$	$f(x) = \cos x$
(0°,0)	(0°,1)
(90°,1)	(90°,0)
(180°,0)	(180°,-1)
(270°,-1)	(270°,0)
(360°,0)	(360°,1)

e.g. $f(x) = \sin (2(x + 45°)) - 2$

- a horizontal compression by a factor of $\dfrac{1}{2}$
- a translation of 45° to the left and 2 units down

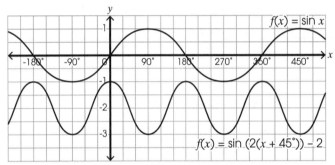

Discrete Functions

Explicit Formula and Recursive Formula

Explicit Formula

$$t_n = a + (n - 1)d$$

↑ nth term   ↑ first term   ↑ common difference

e.g. $a = 4$, $d = 2$

Find t_{25}.

$t_{25} = 4 + (25 - 1)2$
$= 52$

Recursive Formula

$$t_n = t_{n-1} + d$$

↑ nth term   ↑ common difference

e.g. $t_1 = 10$, $d = 3$

Find t_3.

$t_2 = 10 + 3$ $t_3 = 13 + 3$
$= 13$ $= 16$

Pascal's Triangle and Binomial Powers

Pascal's Triangle

```
            1
          1   1
        1   2   1
      1   3   3   1
    1   4   6   4   1
  1   5  10  10   5   1
1   6  15  20  15   6   1
1  7  21  35  35  21  7  1
```

A term in Pascal's triangle

$$t_{n,r}$$

horizontal row number   diagonal row number

- horizontal row starts at row number 0
- diagonal row starts at row number 1
- sum of each row is 2^n
- first and last terms of each row are always 1
- each term is the sum of the two terms immediately above it

$$t_{n,r} = t_{n-1, r-1} + t_{n-1, r}$$

Handy Reference

Binomial Powers

- Coefficients in the expansions of $(a+b)^n$ can be found in rows of n of Pascal's triangle.
- In each expansion, the power of a increases and the power of b decreases.
- The degree of each term is always equal to the exponent of the binomial power.

Pascal's Triangle $(a + b)^n$

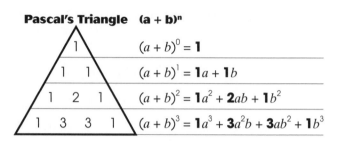

$(a + b)^0 = \mathbf{1}$

$(a + b)^1 = \mathbf{1}a + \mathbf{1}b$

$(a + b)^2 = \mathbf{1}a^2 + \mathbf{2}ab + \mathbf{1}b^2$

$(a + b)^3 = \mathbf{1}a^3 + \mathbf{3}a^2b + \mathbf{3}ab^2 + \mathbf{1}b^3$

Sequences and Series

Arithmetic Sequence

- a sequence where the differences between consecutive terms are constant

$$t_n = a + (n-1)d$$
or
$$t_n = t_{n-1} + d$$

Arithmetic Series

- sum of the terms of an arithmetic sequence

$$S_n = \frac{n}{2}(a + t_n)$$
or
$$S_n = \frac{n}{2}(2a + (n-1)d)$$

Geometric Sequence

- a sequence where the ratios of consecutive terms are constant
- terms are obtained by multiplying the first term a and each subsequent term by a common ratio, r

$$t_n = ar^{n-1}$$

Geometric Series

- sum of the terms of a geometric sequence

$$S_n = \frac{a(r^n - 1)}{r - 1},\ r \neq 1$$

Financial Applications

Simple Interest

- interest calculated on the original principal

interest — principal

$$I = Prt \leftarrow \text{time}$$

interest rate

Compound Interest

- interest that is calculated at regular compounding periods, added to the principal for the following compounding period

amount   compounding period

$$A = P(1 + i)^n$$

principal   interest rate

Present Value of an Annuity

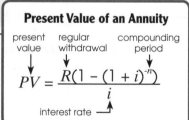

present value   regular withdrawal   compounding period

$$PV = \frac{R(1 - (1 + i)^{-n})}{i}$$

interest rate

Present Value

- the principal invested or borrowed today to result in a given future amount

present value   future value

$$PV = \frac{FV}{(1 + i)^n} \leftarrow \text{compounding period}$$

interest rate

Annuity

- a sum of money paid as a series of regular payments

regular payment   compounding period

total amount

$$A = \frac{R((1 + i)^n - 1)}{i}$$

interest rate

ISBN: 978-1-77149-222-5

1 Basic Skills

1.1 Graphing Systems of Linear Equations

Try This (p. 6)

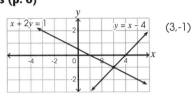

$(3,-1)$

1.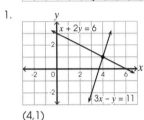

$(4,1)$

2.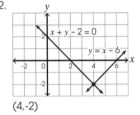

$(4,-2)$

3. $(15,7)$
4. no solutions
5. $(-4,3)$

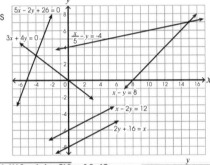

6a. $AB = \sqrt{(6 - (-6))^2 + (-4 - 2)^2} \doteq 13.42$
$CD = \sqrt{(6 - (-2))^2 + (-1 - (-3))^2} \doteq 8.25$

b. midpoint $AB = (\frac{-6 + 6}{2}, \frac{2 + (-4)}{2}) = (0,-1)$

midpoint $CD = (\frac{-2 + 6}{2}, \frac{-3 + (-1)}{2}) = (2,-2)$

c. The point of intersection is $(2,-2)$. So the midpoint of CD falls on the point of intersection.

7. $y = 4x - 1$
$2x + 3(4x - 1) = 11$
$2x + 12x - 3 = 11$
$x = 1$
$y = 4(1) - 1 = 3$
$\therefore (1,3)$

8. $y = \frac{7}{2}x - 7$
$5x - 4(\frac{7}{2}x - 7) = -9$
$5x - 14x + 28 = -9$
$x = \frac{37}{9}$
$y = \frac{7}{2}(\frac{37}{9}) - 7 = \frac{133}{18}$
$\therefore (\frac{37}{9}, \frac{133}{18})$

9. $y = 1 + x$
$-0.5x + 0.25(1 + x) = -1$
$-0.5x + 0.25 + 0.25x = -1$
$x = 5$
$y = 1 + 5 = 6$
$\therefore (5,6)$

10. $8x + y = -16$ ①
$3x - y = 5$ ②
$11x = -11$ ① + ②
$x = -1$
$3(-1) - y = 5$
$y = -8$
$\therefore (-1,-8)$

11. $5x + y = 9$ ①
$10x - 7y = -18$ ②
$9y = 36$ ① × 2 - ②
$y = 4$
$5x + 4 = 9$
$x = 1$
$\therefore (1,4)$

12. $-4x + 9y = 9$ ①
$\frac{1}{6}x - \frac{1}{2}y = -1$ ②
$-3y = -15$ ① + ② × 24
$y = 5$
$-4x + 9(5) = 9$
$x = 9$
$\therefore (9,5)$

13. $2x + 8y = 6$ ①
$\frac{1}{3}x + \frac{4}{3}y = 1$ ②
$0y = 0$ ① - ② × 6
There are infinitely many solutions. The lines have the same slope and y-intercept.

14. $x = \frac{9}{4}y + \frac{22}{4}$
$-7(\frac{9}{4}y + \frac{22}{4}) - 8y = 9$
$y = -2$
$x = \frac{9}{4}(-2) + \frac{22}{4} = 1$
There is one solution: $(1,-2)$.
The lines do not have the same slope or y-intercept.

15. $y = -2x - 4$
$(-2x - 4) + 2 = 2x$
$x = -\frac{1}{2}$
$y = -2(-\frac{1}{2}) - 4 = -3$
There is one solution: $(-\frac{1}{2},-3)$.
The lines do not have the same slope or y-intercept.

16. F   17. T   18. T   19. F

20. Let b be the speed of the boat and w be the speed of the water current.
$2(b + w) = 12 \rightarrow b = 6 - w$ $b = 5$
$3(b - w) = 12 \rightarrow b = 4 + w$ $w = 1$
The speed of the boat in still water is 5 km/h and the speed of the water current is 1 km/h.

21a. $0 = \frac{3 + a}{2}$ $0 = \frac{6 + b}{2}$
$a = -3$ $b = -6$
The coordinates are $(-3,-6)$.

b. $AC = \sqrt{(3 - (-3))^2 + (6 - (-6))^2} = \sqrt{180}$
Side length: $x^2 + x^2 = (\sqrt{180})^2$
$x = \sqrt{90}$
Perimeter: $4x = 4\sqrt{90} \doteq 37.95$
The perimeter of square $ABCD$ is 37.95 units.

22. Point of intersection: $2(3y - 6) + y = -5$
$y = 1$
$x = 3(1) - 6 = -3$ $\therefore (-3,1)$
Slope of $l_1 = -2$; $l_\perp = \frac{1}{2}$
$y = \frac{1}{2}x + b$
$1 = \frac{1}{2}(-3) + b$
$b = \frac{5}{2}$
The equation is $y = \frac{1}{2}x + \frac{5}{2}$.

1.2 Exponent Rules and Polynomials

1. $= a^8$
2. $= a^2b$
3. $= \frac{1}{a^3b^3}$
4. $= \frac{a^4b^6}{c^4}$
5. $= 9a^2b^6$
6. $= \frac{2}{81a^3b^{18}}$

7. $= \frac{2^{-2} \times 3^2 \times 5^1}{2^2 \times 3^2 \times 5^2}$
$= \frac{1}{2^4 \times 5}$

8. $= \frac{2^{-3} \times 2^{-4}}{2^{-2} \times 3^{-2} \times 2^{-2} \times 3^{-2}}$
$= \frac{3^4}{2^3}$

9. $= \frac{2^2 \times 3^{10} \times 3^{-4}}{2^3 \times 3^6 \times 3^{-2}}$
$= \frac{3^2}{2}$

10. $= \frac{4^{-1} \times 2^6}{2^3} + \frac{3^1 \times 9^{-1}}{3^{-2}}$
$= 2 + 3$
$= 5$

11. $= \frac{(-1)^{-2} \times 2^6 \times 2^{-5}}{2^{-2} \times 3^{-6} \times 3^{10}}$
$= \frac{2^3}{3^4}$

12. $= \frac{10^6 \times 2^2 \times 5^{12}}{2^2 \times 5^{-4} \times 10^4 \times 5^6}$
$= 5^{10} \times 10^2$

13. $= 14x^2 + 28x + 4x + 8$
$= 14x^2 + 32x + 8$

14. $= -3x^2 + 12x + x - 4$
$= -3x^2 + 13x - 4$

15. $= 2y^2 - 12y + 5y - 30$
    $= 2y^2 - 7y - 30$

16. $= -2y^2 + y + 6y - 3$
    $= -2y^2 + 7y - 3$

17. $= 6m^2 + 4mn - 3mn - 2n^2$
    $= 6m^2 + mn - 2n^2$

18. $= -2m^2 + 6mn + mn - 3n^2$
    $= -2m^2 + 7mn - 3n^2$

19. $= 5m^2 - 15mn - mn + 3n^2$
    $= 5m^2 - 16mn + 3n^2$

20. GCF: $4x$; x ; $2y$

21. GCF: $3ab$; $-ab$; $2b$; $5a$

22. GCF: $2m^2n^2$
    $= 2m^2n^2(3m - n + 2mn)$

23. GCF: $5ab$
    $= 5ab(2c - ac^2 + 3b)$

24. GCF: $3xy$
    $= 3xy(3z - x + 2z^2)$

25. GCF: $8m^2n^2$
    $= 8m^2n^2(2 - n^2 - 3m^2)$

26. GCF: $x + y$
    $= (x + y)(3x - 4)$

27. GCF: $a - b$
    $= (a - b)(a + b + 3a - 3b)$
    $= (a - b)(4a - 2b)$
    $= 2(a - b)(2a - b)$

28. GCF: $(x - y)^2$
    $= (x - y)^2(2xy - 3)$

29. GCF: $3(a + b)$
    $= 3(a + b)(a(a + b) - 1 + 3b)$
    $= 3(a + b)(a^2 + ab + 3b - 1)$

30. $= 3p^2 + 3pq - p^2 + pq$
    $= 2p^2 + 4pq$
    $= 2p(p + 2q)$

31. $= a^2 - ab + ab + b^2$
    $= a^2 + b^2$

32. $= m^3 + m^2 - m + m^2 - m^3$
    $= 2m^2 - m$
    $= m(2m - 1)$

33. $= x^3y + x^2y^2 - x^2y^2 + xy^3$
    $= x^3y + xy^3$
    $= xy(x^2 + y^2)$

34. $= p^2 + 2pq + q^2 - p^2 + 3pq$
    $= 5pq + q^2$
    $= q(5p + q)$

35. $= a^2b - ab^2 + abc - bc - abc$
    $= a^2b - ab^2 - bc$
    $= b(a^2 - ab - c)$

36. $= \dfrac{m^2 - mn + n^2 - mn - m^2 - 2mn - n^2}{mn}$
    $= \dfrac{-4mn}{mn}$
    $= -4$

37. $= \dfrac{p^2q - 3p^2 - p^2q - 4pq - 3p^2 - 2pq}{3p^2 - 3pq + pq - q^2}$
    $= \dfrac{-6p^2 - 6pq}{3p^2 - 2pq - q^2}$
    $= \dfrac{-6p(p + q)}{(3p + q)(p - q)}$

38. $2^{-2}(x + y)^2$
    $= \dfrac{(x + y)^2}{2^2}$
    $= (\dfrac{x + y}{2})^2$
    Yes, they are equivalent.

39. $p^2q^0 - (p + q)^2$
    $= p^2 - p^2 - 2pq - q^2$
    $= -2pq - q^2$
    $= -q(2p + q)$
    No, they are not equivalent.

40. $(i + j)^2 - (i - j)^2$
    $= i^2 + 2ij + j^2 - i^2 + 2ij - j^2$
    $= 4ij$
    No, they are not equivalent.

41. $n(\dfrac{m + n}{2})^{-2} - \dfrac{4}{m + n}$
    $= \dfrac{4n}{(m + n)^2} - \dfrac{4}{m + n}$
    $= -4m(m + n)^{-2}$
    Yes, they are equivalent.

42. $p \times p \times p \times p - 3^2 \times p \times p$
    $= p^4 - 3^2p^2$
    $= p^2(p^2 - 3^2)$
    $= p^2(p - 3)(p + 3)$
    No, they are not equivalent.

43. $\dfrac{x^2}{x + y} - x$
    $= \dfrac{x^2}{x + y} - \dfrac{x(x + y)}{x + y}$
    $= \dfrac{-xy}{x + y}$

    $y - \dfrac{y^2}{x + y}$
    $= \dfrac{y(x + y)}{x + y} - \dfrac{y^2}{x + y}$
    $= \dfrac{xy}{x + y}$
    No, they are not equivalent.

44. $\dfrac{(p^2 + p) + (p + 1) + (p + 1)}{p + 1}$
    $= \dfrac{p^2 + 3p + 2}{p + 1}$
    $= \dfrac{(p + 1)(p + 2)}{p + 1}$
    $= p + 2$
    Each piece will be $(p + 2)$ long.

45. $\dfrac{0.25(8y + 1)(y - 1) - 2(y - 1)}{0.25}$
    $= (8y^2 - 7y - 1) - 8(y - 1)$
    $= 8y^2 - 15y + 7$
    $= (8y - 7)(y - 1)$
    Kevin has $(8y - 7)(y - 1)$ quarters.

46a. $\pi r^2 - \pi(r - s)^2$
    $= \pi r^2 - \pi r^2 + 2\pi rs - \pi s^2$
    $= 2\pi rs - \pi s^2$
    $= \pi s(2r - s)$
    The area of the ring is
    $\pi s(2r - s)$.

b. $2\pi r + 2\pi(r - s)$
    $= 2\pi(2r - s)$
    $2\pi(2r - s)$ of ribbon is
    needed.

47a. $\dfrac{x^2 + 2xy + 4xy + 8y^2}{0.5x + 2y}$
    $= \dfrac{(x + 4y)(x + 2y)}{0.5(x + 4y)}$
    $= \dfrac{x + 2y}{0.5}$
    $= 2(x + 2y)$
    The ratio is $2(x + 2y)$.

b. $\dfrac{x^2 + 2xy + xy + 2y^2}{2(x + 2y)}$
    $= \dfrac{(x + 2y)(x + y)}{2(x + 2y)}$
    $= \dfrac{x + y}{2}$
    $= 0.5(x + y)$
    The length of the
    corresponding side of
    Figure A is $0.5(x + y)$.

1.3 Factorization

Try This (p. 14)

$= (x + 7)(x - 3)$

$= 5x^2 - 10x + 7x - 14$
$= 5x(x - 2) + 7(x - 2)$
$= (x - 2)(5x + 7)$

1. $= 6x^2 + 15x - 16x - 40$
   $= 3x(2x + 5) - 8(2x + 5)$
   $= (2x + 5)(3x - 8)$

2. $= (x + 3)(x - 5)$

3. $= 3x^2 - 9x - x + 3$
   $= 3x(x - 3) - 1(x - 3)$
   $= (x - 3)(3x - 1)$

4. $= 4x^2 + 8x + 3x + 6$
   $= 4x(x + 2) + 3(x + 2)$
   $= (x + 2)(4x + 3)$

5. $= (x + 7y)(x - 5y)$

6. $= (x - 30y)(x + 3y)$

7. $= 12x^2 + 4x - 9x - 3$
   $= 4x(3x + 1) - 3(3x + 1)$
   $= (3x + 1)(4x - 3)$

8. $= 10x^2 + 11xy - 6y^2$
   $= 10x^2 - 4xy + 15xy - 6y^2$
   $= 2x(5x - 2y) + 3y(5x - 2y)$
   $= (5x - 2y)(2x + 3y)$

9. $= x^2 + 8x - 20$
   $= (x + 10)(x - 2)$

10. No, she did not do the work correctly.
    $-2x + x^2 + 6$
    $= x^2 - 2x + 6$
    The polynomial cannot be factored any further.

11. $= (x - 5)^2$

12. $= (9x - 2y)^2$

13. $= (2x - 3y)^2$

14. $= (x + 6)^2$

15. $= (3x + 4y^2)^2$

16. $= (2x^2 - 11y)^2$

17. No

18. Yes ; $= (2x - 1)(2x + 1)$

19. No

20. Yes ; $= (xy - 2)(xy + 2)$

21. No

22. No

23. Yes ; $= (5x - 6y)(5x + 6y)$

24. Yes ; $= (1 - 7x)(1 + 7x)$

25. The possible values are -22 and 22.

26. $m^2 - 4n^2 = (m - 2n)(m + 2n)$

Try This (p. 16)

$6x$
x ; $3x^2$; $7x$; 6
x ; $3x - 2$; $x + 3$

27. $= 3(6x^2 + 5x - 4)$
    $= 3(2x - 1)(3x + 4)$

28. $= y(x^2 + 8x + 15)$
    $= y(x + 3)(x + 5)$

29. $= x^2(x - 7y) - 3y(x - 7y)$
    $= (x - 7y)(x^2 - 3y)$

30. $= (4x^2 - 1)(4x^2 + 1)$
    $= (2x - 1)(2x + 1)(4x^2 + 1)$

31. $= 2(x^4 + 6x^2 + 9)$
    $= 2(x^2 + 3)^2$

32. $= (16x^2 - 9)(16x^2 + 9)$
    $= (4x - 3)(4x + 3)(16x^2 + 9)$

33. $= 5(x^4 - 16y^4)$
    $= 5(x^2 - 4y^2)(x^2 + 4y^2)$
    $= 5(x - 2y)(x + 2y)(x^2 + 4y^2)$

34. $= y(4x^2 - 19x - 5)$
    $= y(4x + 1)(x - 5)$

ISBN: 978-1-77149-222-5

35. $= k(x^4 - y^4)$
$= k(x^2 - y^2)(x^2 + y^2)$
$= k(x - y)(x + y)(x^2 + y^2)$

36. k can be -4 or -5.
If $k = -4$, the factored form is $x(x^2 - 2)^2$.
If $k = -5$, the factored form is $x(x - 1)(x + 1)(x + 2)(x - 2)$.

37. No, because the binomial can still be factored.
$$\frac{x^4}{2} - 8$$
$$= \frac{1}{2}(x^4 - 16)$$
$$= \frac{1}{2}(x^2 - 4)(x^2 + 4)$$
$$= \frac{1}{2}(x - 2)(x + 2)(x^2 + 4)$$

1.4 Simple Quadratic Equations

1. **A** $y = x^2$ **B** $y = x^2 - 6x + 5$

A x	y
-3	9
-2	4
-1	1
0	0
1	1
2	4
3	9

B x	y
0	5
1	0
2	-3
3	-4
4	-3
5	0
6	5

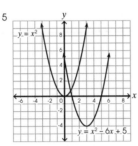

A: opens upward ; minimum point at (0,0) ;
vertex at (0,0) ; axis of symmetry at $x = 0$
B: opens upward ; minimum point at (3,-4) ;
vertex at (3,-4) ; axis of symmetry at $x = 3$

2.

x	-3	-2	-1	0	1	2	3
$f(x) = x^2$	9	4	1	0	1	4	9
$g(x) = \frac{1}{2}x^2$	4.5	2	0.5	0	0.5	2	4.5
$h(x) = 2x^2$	18	8	2	0	2	8	18

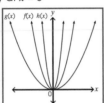

$\frac{1}{2}$; compressed ; 2 ; stretched
a. compression   b. stretch   c. stretch

3.

x	-3	-2	-1	0	1	2	3
$f(x) = x^2$	9	4	1	0	1	4	9
$g(x) = -x^2$	-9	-4	-1	0	-1	-4	-9

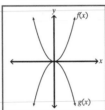

upward ; downward
a. opens downward
b. opens upward
c. opens downward

4.
vertex: (4,3)
axis of symmetry: $x = 4$
direction of opening:
opens upward

5.
vertex: (-3,-6)
axis of symmetry: $x = -3$
direction of opening:
opens downward

6.
vertex: (1,0)
axis of symmetry: $x = 1$
direction of opening:
opens downward

7.
vertex: $(\frac{1}{2}, 1)$
axis of symmetry: $x = \frac{1}{2}$
direction of opening:
opens upward

8.
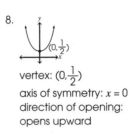
vertex: $(0, \frac{1}{2})$
axis of symmetry: $x = 0$
direction of opening:
opens upward

9.
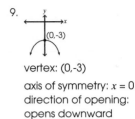
vertex: (0,-3)
axis of symmetry: $x = 0$
direction of opening:
opens downward

1.5 Triangles and Trigonometric Ratios

1. $y \doteq 14.97$
$\sin \theta \doteq 0.56$ $\sin \beta \doteq 0.83$
$\cos \theta \doteq 0.83$ $\cos \beta \doteq 0.56$
$\tan \theta \doteq 0.67$ $\tan \beta \doteq 1.50$

2. $y \doteq 9.76$
$\sin \theta \doteq 0.79$ $\sin \beta \doteq 0.61$
$\cos \theta \doteq 0.61$ $\cos \beta \doteq 0.79$
$\tan \theta \doteq 1.28$ $\tan \beta \doteq 0.78$

3. 76°   4. 37°   5. 51°
6. 60°   7. 49°   8. 16°
9. 44°   10. 18°   11. 0.53
12. 0.71   13. 0.53   14. 0.97
15. 0.97   16. 0.81   17. 0.53 ; 0.85

18. $\cos 37° = \frac{6.5}{x}$ $\tan 37° = \frac{y}{6.5}$ $\tan \theta = \frac{6.5}{4.9}$
$x \doteq 8.14$ $y \doteq 4.90$ $\theta \doteq 53°$

19. $\sin 42° = \frac{x}{15}$ $\cos 42° = \frac{y}{15}$ $\sin \theta = \frac{11.15}{15}$
$x \doteq 10.04$ $y \doteq 11.15$ $\theta \doteq 48°$

20. $\cos 30° = \frac{x}{\sqrt{80}}$ $\sin 30° = \frac{y}{\sqrt{80}}$ $\sin \theta = \frac{7.75}{\sqrt{80}}$
$x \doteq 7.75$ $y \doteq 4.47$ $\theta \doteq 60°$

21. $\cos \theta = \frac{7}{9}$ $\cos \beta = \frac{7}{9}$ $\sin 39° = \frac{h}{9}$
$\theta \doteq 39°$ $\beta \doteq 39°$ $h \doteq 5.66$

22. $\cos \theta = \frac{14.5}{16}$ $\sin \beta = \frac{14.5}{16}$
$\theta \doteq 25°$ $\beta \doteq 65°$

23. $\tan \theta = \frac{10}{12}$ $\tan \beta = \frac{10}{(6 + 12)}$
$\theta \doteq 40°$ $\beta \doteq 29°$
$\cos 40° = \frac{12}{x}$ $\sin 29° = \frac{10}{y}$
$x \doteq 15.66$ $y \doteq 20.63$

24. $\tan 34° = \frac{x}{8.5}$ $\sin 28° = \frac{5.73}{z}$ $\tan 28° = \frac{5.73}{8.5 + y}$
$x \doteq 5.73$ $z \doteq 12.21$ $y \doteq 2.28$

25a. $\sin 60° = \frac{2.5}{l}$
$l \doteq 2.89$
The ladder is 2.89 m long.

b. $\tan 60° = \frac{2.5}{d}$
$d \doteq 1.44$
The ladder is 1.44 m away from the wall.

26a. $\tan 36° = \frac{x}{180}$ $\tan 24° = \frac{y}{180}$
$x \doteq 130.78$ $y \doteq 80.14$
$130.78 + 80.14 = 210.92$
The tower is 210.92 m tall.

b. $\cos 36° = \frac{180}{d}$
$d \doteq 222.49$
The shortest distance is 222.49 m.

27a. $\cos 53° = \frac{9}{a}$ $\cos 36° = \frac{7}{b}$
$a \doteq 14.95$ $b \doteq 8.65$
Bird B will get the apple first.

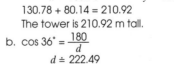

b. $\tan 53° = \frac{x}{9}$ $\tan 36° = \frac{y}{7}$
$x \doteq 11.94$ $y \doteq 5.09$
$11.94 + 5.09 = 17.03$
The two trees are 17.03 m apart.

ISBN: 978-1-77149-222-5

2 Equivalent Algebraic Expressions

2.1 Adding and Subtracting Polynomials

Try This (p. 22)

$$f(x) = 2x^2 - 3x - x - x^2 + 1 \qquad g(x) = -x + x^2 - 3x + 1$$
$$= x^2 - 4x + 1 \qquad\qquad = x^2 - 4x + 1$$

are
1. not equivalent
2. not equivalent
3. not equivalent
4. equivalent
5. equivalent
6. A, B, D

7-12. (Check Questions 7, 10, 11, and 12.)

13. $3x(-5 - x) + 2(3 - x) = -3x^2 - 17x + 6$
   $3(x^2 + 5) + x - 9(2x + 1) = 3x^2 - 17x + 6$
   $\therefore$ not equivalent
   Substitute $x = 1$,
   $3(1)(-5 - 1) + 2(3 - 1) = -14$
   $3(1^2 + 5) + 1 - 9(2(1) + 1) = -8$
   $\therefore$ not equivalent

14. $x(2 + x) - 3(x^2 - 1) + 2(-2 - 3x) = -(x + 1)^2 + m$
   $-2x^2 - 4x - 1 = -x^2 - 2x - 1 + m$
   $m = -x^2 - 2x$

15. No, she is incorrect.
   $f(x) = -4x^2 + 2x + 2 \qquad g(x) = x + 2$
   $f(x) \neq g(x)$

16. (Suggested answer)
   $f(x) = x^2 - 1 \qquad f(1) = 0 \qquad f(-1) = 0$
   $g(x) = -x^2 + 1 \qquad g(1) = 0 \qquad g(-1) = 0$

17a. $f(x) = 4x^2 - 2x$
   $g(x) = 5x^2 + x - 2$
   $h(x) = 2x^2 - 2x$
   Since $f(x) \neq g(x) \neq h(x)$, it is a scalene triangle.
   b. $(4x^2 - 2x) + (5x^2 + x - 2) + (2x^2 - 2x)$
   $= 11x^2 - 3x - 2$
   For $x = 5$, $11(5)^2 - 3(5) - 2 = 258$.
   The perimeter is $(11x^2 - 3x - 2)$ units.
   If x equals 5, the perimeter is 258 units.

18a. Let n represent the number of guests.
   For $0 \leq n \leq 100$,
   $C(n) = (300 + 10n) + (100 + 5n)$
   $= 400 + 15n$
   For $n > 100$,
   $C(n) = (300 + 10n) + (100 + 5n) - 7n$
   $= 400 + 8n$
   b. \$1825 ; \$2000
   c. $C(n) = 200 + 150 + 9n + 50 + 6n = 400 + 15n$
   It is equivalent to Burger Palace's when $0 \leq n \leq 100$.
   d. They should choose Burger Palace. The cost will be \$2000.

19a. $h_1(t) - h_2(t) = (-5(t - 10)^2 + 1500) - (100(6 - t) - t(5t - 200) + 400)$
   $= (-5t^2 + 100t + 1000) - (-5t^2 + 100t + 1000)$
   $= 0$
   b. Since the difference is 0, it means the altitudes of the two rockets were equal.
   c. $0 = -5(t - 10)^2 + 1500$
   $(t - 10)^2 = 300$
   $t = 10 \pm \sqrt{300}$
   $t \doteq 27.32$ or $t \doteq -7.32$
   (not applicable)
   It took the rockets 27.32 s to reach the ground.

2.2 Multiplying and Factoring Polynomials

1. $6x^2 ; 12x ; 15x ; 30$
   $6x^2 + 10x^2 + 12x - 15x - 30$
   $-4x^3 + 16x^2 - 3x - 30$

2. $= (3x^2 - 5x - 28)(-x - 5)$
   $= -3x^3 + 5x^2 + 28x - 15x^2 + 25x + 140$
   $= -3x^3 - 10x^2 + 53x + 140$
3. $a^3 - 11a^2 + 38a - 40$
4. $5b^2 - 5b - 59$
5. $m^3 - m^2 + 6m - 12$
6. $-n^3 - 5n^2 + 11n + 3$
7a. equivalent   b. not equivalent   c. equivalent
8a. $((x + 2)^2 - 4)(x + 3) \div 2 = \frac{1}{2}x^3 + \frac{7}{2}x^2 + 6x$
   The area is $\frac{1}{2}x^3 + \frac{7}{2}x^2 + 6x$.
   b. $((x + 2)^2 - 4) + (x + 3) + (5x + 3) = x^2 + 10x + 6$
   The perimeter is $x^2 + 10x + 6$.
9. $2x^2 ; 6 ; x ; 2 ; x ; 2 ; x ; 2$
10. $27 ; 2 ; 2x ; 9 ; 2x ; 9 ; 2x ; 9 ; 1$
11. • $25 ; 64 ; 5 ; 8 ; 5 ; 8$
   • $2x ; 7 ; 2x ; 7$
   • $25 ; 30 ; 9 ; 5x ; 30 ; 3 ; 5x ; 3$
   • prime
12. $2x(2x - 1)(x - 1)$
13. $(2y + 3x)(4y - 7x)$
14. $5(x^2 - 9x + 70)$
15. $3(4xy - 3)(4xy + 3)$
16. $(m + 3)(m - 2)(m + 2)$
17. $(p - 3)(q - 2)$
18. prime
19. $(w - 2)(w + 2)(w^2 + 4)$
20. $= 2x^5 - 26x^3 + 72x$
   $= 2x(x^4 - 13x^2 + 36)$
   $= 2x(x^2 - 4)(x^2 - 9)$
   $= 2x(x - 2)(x + 2)(x - 3)(x + 3)$
21. $= 9a^2 - b^2 - 2b - 1$
   $= 9a^2 - (b^2 + 2b + 1)$
   $= (3a)^2 - (b + 1)^2$
   $= (3a + b + 1)(3a - b - 1)$
22. $= x^2 + 2x - 3 - 2x^2 + 27$
   $= -x^2 + 2x + 24$
   $= (x + 4)(-x + 6)$
   $= -(x + 4)(x - 6)$
23. $= x^3 - 2x^2 - x - x^2 + 2x + 1 - 4$
   $= x^3 - 3x^2 + x - 3$
   $= x^2(x - 3) + (x - 3)$
   $= (x^2 + 1)(x - 3)$
24. $= (p - q)(p^2 - 1) + pq(p - q)$
   $= (p - q)(p^2 + pq - 1)$
25. $= -x + x^3 + 5x^2 - 5$
   $= x^3 + 5x^2 - x - 5$
   $= x^2(x + 5) - (x + 5)$
   $= (x^2 - 1)(x + 5)$
   $= (x - 1)(x + 1)(x + 5)$
26a. $2(5x + 2)(x + 2)$
   b. $2(5x^2 + 6x + 2)(3x + 1)$
27. Area before: $(2b)b \div 2 = b^2$
   Area after: $(2b + 1)(b - 1) \div 2 = b^2 - \frac{b}{2} - \frac{1}{2}$
   Difference: $b^2 - \frac{b}{2} - \frac{1}{2} - b^2 = -\frac{b}{2} - \frac{1}{2}$
   Since the expression is negative, the area of the triangle decreases.
28a. $(2x - 3y)(4x^2 + 9y^2)$
   $= 8x^3 + 18xy^2 - 12x^2y - 27y^3$
   $(2x)^3 - (3y)^3$
   $= 8x^3 - 27y^3$
   The expressions are not equivalent.
   b. $(2x)^3 - (3y)^3$
   $= (2x - 3y)((2x)^2 + (2x)(3y) + (3y)^2)$
   $= (2x - 3y)(4x^2 + 6xy + 9y^2)$

2.3 Multiplying and Dividing Rational Expressions

Try This (p. 29)

$$= \frac{1}{3x} ; x \neq 0 \qquad\qquad = \frac{3(1 - 3x)}{6(x - 1)}$$
$$= \frac{1 - 3x}{2x - 1} ; x \neq 1$$

1. $= \frac{-3(4 + x)}{3x}$
   $= \frac{-(4 + x)}{x} ; x \neq 0$
2. $= \frac{x - 1}{x + 3} ; x \neq -3, 1$
3. $= -\frac{2}{x} ; x \neq 0$
4. $= \frac{6x(x - 1)}{x^2}$
   $= \frac{6(x - 1)}{x} ; x \neq 0$

ISBN: 978-1-77149-222-5

5. $= \dfrac{3x^2y^2}{3xy(3x + 4y)}$

   $= \dfrac{xy}{3x + 4y}$; $x \neq 0, -\dfrac{4y}{3}$

   $\quad\quad\quad\quad\quad y \neq 0$

6. $= \dfrac{3x(y^2 - 4)}{x(y^2 - y - 2)}$

   $= \dfrac{3x(y - 2)(y + 2)}{x(y - 2)(y + 1)}$

   $= \dfrac{3(y + 2)}{y + 1}$; $x \neq 0, y \neq -1, 2$

7. $= \dfrac{6x^2y - 9xy^2}{8x - 12y}$

   $= \dfrac{3xy(2x - 3y)}{4(2x - 3y)}$

   $= \dfrac{3xy}{4}$; $x \neq \dfrac{3y}{2}$

8. $= \dfrac{(m + 1)(m - 2)(m - 1)}{(m - 1)(m + 1)(m - 3)}$

   $= \dfrac{m - 2}{m - 3}$; $m \neq -1, 1, 3$

9. $= \dfrac{7a(a - 4)}{(a - 4)(5a^2)}$

   $= \dfrac{7}{5a}$; $a \neq 0, 4$

10. $= \dfrac{16n(n + 1)}{40(n + 1)}$

    $= \dfrac{2n}{5}$; $n \neq -1$

Try This (p. 30)

$= \dfrac{(x - 10)(x + 1)}{(x + 1)}$

$= x - 10$

Domain: $\{x \in \mathbb{R} \mid x \neq -1\}$

11. $= \dfrac{x^3}{x(x + 1)}$

    $= \dfrac{x^2}{x + 1}$

    $\{x \in \mathbb{R} \mid x \neq 0, -1\}$

12. $= \dfrac{x + 2}{(x - 2)(x + 2)}$

    $= \dfrac{1}{x - 2}$

    $\{x \in \mathbb{R} \mid x \neq -2, 2\}$

13. $= \dfrac{x - 3}{-5(x - 3)}$

    $= -\dfrac{1}{5}$

    $\{x \in \mathbb{R} \mid x \neq 3\}$

14. $= \dfrac{2x(x + 5)}{-3(x + 5)}$

    $= -\dfrac{2x}{3}$

    $\{x \in \mathbb{R} \mid x \neq -5\}$

15. $= \dfrac{4(x^2 - 4)}{(x + 3)(x - 2)}$

    $= \dfrac{4(x - 2)(x + 2)}{(x + 3)(x - 2)}$

    $= \dfrac{4(x + 2)}{x + 3}$

    $\{x \in \mathbb{R} \mid x \neq -3, 2\}$

16. $= \dfrac{2x(x - 1)}{(x - 1)^3}$

    $= \dfrac{2x}{(x - 1)^2}$

    $\{x \in \mathbb{R} \mid x \neq 1\}$

17. $= \dfrac{(m - 1)^2}{2(m + 9)(m - 1)}$

    $= \dfrac{m - 1}{2(m + 9)}$

    $\{m \in \mathbb{R} \mid m \neq -9, 1\}$

18. $= \dfrac{(t - 5)(t - 6)(t - 5)}{(t - 6)(t + 6)}$

    $= \dfrac{(t - 5)^2}{t + 6}$

    $\{t \in \mathbb{R} \mid t \neq -6, 5, 6\}$

19. $= \dfrac{5a^2(a - 1)(a + 1)}{20a(a + 1)}$

    $= \dfrac{a(a - 1)}{4}$

    $\{a \in \mathbb{R} \mid a \neq 0, -1\}$

20. $= \dfrac{3(w - 4)(w + 5)(w - 3)}{(w - 4)(w + 4)(w + 1)}$

    $= \dfrac{3(w + 5)(w - 3)}{(w + 4)(w + 1)}$

    $\{w \in \mathbb{R} \mid w \neq -4, -1, 4\}$

21A: $= \dfrac{(x - 2)(x - 3)}{x - 2}$

   $= x - 3$

   $x \neq 2$

   $\{x \in \mathbb{R} \mid x \neq 2\}$

B: $= \dfrac{(2x + 5)(x - 1)}{2x + 5}$

   $= x - 1$

   $x \neq -\dfrac{5}{2}$

   $\{x \in \mathbb{R} \mid x \neq -\dfrac{5}{2}\}$

C: $= \sqrt{x - 1} \times \dfrac{3(x - 6)}{(x - 6)}$

   $= 3\sqrt{x - 1}$

   $x \geq 1, x \neq 6$

   $\{x \in \mathbb{R} \mid x \geq 1, x \neq 6\}$

D: $= \dfrac{(x + 1)(x - 1)}{(x - 2)(x - 1)}$

   $= \dfrac{x + 1}{x - 2}$

   $x \neq 1, 2$

   $\{x \in \mathbb{R} \mid x \neq 1, 2\}$

E: $= \dfrac{(x + 2)(x + 1)}{(x + 1)(x - 3)}$

   $= \dfrac{x + 2}{x - 3}$

   $x \neq -1, 3$

   $\{x \in \mathbb{R} \mid x \neq -1, 3\}$

F: $= \dfrac{(x^2 + 1)(x^2 - 1)}{x - 1}$

   $= \dfrac{(x^2 + 1)(x + 1)(x - 1)}{x - 1}$

   $= (x^2 + 1)(x + 1)$

   $x \neq 1$

   $\{x \in \mathbb{R} \mid x \neq 1\}$

C ; A ; E ;
D ; F ; B

22a. $(x^2 - 2x)\left(\dfrac{3x^2 + 6x}{x - 2}\right)$

   $= \dfrac{3x^2(x - 2)(x + 2)}{x - 2}$

   $= 3x^2(x + 2)$; $x \neq 2$

   The area of the rectangle is $3x^2(x + 2)$.

b. $\dfrac{x^2 - 2x}{\left(\dfrac{3x^2 + 6x}{x - 2}\right)} = \dfrac{x(x - 2)(x - 2)}{3(x + 2)}$

   $= \dfrac{(x - 2)^2}{3(x + 2)}$; $x \neq -2, 0, 2$

   The ratio is $\dfrac{(x - 2)^2}{3(x + 2)}$.

23a. height: $\dfrac{1}{2}(x^2 + 3x + 2) \times 2 \div \dfrac{x^2 - 1}{x + 2}$

   $= (x + 2)(x + 1) \times \dfrac{x + 2}{(x + 1)(x - 1)}$

   $= \dfrac{(x + 2)^2}{x - 1}$; $x \neq -2, -1, 1$

   The height is $\dfrac{(x + 2)^2}{x - 1}$.

b. $\dfrac{1}{2}(x^2 + 3x + 2)\left(\dfrac{x + 5}{x + 1}\right)$

   $= \dfrac{(x + 2)(x + 1)(x + 5)}{2(x + 1)}$

   $= \dfrac{(x + 2)(x + 5)}{2}$; $x \neq -1$

   The volume is $\dfrac{(x + 2)(x + 5)}{2}$.

24a. $(x^3 - 6x^2 - 4x + 24) \div (x - 2) \div (x - 6)$

   $= \dfrac{(x - 2)(x + 2)(x - 6)}{(x - 2)(x - 6)}$

   $= x + 2$; $x \neq 2, 6$

   The height of the prism is $x + 2$.

b. $\dfrac{x + 2}{x^3 - 6x^2 - 4x + 24}$

   $= \dfrac{x + 2}{(x - 2)(x + 2)(x - 6)}$

   $= \dfrac{1}{(x - 2)(x - 6)}$; $x \neq 2, 6$

   The ratio is $\dfrac{1}{(x - 2)(x - 6)}$.

25. (Suggested answers) $\dfrac{(x - 3y)(y - 4x)}{x - 3y}$ and $\dfrac{(x - 3y)^2(y - 4x)}{(x - 3y)^2}$

26. (Suggested answers)

   $\dfrac{1}{(x + 1)(x - 1)(x - 3)}$ and $\dfrac{x}{(x + 1)(x - 1)(x - 3)}$

2.4 Simplifying Rational Expressions

1. $= \dfrac{3m - n + 2n - 5m}{n}$

   $= \dfrac{-2m + n}{n}$

2. $= \dfrac{y^2 - y - y + 2y^2}{3y - 2}$

   $= \dfrac{3y^2 - 2y}{3y - 2}$

   $= \dfrac{y(3y - 2)}{3y - 2}$

   $= y$

3. $= \dfrac{4xy + (x - y)^2}{x + y}$

   $= \dfrac{4xy + x^2 - 2xy + y^2}{x + y}$

   $= \dfrac{x^2 + 2xy + y^2}{x + y}$

   $= \dfrac{(x + y)^2}{x + y}$

   $= x + y$

4. $= \dfrac{p^2 - 3p - 54}{p - 9}$

   $= \dfrac{(p - 9)(p + 6)}{p - 9}$

   $= p + 6$

5. $= \dfrac{5v^2 - 5v}{1 - v}$

   $= \dfrac{-5v(1 - v)}{1 - v}$

   $= -5v$

6. $= \dfrac{a^2 - 30 + a}{a + 6}$

   $= \dfrac{(a + 6)(a - 5)}{a + 6}$

   $= a - 5$

7. $= \dfrac{b - 8}{b^2 + b - 72}$

   $= \dfrac{b - 8}{(b - 8)(b + 9)}$

   $= \dfrac{1}{b + 9}$

8. $= \dfrac{x^2 + 1 - 2x}{x - 1}$

   $= \dfrac{(x - 1)^2}{x - 1}$

   $= x - 1$

9. $= \dfrac{y - 5 + 2}{y^2 - 3y}$

$= \dfrac{y - 3}{y(y - 3)}$

$= \dfrac{1}{y}$

10. $= \dfrac{2 - 5k}{k + 3} - \dfrac{5 - 4k}{k + 3}$

$= \dfrac{2 - 5k - 5 + 4k}{k + 3}$

$= \dfrac{-3 - k}{k + 3}$

$= \dfrac{-(k + 3)}{k + 3}$

$= -1$

11. $= \dfrac{10}{2x + 10} + \dfrac{2x}{2x + 10}$

$= \dfrac{2x + 10}{2x + 10}$

$= 1$

12. $= \dfrac{m - 4n + 4m + 4n}{9mn}$

$= \dfrac{5m}{9mn}$

$= \dfrac{5}{9n}$

13. $= \dfrac{1 - t^2}{(t - 1)^2}$

$= \dfrac{(1 - t)(1 + t)}{(t - 1)^2}$

$= \dfrac{-(t - 1)(t + 1)}{(t - 1)^2}$

$= -\dfrac{t + 1}{t - 1}$

14A. $-\dfrac{x - 7}{x + 6}$; $x \neq -6, 7$ B: y^2 ; $y \neq 1$

C: $-\dfrac{x - y}{x + y}$; $x \neq -y, y$ D: $\dfrac{2(x + y)}{2x + y}$; $x \neq -\dfrac{y}{2}$

15. $= \dfrac{2p - 3}{(p - 2)(p - 3)} - \dfrac{5}{(p - 3)(p + 3)}$ LCM: $(p - 2)(p - 3)(p + 3)$

$= \dfrac{(2p - 3)(p + 3)}{(p - 2)(p - 3)(p + 3)} - \dfrac{5(p - 2)}{(p - 2)(p - 3)(p + 3)}$

$= \dfrac{2p^2 + 6p - 3p - 9 - 5p + 10}{(p - 2)(p - 3)(p + 3)}$

$= \dfrac{2p^2 - 2p + 1}{(p - 2)(p - 3)(p + 3)}$; $p \neq -3, 2, 3$

16. LCM: $(x + 4)(x - 4)$

$= \dfrac{16}{(x + 4)(x - 4)} + \dfrac{2(x - 4)}{(x + 4)(x - 4)}$

$= \dfrac{2x - 8 + 16}{(x + 4)(x - 4)}$

$= \dfrac{2x + 8}{(x + 4)(x - 4)}$

$= \dfrac{2(x + 4)}{(x + 4)(x - 4)}$

$= \dfrac{2}{x - 4}$; $x \neq -4, 4$

17. LCM: $(m + 3)(m + 4)(m + 1)$

$= \dfrac{3m(m + 1)}{(m + 3)(m + 4)(m + 1)} - \dfrac{4m(m + 3)}{(m + 3)(m + 4)(m + 1)}$

$= \dfrac{3m^2 + 3m - 4m^2 - 12m}{(m + 3)(m + 4)(m + 1)}$

$= \dfrac{-m^2 - 9m}{(m + 3)(m + 4)(m + 1)}$

$= \dfrac{-m(m + 9)}{(m + 3)(m + 4)(m + 1)}$; $m \neq -1, -3, -4$

18. LCM: $(a - 3)(a - 5)$

$= \dfrac{4(a - 5)}{(a - 3)(a - 5)} + \dfrac{a(a - 3)}{(a - 3)(a - 5)}$

$= \dfrac{4a - 20 + a^2 - 3a}{(a - 3)(a - 5)}$

$= \dfrac{a^2 + a - 20}{(a - 3)(a - 5)}$

$= \dfrac{(a + 5)(a - 4)}{(a - 3)(a - 5)}$; $a \neq 3, 5$

19. LCM: $(x + 2)(x - 3)(3x + 1)$

$= \dfrac{x + 1}{(x + 2)(x - 3)} + \dfrac{x}{(3x + 1)(x - 3)}$

$= \dfrac{(x + 1)(3x + 1) + x(x + 2)}{(x + 2)(x - 3)(3x + 1)}$

$= \dfrac{3x^2 + 4x + 1 + x^2 + 2x}{(x + 2)(x - 3)(3x + 1)}$

$= \dfrac{4x^2 + 6x + 1}{(x + 2)(x - 3)(3x + 1)}$; $x \neq -2, 3, -\dfrac{1}{3}$

20. LCM: $(a - 2)^3$

$= \dfrac{4(a - 2)^2}{(a - 2)^3} - \dfrac{81}{(a - 2)^3}$

$= \dfrac{4a^2 - 16a + 16 - 81}{(a - 2)^3}$

$= \dfrac{4a^2 - 16a - 65}{(a - 2)^3}$

$= \dfrac{(2a + 5)(2a - 13)}{(a - 2)^3}$; $a \neq 2$

21. LCM: $(m + 2)(m + 3)$

$= \dfrac{(-3m - 1) + (m - 3)(m + 3)}{(m + 2)(m + 3)}$

$= \dfrac{-3m - 1 + m^2 - 9}{(m + 2)(m + 3)}$

$= \dfrac{m^2 - 3m - 10}{(m + 2)(m + 3)}$

$= \dfrac{(m - 5)(m + 2)}{(m + 2)(m + 3)}$

$= \dfrac{m - 5}{m + 3}$; $m \neq -2, -3$

22. $= 6x - 4x$

$= 2x$; $x \neq 0, y \neq 0$

23. $= \dfrac{(x - 1)(x + 1)}{(x + 1)} - \left(\dfrac{6x}{x + 1}\right)\left(\dfrac{(x + 1)(x - 1)}{x}\right)$

$= (x - 1) - 6(x - 1)$

$= -5(x - 1)$; $x \neq -1, 0, 1$

24. $= \dfrac{z}{z - 2} - \dfrac{4(z + 2)^2}{z + 2}$

$= \dfrac{z}{z - 2} - 4(z + 2)$

$= \dfrac{z}{z - 2} - \dfrac{4(z + 2)(z - 2)}{z - 2}$

$= \dfrac{z - 4(z^2 - 4)}{z - 2}$

$= \dfrac{-4z^2 + z + 16}{z - 2}$; $z \neq -2, 2$

25. $= \dfrac{b}{b - 2a} - \dfrac{12}{(b - 4a)(b - 2a)}$

$= \dfrac{b(b - 4a) - 12}{(b - 4a)(b - 2a)}$

$= \dfrac{b^2 - 4ab - 12}{(b - 4a)(b - 2a)}$; $b \neq 4a, 2a$

26. $= \dfrac{(2x + 5)(x + 4)}{(2x + 5)(x + 6)} \times \dfrac{(x - 4)(x + 4)}{(x + 4)^2} \times \dfrac{6(x + 5)}{x - 4}$

$= \dfrac{6(x + 5)}{(x + 6)}$; $x \neq -6, -5, -4, -2.5, 4$

27. $= \dfrac{5(m - n)}{10} \times \dfrac{6}{(m - n)(m + n)} + \dfrac{3mn}{(m + n)^2}$

$= \dfrac{3(m + n) + 3mn}{(m + n)^2}$

$= \dfrac{3(m + mn + n)}{(m + n)^2}$; $m \neq -n, n$

28. $= \dfrac{4a}{(a + 1)^2} - \dfrac{(2a + 3)(a - 5)}{(a - 1)(a + 1)(2a - 3)} \times \dfrac{-3(a - 1)}{2(a - 5)}$

$= \dfrac{8a(2a - 3) + 3(2a + 3)(a + 1)}{2(2a - 3)(a + 1)^2}$

$= \dfrac{22a^2 - 9a + 9}{2(2a - 3)(a + 1)^2}$; $a \neq -1, 1, \dfrac{3}{2}, 5$

29. $= \dfrac{4(p - 4)}{5(p + 3)} \times \dfrac{(3p + 1)(p + 3)}{2(p + 2)} \times \dfrac{(p + 2)^2}{(3p + 1)(p - 4)}$

$= \dfrac{2(p + 2)}{5}$; $p \neq -3, -2, -\dfrac{1}{3}, 4$

30. $= \dfrac{(x + 6)(x - 2)}{x(x - 2)} \times \dfrac{(x + 2)(x - 1)}{3(x - 2)} + \dfrac{1}{x} + \dfrac{3x}{x - 2}$

$= \dfrac{(x - 1)(x + 6) + 3(x - 2) + 9x^2}{3x(x - 2)}$

$= \dfrac{2(5x^2 + 4x - 6)}{3x(x - 2)}$; $x \neq -2, 0, 1, 2$

31. $= \dfrac{2}{(n - 2)(n + 1)} \times \dfrac{(n + 4)(n - 2)}{10n} \times \dfrac{n(n + 1)}{(n + 4)(n - 3)}$

$= \dfrac{1}{5(n - 3)}$; $n \neq -4, -1, 0, 2, 3$

32. $f(x) = \dfrac{x^2 - 2x - 3}{x^2 + 2x - 3} \div \dfrac{x^2 + 4x + 3}{x^2 - 4x + 3} + \dfrac{x - 3}{x^2 + 4x + 3}$

$= \dfrac{(x + 1)(x - 3)}{(x + 3)(x - 1)} \times \dfrac{(x + 3)(x + 1)}{(x - 3)(x - 1)} + \dfrac{x - 3}{x^2 + 4x + 3}$

$= \dfrac{(x + 1)^2}{(x - 1)^2} + \dfrac{x - 3}{(x + 1)(x + 3)}$ ← forgot to multiply the reciprocal
← should find the LCD to do the addition

$= \dfrac{(x + 1)(x - 3)}{(x - 1)^2(x + 3)}$; $x \neq 1$ ← some restrictions missing

$= \dfrac{(x + 1)(x - 3)}{(x + 3)(x - 1)} \times \dfrac{(x - 3)(x - 1)}{(x + 3)(x + 1)} + \dfrac{x - 3}{x^2 + 4x + 3}$

$= \dfrac{(x - 3)^2}{(x + 3)^2} + \dfrac{x - 3}{(x + 3)(x + 1)}$

$= \dfrac{(x - 3)^2(x + 1) + (x - 3)(x + 3)}{(x + 3)^2(x + 1)}$

$= \dfrac{(x - 3)((x - 3)(x + 1) + (x + 3))}{(x + 3)^2(x + 1)}$

$= \dfrac{(x - 3)(x^2 - x)}{(x + 3)^2(x + 1)}$

$= \dfrac{x(x - 1)(x - 3)}{(x + 3)^2(x + 1)}$; $x \neq -3, -1, 1, 3$

33. Area $= \dfrac{(5x + y)^2}{(2x - 2y)^2}$ Perimeter $= \sqrt{\dfrac{(5x + y)^2}{(2x - 2y)^2}} \times 4$

$= \dfrac{4(5x + y)}{2x - 2y}$

$= \dfrac{2(5x + y)}{x - y}$; $x \neq y$

The perimeter is $\dfrac{2(5x + y)}{x - y}$ and the restriction is $x \neq y$.

34a. Area $= (3x - 6 + x^2 + 3x - 10) \times 4x \div 2$

$= (x^2 + 6x - 16) \times 4x \div 2$

$= 2x(x - 2)(x + 8)$

The area is $2x(x - 2)(x + 8)$.

b. $y^2 = ((x^2 + 3x - 10) - (3x - 6))^2 + (4x)^2$

$y^2 = (x^2 - 4)^2 + (4x)^2$

$y^2 = x^4 + 8x^2 + 16$

$y^2 = (x^2 + 4)^2$

$y = x^2 + 4$

The side length is $y = x^2 + 4$.

35. $f(x) = \dfrac{60x}{x - 1} - \dfrac{80x}{x + 2} = \dfrac{60x(x + 2) - 80x(x - 1)}{(x - 1)(x + 2)}$

$= \dfrac{60x^2 + 120x - 80x^2 + 80x}{(x - 1)(x + 2)}$

$= \dfrac{-20x^2 + 200x}{(x - 1)(x + 2)}$

$= \dfrac{20x(10 - x)}{(x - 1)(x + 2)}$

For $(x - 1)$ hours, $x - 1 > 0$, so $x > 1$.

$f(x) = \dfrac{20(10 - x)}{(x - 1)(x + 2)} > 0$; $10 - x > 0$, $x < 10$.

∴ The restriction is $1 < x < 10$.

36a. Solid A: $\dfrac{1}{3}\pi r^2 h + \pi r^2 h = \dfrac{4}{3}\pi r^2 h$

Solid B: $\dfrac{1}{3}\pi r^2(2h) = \dfrac{2}{3}\pi r^2 h$

b. $\dfrac{4}{3}\pi r^2 h : \dfrac{2}{3}\pi r^2 h = 2:1$

The ratio is 2:1.

37a. $\dfrac{1}{R} = \dfrac{1}{x + 2} + \dfrac{1}{y - 3}$

$\dfrac{1}{R} = \dfrac{(y - 3) + (x + 2)}{(x + 2)(y - 3)}$

$\dfrac{1}{R} = \dfrac{x + y - 1}{(x + 2)(y - 3)}$

$R = \dfrac{(x + 2)(y - 3)}{x + y - 1}$; $x + y \neq 1$, $x \neq -2$, $y \neq 3$

b. $\dfrac{1}{R} = \dfrac{1}{x} + \dfrac{1}{4x^2 - x}$

$\dfrac{1}{R} = \dfrac{(4x - 1) + 1}{x(4x - 1)}$

$\dfrac{1}{R} = \dfrac{4}{4x - 1}$

$R = \dfrac{4x - 1}{4}$; $x \neq 0, \dfrac{1}{4}$

38. $W = F \times d$

$d = W \div F$

$d = \dfrac{2(16x^2 - 1)}{x - 1} \div \dfrac{8x^2 - 10x - 3}{x - 1}$

$d = \dfrac{2(4x - 1)(4x + 1)}{x - 1} \times \dfrac{x - 1}{(2x - 3)(4x + 1)}$

$d = \dfrac{2(4x - 1)}{2x - 3}$; $x \neq -\dfrac{1}{4}, \dfrac{3}{2}, 1$

The distance moved is $\dfrac{2(4x - 1)}{2x - 3}$ and the restrictions are $x \neq -\dfrac{1}{4}, \dfrac{3}{2}, 1$.

3   Quadratic Functions

3.1   The Domain and Range of a Function

Try This (p. 38)

This is not a function; 2 maps to both 8 and 10.

{(2,8), (2,10), (3,9), (4,10), (5,11)}

{2, 3, 4, 5}

{8, 9, 10, 11}

1A: yes   B: yes

{(-5,3), (-2,3), (2,6), (5,3)}   {(-4,1), (3,2), (-2,2.5), (2,-1)}

{-5, -2, 2, 5}   {-4, -2, 2, 3}

{3, 6}   {-1, 1, 2, 2.5}

Try This (p. 39)

 This vertical line intersects the relation at only one point.

is

2A: ✔   B: ✔   C: ✗   D: ✔   E: ✗

3.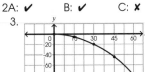

yes

4.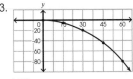

x	4	8	12	16	20
y	0	±2	±2.8	±3.5	±4

no

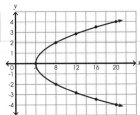

Try This (p. 40)

{1, 2, 5, 6}

{10, 14, 21, 28}

This is a function because each element of the domain maps to one element in the range.

5. {2, 3, 8, 11, 25}

{6, 9, 16, 19, 33}

Yes ; Each element of the domain maps to one element in the range.

6. {5, 8, 9, 12}

{72, 88, 96, 107, 127}

No ; The value 5 maps to both 72 and 88.

7. {1, 2, 4, 8}

{4, 6, 7, 9}

No ; The value 2 maps to both 6 and 9.

8. {-5, -4, -3, -1, 2}

{-9, -8, -6, 0, 6}

Yes ; Each element of the domain maps to one element in the range.

Try This (p. 41)

$\{x \in \mathbb{R} \mid -4 \leq x \leq 4\}$

$\{y \in \mathbb{R} \mid -4 \leq y \leq 4\}$

9. C ; A ; B
   D: $\{x \in \mathbb{R} \mid x \geq -2\}$ E: $\{x \in \mathbb{R} \mid x \neq 4\}$
       $\{y \in \mathbb{R} \mid y \geq 3\}$ $\{y \in \mathbb{R} \mid y \neq 0\}$
   F: $\{x \in \mathbb{R}\}$
       $\{y \in \mathbb{R} \mid y \leq 9\}$

10.
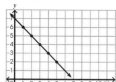

x	1	2	3	4	5
y	6	5	4	3	2

$\{x \in \mathbb{R}\}$
$\{y \in \mathbb{R}\}$

11.
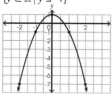

x	-2	-1	0	1	2
y	-7	-1	1	-1	-7

$\{x \in \mathbb{R}\}$
$\{y \in \mathbb{R} \mid y \leq -1\}$

12. (Suggested graph)

$\{x \in \mathbb{R}\}$
$\{y \in \mathbb{R} \mid y < 3\}$

13. (Suggested graph)

$\{x \in \mathbb{R} \mid x > -1\}$
$\{y \in \mathbb{R} \mid y > -1\}$

3.2 Function Notation

Try This (p. 43)

-2 ; -2 ; -2 ; = 8 - 2 - 4 ; = 2 ; 2

1. $f(2) = -3(2)^2 - 2 + 2 = -12$
   $f(0) = -3(0)^2 - 0 + 2 = 2$
   $f(-\frac{1}{3}) = -3(-\frac{1}{3})^2 - (-\frac{1}{3}) + 2 = 2$

2. $f(2) = (3(2) - 1)^2 - 1 = 24$
   $f(0) = (3(0) - 1)^2 - 1 = 0$
   $f(-\frac{1}{3}) = (3(-\frac{1}{3}) - 1)^2 - 1 = 3$

3. $f(2) = 1 - \frac{1}{2 - 1} = 0$
   $f(0) = 1 - \frac{1}{0 - 1} = 2$
   $f(-\frac{1}{3}) = 1 - \frac{1}{-\frac{1}{3} - 1} = 1\frac{3}{4}$

4a. $\frac{2}{3}$ b. 2
c. $\frac{b}{b + 1}$ d. $\frac{b - 1}{b}$

5a. $1\frac{2}{3}$ b. -1
c. $\frac{b^2 + b - 1}{b + 1}$ d. $\frac{b^2 - b - 1}{b}$

6a. $2\frac{1}{3}$ b. 3
c. $\frac{b^2 + 2b - 1}{b + 1}$ d. $-b + 2$

7.
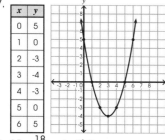

x	y
0	5
1	0
2	-3
3	-4
4	-3
5	0
6	5

	from the graph	by evaluation
$f(0)$	5	5
$f(\frac{1}{2})$	$2\frac{1}{4}$	$2\frac{1}{4}$
$f(\frac{5}{2})$	$-3\frac{3}{4}$	$-3\frac{3}{4}$
$f(4\frac{1}{2})$	$-1\frac{3}{4}$	$-1\frac{3}{4}$
$f(6)$	5	5

8. $15 - \frac{18}{2} = 6$; 6°C

$15 - \frac{d}{2}$; $d = 26$; 26 m

9. Let E represent the money earned and s represent the total sales.
   $E(s) = 40 + 0.1s$
   • $s = 250$,
   $E(250) = 40 + 0.1(250) = 65$
   Alice will earn $65.
   • $E(s) = 58$,
   $58 = 40 + 0.1s$
   $s = 180$
   The total sales will be $180.

10. Let T represent the average temperature and d represent the distance.
    $T(d) = 40 - 2(\frac{d}{80})$
    $T(d) = 40 - \frac{d}{40}$
    • $d = 270$,
    $T(270) = 40 - \frac{270}{40} = 33.25$
    The average temperature is 33.25°C.
    • $T(d) = 28$,
    $28 = 40 - \frac{d}{40}$
    $d = 480$
    The place is 480 km north of the equator.

11. Let V represent the value of the car and t represent the time.
    $V(t) = 32\,000 - 1200(\frac{t}{6})$
    $V(t) = 32\,000 - 200t$
    • $V(t) = 15\,000$,
    $15\,000 = 32\,000 - 200t$
    $t = 85$
    It will take 85 months.
    • $t = 48$,
    $V(48) = 32\,000 - 200(48) = 22\,400$
    The value of the car will be $22\,400.

12a. $A(d) = \pi(\frac{3}{2}d)^2 - \pi(\frac{d}{2})^2$
     $A(d) = 2\pi d^2$
 b. $A(4) = 2 \times 3.14 \times 4^2 = 100.48$
    The area of the ring is 100.48 cm².
 c. $A(d) = 628$
    $628 = 2 \times 3.14 \times d^2$
    $d = 10$
    The diameter of the inner circle is 10 cm.

13a. $20\,500   b. $4214.29   c. 18 years

3.3 Maximum or Minimum Values of Quadratic Functions

1. 6 ;
   3 ; 3 ;
   3 ; 18 ;
   3 ; 1 ;
   2 ; -1 ;
   (-3,-1) ; up ; min. ; -1

2. $= x^2 + 5x + (\frac{5}{2})^2 - (\frac{5}{2})^2 + 3$
   $= (x + \frac{5}{2})^2 - \frac{13}{4}$
   vertex at $(-\frac{5}{2}, -\frac{13}{4})$; opens up ;
   min. value of $-\frac{13}{4}$

3. $= -(x^2 - 9x + (-\frac{9}{2})^2) + (-\frac{9}{2})^2 - 20$
   $= -(x - \frac{9}{2})^2 + \frac{1}{4}$
   vertex at $(\frac{9}{2}, \frac{1}{4})$; opens down ; max. value of $\frac{1}{4}$

4. $= 3(x^2 + 2x + (\frac{2}{2})^2) - 3(\frac{2}{2})^2 + 5$
   $= 3(x + 1)^2 + 2$
   vertex at (-1,2) ; opens up ; min. value of 2

5. $= -\frac{1}{2}(x^2 - 8x + (-\frac{8}{2})^2) + \frac{1}{2}(-\frac{8}{2})^2 + 1$
   $= -\frac{1}{2}(x - 4)^2 + 9$
   vertex at (4,9) ; opens down ; max. value of 9

6. $= x^2 - \frac{1}{2}x + (-\frac{\frac{1}{2}}{2})^2 - (-\frac{\frac{1}{2}}{2})^2$
   $= (x - \frac{1}{4})^2 - \frac{1}{16}$
   vertex at $(\frac{1}{4}, -\frac{1}{16})$; opens up ; min. value of $-\frac{1}{16}$

7. $= -\frac{1}{3}(x^2 + 9x + (\frac{9}{2})^2) + \frac{1}{3}(\frac{9}{2})^2 + 3$
   $= -\frac{1}{3}(x + \frac{9}{2})^2 + \frac{39}{4}$
   vertex at $(-\frac{9}{2}, \frac{39}{4})$; opens down ; max. value of $\frac{39}{4}$

8. 2 ;
   x ; 2 ;
   0 ; 2 ;
   0 ; 2 ; 1 ;
   1 ; 1 ;
   3 ;
   (1,3) ; up ; min. ; 3

9. $= 3x(x - 2) + 1$
   $x = 0$ or $x = 2$
   $x_{\text{vertex}} = \frac{0 + 2}{2} = 1$
   $f(1) = 3(1)^2 - 6(1) + 1 = -2$
   vertex at (1,-2) ; opens up ; min. value of -2

10. $= -2x^2 - 5x + 8$
    $= -2x(x + \frac{5}{2}) + 8$
    $x = 0$ or $x = -\frac{5}{2}$
    $x_{\text{vertex}} = \frac{0 + (-\frac{5}{2})}{2} = -\frac{5}{4}$
    $f(-\frac{5}{4}) = -2(-\frac{5}{4} + 1)^2 - (-\frac{5}{4}) + 10 = \frac{89}{8}$
    vertex at $(-\frac{5}{4}, \frac{89}{8})$; opens down ; max. value of $\frac{89}{8}$

11. $= -x(x + 3) - 2$
    $x = 0$ or $x = -3$
    $x_{\text{vertex}} = \frac{0 + (-3)}{2} = -\frac{3}{2}$
    $f(-\frac{3}{2}) = -(-\frac{3}{2})^2 - 2 - 3(-\frac{3}{2}) = \frac{1}{4}$
    vertex at $(-\frac{3}{2}, \frac{1}{4})$; opens down ; max. value of $\frac{1}{4}$

12. $= -4x(x - 4) + 1$
    $x = 0$ or $x = 4$
    $x_{\text{vertex}} = \frac{0 + 4}{2} = 2$
    $f(2) = -4(2)^2 + 16(2) + 1 = 17$
    vertex at (2,17) ; opens down ; max. value of 17

13. $= 2x(x + \frac{5}{2}) + \frac{1}{2}$
    $x = 0$ or $x = -\frac{5}{2}$
    $x_{\text{vertex}} = \frac{0 + (-\frac{5}{2})}{2} = -\frac{5}{4}$
    $f(-\frac{5}{4}) = \frac{1}{2} + 5(-\frac{5}{4}) + 2(-\frac{5}{4})^2 = -\frac{21}{8}$
    vertex at $(-\frac{5}{4}, -\frac{21}{8})$; opens up ; min. value of $-\frac{21}{8}$

14. $= \frac{1}{2}x(x - 4)$
    $x = 0$ or $x = 4$
    $x_{\text{vertex}} = \frac{0 + 4}{2} = 2$
    $f(2) = \frac{1}{2}(2)^2 - 2(2) = -2$
    vertex at (2,-2) ; opens up ; min. value of -2

15. by completing the square:
    $f(x) = 2(x^2 - \frac{1}{2}x + (-\frac{1}{4})^2) - 2(-\frac{1}{4})^2 + 1$
    $= 2(x - \frac{1}{4})^2 + \frac{7}{8}$ Vertex: $(\frac{1}{4}, \frac{7}{8})$
    by partial factoring:
    $= 2x(x - \frac{1}{2}) + 1$
    $x = 0$ or $x = \frac{1}{2}$
    $x_{\text{vertex}} = \frac{0 + \frac{1}{2}}{2} = \frac{1}{4}$
    $y_{\text{vertex}} = 2(\frac{1}{4})^2 - (\frac{1}{4}) + 1 = \frac{7}{8}$ Vertex: $(\frac{1}{4}, \frac{7}{8})$

16. by completing the square:
    $f(x) = -(x^2 - 3x + (-\frac{3}{2})^2) + (-\frac{3}{2})^2 + 3$
    $= -(x - \frac{3}{2})^2 + \frac{21}{4}$ Vertex: $(\frac{3}{2}, \frac{21}{4})$
    by partial factoring:
    $= -x(x - 3) + 3$
    $x = 0$ or $x = 3$
    $x_{\text{vertex}} = \frac{0 + 3}{2} = \frac{3}{2}$
    $y_{\text{vertex}} = 3(\frac{3}{2}) - (\frac{3}{2})^2 + 3 = \frac{21}{4}$ Vertex: $(\frac{3}{2}, \frac{21}{4})$

17. $f(x) = 2(x^2 - 2x) - 3$
    $= 2(x - 1)^2 - 2 - 3$
    $= 2(x - 1)^2 - 5$
    Vertex: (1,-5)

    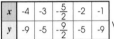

x	-1	0	1	2	3
y	3	-3	-5	-3	3

    The minimum value is -5.

18. $f(x) = -2x(x + 5) - 17$
    $x = 0$ or $x = -5$
    $x_{\text{vertex}} = \frac{0 + (-5)}{2} = -\frac{5}{2}$
    $y_{\text{vertex}} = -2(-\frac{5}{2})^2 - 10(-\frac{5}{2}) - 17 = -\frac{9}{2}$

x	-4	-3	$-\frac{5}{2}$	-2	-1
y	-9	-5	$-\frac{9}{2}$	-5	-9

    Vertex: $(-\frac{5}{2}, -\frac{9}{2})$

    The maximum value is $-\frac{9}{2}$.

19. (48 – x) ; (48 – x)
    $x = 0$ or $x = 48$
    $x_{\text{vertex}} = \frac{0 + 48}{2} = 24$
    $y_{\text{vertex}} = (24)(48 - 24) = 576$
    The greatest possible product is 576.
    The two numbers are 24 and 24.

20. The x-coordinates of the vertices
    for all three functions are the
    same. The value is 3.

21. $C(x) = 2100 - 8x + 0.01x^2$
    $= 0.01(x^2 - 800x + 400^2) - 0.01(400)^2 + 2100$
    $= 0.01(x - 400)^2 + 500$
    vertex at (400,500) ; opens up ; min. value of 500
    400 baseballs should be produced each day.

22. $P(x) = -0.5(x^2 - 80x + 40^2) + 0.5(40)^2 - 350$
    $= -0.5(x - 40)^2 + 450$
    vertex at (40,450) ; opens down ; max. value of 450
    The company has to sell 40 pairs of shoes each day.

23. $A(x) = x(100 - x)$
    $= -(x^2 - 100x)$
    $= -(x^2 - 100x + 50^2) + 50^2$
    $= -(x - 50)^2 + 2500$

    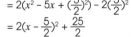

    The dimensions are 50 m by 50 m. The area is 2500 m².

24. $A(x) = x^2 + (5 - x)^2$
    $= x^2 + 25 - 10x + x^2$
    $= 2x^2 - 10x + 25$
    $= 2(x^2 - 5x + (\frac{5}{2})^2) - 2(\frac{5}{2})^2 + 25$
    $= 2(x - \frac{5}{2})^2 + \frac{25}{2}$

    $A(x)$ has a minimum value of $\frac{25}{2}$ when $x = \frac{5}{2}$.
    The length of each piece is 10 m.

25. $R(x) = (50 - x)(600 + 15x)$
    $= 30\,000 + 750x - 600x - 15x^2$
    $= -15(x^2 - 10x) + 30\,000$
    $= -15(x^2 - 10x + 5^2) + 15 \times 5^2 + 30\,000$
    $= -15(x - 5)^2 + 30\,375$
    The maximum revenue will be $30\,375. The price of the sweatshirt will be $45.

3.4 Operations with Radicals

1. $4 ; 4 ; 2\sqrt{3}$ 2. $16 ; 16 ; 4\sqrt{2}$ 3. $2\sqrt{5}$
4. $5\sqrt{3}$ 5. $4\sqrt{7}$ 6. $2\sqrt{2}$
7. $10\sqrt{2}$ 8. $2\sqrt{6}$ 9. $6\sqrt{10}$
10. $4\sqrt{5}$ 11. $\frac{3}{2}\sqrt{15}$ 12. $-3\sqrt{5}$
13. $-40\sqrt{5}$ 14. 54 15. 32
16. 3 17. $-2\sqrt{2}$ 18. $\frac{7}{3}$
19. $-6\sqrt{50}$ 20. $\frac{3\sqrt{2}}{2} \times \frac{2 \times 3\sqrt{3}}{3}$ 21. $3 \times 3\sqrt{21} \times \frac{\sqrt{15}}{9}$
    $= -30\sqrt{2}$ $= 3\sqrt{6}$ $= -3\sqrt{35}$
22. $-84\sqrt{2}$ 23. $-5\sqrt{30}$ 24. $13\sqrt{2}$
25. $-30\sqrt{10}$ 26. -36 27. $9\sqrt{5}$

Try This (p. 51)

$4 ; 2 ; 9 ; 2 ;$
$2 ; 2 ; 3 ; 2 ;$
$6\sqrt{2} + 15\sqrt{2} ; = 21\sqrt{2}$

28. $-5\sqrt{2}$ 29. $8\sqrt{5}$ 30. $20\sqrt{6}$
31. $-22\sqrt{3}$ 32. $-\frac{7\sqrt{5}}{2}$ 33. $\frac{17\sqrt{2}}{2}$
34. $= 9\sqrt{6} + 18\sqrt{7} + 20\sqrt{6} + 6\sqrt{7}$
    $= 29\sqrt{6} + 24\sqrt{7}$
35. $= -4\sqrt{3} + 48\sqrt{2} - 21\sqrt{3} - 24\sqrt{2}$
    $= 24\sqrt{2} - 25\sqrt{3}$
36. $4\sqrt{3} ; 6$ 37. $= 3 \times 5 - 2\sqrt{10}$ 38. $= -9\sqrt{2} + 6\sqrt{10}$
                $= 15 - 2\sqrt{10}$
39. $-23 + 3\sqrt{15}$ 40. 1 41. $6\sqrt{5} - 3\sqrt{10}$
42. $-7\sqrt{5} + \sqrt{6}$
43. $3 ; 3 ; 3 ; 3 ;$ 44. $-9 - 11\sqrt{6}$
    $15 ; 5\sqrt{3} ; 3\sqrt{12} ; \sqrt{36} ;$ 45. $9 - 9\sqrt{7}$
    $15 + 5\sqrt{3} - 6\sqrt{3} - 6 ;$ 46. $28 + 10\sqrt{3}$
    $= 9 - \sqrt{3}$ 47. 86
48. $-6\sqrt{2}$ 49. $-10 + 5\sqrt{6}$ 50. $-8 - 4\sqrt{6}$
51. $l_1 : \sqrt{(2 - (-2))^2 + (-3 - 5)^2} = \sqrt{80} = 4\sqrt{5}$
    $l_2 : \sqrt{(6 - 10)^2 + (-1 - (-2))^2} = \sqrt{17}$
    Difference: $4\sqrt{5} - \sqrt{17}$
    The lengths of the segments are $4\sqrt{5}$ and $\sqrt{17}$.
    The difference is $4\sqrt{5} - \sqrt{17}$.
52. Perimeter: $\sqrt{18} + 2\sqrt{2} - 1 + 2\sqrt{2} + 1 = 3\sqrt{2} + 4\sqrt{2} = 7\sqrt{2}$
    Area: $(2\sqrt{2} - 1)(2\sqrt{2} + 1) \div 2 = (8 + 2\sqrt{2} - 2\sqrt{2} - 1) \div 2 = 3.5$
    The perimeter is $7\sqrt{2}$ and the area is 3.5.
53. $\sqrt{(\sqrt{k} + 1)^2 + (\sqrt{k} - 1)^2} = \sqrt{k + 2\sqrt{k} + 1 + k - 2\sqrt{k} + 1}$
    $= \sqrt{2k + 2}$
    The length of its diagonal is $\sqrt{2k + 2}$ cm.

3.5 Solving Quadratic Equations

Try This (p. 53)

$4 ; 2 ;$
$4 ; 2 ;$
$4 ; 2 ;$
$x = 4 ; x = 2$

1. $(x + 5)(x - 2) = 0$ 2. $3(x - 4)(x + 4) = 0$
   $x = -5$ or $x = 2$ $x = 4$ or $x = -4$
3. $2(3x + 2)(x - 2) = 0$ 4. $(x + 6)(x - 2) = 0$
   $x = -\frac{2}{3}$ or $x = 2$ $x = -6$ or $x = 2$
5. $(4x - 1)(7x + 1) = 0$ 6. $(3x - 1)(5x - 1) = 0$
   $x = \frac{1}{4}$ or $x = -\frac{1}{7}$ $x = \frac{1}{3}$ or $x = \frac{1}{5}$

7. $(3x + 2)(4x + 5) = 0$ 8. $(6x + 7)(2x + 3) = 0$
   $x = -\frac{2}{3}$ or $x = -\frac{5}{4}$ $x = -\frac{7}{6}$ or $x = -\frac{3}{2}$
9. $(x + 7)(x + 11) = 0$
   $x = -7$ or $x = -11$
10. $7x + 3x^2 - 9x - 16 = 0$ 11. $-7x^2 + 7x + x^2 + 6x - 5 = 0$
    $3x^2 - 2x - 16 = 0$ $-6x^2 + 13x - 5 = 0$
    $(3x - 8)(x + 2) = 0$ $(-2x + 1)(3x - 5) = 0$
    $x = \frac{8}{3}$ or $x = -2$ $x = \frac{1}{2}$ or $x = \frac{5}{3}$
12. $(3(y + 3) + 4)(3(y + 3) - 7) = 0$
    $3(y + 3) + 4 = 0$ or $3(y + 3) - 7 = 0$
            $y = -\frac{13}{3}$ $y = -\frac{2}{3}$
13. $(-3(2y) + 4)(2(2y) + 1) = 0$
    $-3(2y) + 4 = 0$ or $2(2y) + 1 = 0$
            $y = \frac{2}{3}$ $y = -\frac{1}{4}$

Try This (p. 54)

$5 ; -2 ; -11 ;$
$(-2) ; (-2) ; (5) ; (-11) ; (5) ;$
$= \frac{2 \pm 4\sqrt{14}}{10} ; = \frac{1 \pm 2\sqrt{14}}{5}$

14. $x = \frac{-(-6) \pm \sqrt{(-6)^2 - 4(2)(-17)}}{2(2)}$
    $= \frac{6 \pm \sqrt{172}}{4}$
    $= \frac{3 + \sqrt{43}}{2}$ or $\frac{3 - \sqrt{43}}{2}$
15. $x = \frac{-13 \pm \sqrt{13^2 - 4(-1)(-9)}}{2(-1)}$
    $= \frac{-13 \pm \sqrt{133}}{-2}$
    $= \frac{13 + \sqrt{133}}{2}$ or $\frac{13 - \sqrt{133}}{2}$
16. $x = \frac{-(-7) \pm \sqrt{(-7)^2 - 4(3)(-8)}}{2(3)}$
    $= \frac{7 \pm \sqrt{145}}{6}$
    $= \frac{7 + \sqrt{145}}{6}$ or $\frac{7 - \sqrt{145}}{6}$
17. $n = 2$ or $-\frac{3}{2}$ 18. $n = \frac{1 + 2\sqrt{3}}{3}$ or $\frac{1 - 2\sqrt{3}}{3}$
19. $y = \frac{1 + \sqrt{37}}{4}$ or $\frac{1 - \sqrt{37}}{4}$ 20. $y = \frac{-5 + 3\sqrt{17}}{4}$ or $\frac{-5 - 3\sqrt{17}}{4}$
21. $a = \frac{1 + \sqrt{19}}{3}$ or $\frac{1 - \sqrt{19}}{3}$ 22. $a = \frac{-5 + \sqrt{65}}{4}$ or $\frac{-5 - \sqrt{65}}{4}$
23. $m = \frac{-3 + \sqrt{13}}{2}$ or $\frac{-3 - \sqrt{13}}{2}$ 24. $m = 2 - \frac{\sqrt{2}}{2}$ or $2 + \frac{\sqrt{2}}{2}$
25. $2 ; (5)(-2)$ 26. $b^2 - 4ac$
    $44 > 0$ $= 2^2 - 4(\frac{1}{3})(-6)$
    2 $= 12 > 0$
                2 zeros
27. 2 zeros   28. 0 zeros   29. 1 zero
30. 2 zeros   31. 2 zeros   32. 1 zero
33a. $k > 5$ b. $k = 0$ or $k = -12$ c. $k < -\frac{1}{4}$
34. break even: $f(x) = 0$
    $-5x^2 + 520x + 9600 = 0$
    $-5(x^2 - 104x - 1920) = 0$
    $-5(x + 16)(x - 120) = 0$
    $x = 120$ or $x = -16$ (not applicable)
    120 computers are sold to reach a break-even point.
35. $h(t) = -5t^2 + 20t + 1 = 0$
    $t = \frac{-20 \pm \sqrt{20^2 - 4(-5)(1)}}{2(-5)}$
    $= \frac{-20 \pm \sqrt{420}}{-10}$
    $= 4.05$ or -0.05 (not applicable)
    The ball hits the ground 4.05 s after the throw.

36. x ; $x - 3$
x ; $x - 3$
$x^2 - 3x - 30 = 0$
$x = \dfrac{-(-3) \pm \sqrt{(-3)^2 - 4(1)(-30)}}{2(1)}$
$= \dfrac{3 \pm \sqrt{129}}{2}$
$= 7.18$ or -4.18 (not applicable)
The dimensions of the rectangle are 7.18 cm and 4.18 cm.

37. Total distance: $x(x) + (x - 1)(x - 1) = 11.5$
$2x^2 - 2x - 10.5 = 0$
$x = \dfrac{-(-2) \pm \sqrt{(-2)^2 - 4(2)(-10.5)}}{2(2)}$
$= \dfrac{2 \pm \sqrt{88}}{4}$
$= \dfrac{1 \pm \sqrt{22}}{2}$
$= 2.85$ or -1.85 (not applicable)
The value of x is 2.85.

38. Let x and $x + 1$ be the two consecutive integers.
$x^2 + (x + 1)^2 = 545$
$2x^2 + 2x - 544 = 0$
$2(x^2 + x - 272) = 0$
$2(x - 16)(x + 17) = 0$
$x = 16$ or $x = -17$
When $x = 16$, $x + 1 = 17$.
When $x = -17$, $x + 1 = -16$.
The integers could be "16 and 17" or "-16 and -17".

39. Let x be the perimeter of one of the squares.
$(\dfrac{x}{4})^2 + (\dfrac{40 - x}{4})^2 = 68$
$2x^2 - 80x + 512 = 0$
$2(x^2 - 40x + 256) = 0$
$2(x - 8)(x - 32) = 0$
$x = 8$ or $x = 32$
The perimeters are 8 cm and 32 cm.

40. $f(x) = k - (x - 2)(-x + 1)$
$= k - (-x^2 + 3x - 2)$
$= x^2 - 3x + 2 + k$
$b^2 - 4ac = (-3)^2 - 4(1)(2 + k)$
$= 9 - 8 - 4k$
$= 1 - 4k$

No. of Zeros

If $1 - 4k > 0$; $k < \dfrac{1}{4}$ 2
If $1 - 4k = 0$; $k = \dfrac{1}{4}$ 1
If $1 - 4k < 0$; $k > \dfrac{1}{4}$ 0

There are 2 zeros for $k < \dfrac{1}{4}$, 1 zero for $k = \dfrac{1}{4}$, and no zeros for $k > \dfrac{1}{4}$.

3.6 Families of Quadratic Functions

Try This (p. 57)

Roots: -2 and 3
Factors: $(x + 2)$ and $(x - 3)$
Equation: $f(x) = a(x + 2)(x - 3)$
Three members: $f(x) = -(x + 2)(x - 3)$
$f(x) = (x + 2)(x - 3)$
$f(x) = 2(x + 2)(x - 3)$

1.

Zeros at	4 and 7	-4 and 6	-2
Roots	4 and 7	-4 and 6	-2
Factors	$(x - 4)$ and $(x - 7)$	$(x + 4)$ and $(x - 6)$	$(x + 2)$
Equation	$f(x) = a(x - 4)(x - 7)$	$f(x) = a(x + 4)(x - 6)$	$f(x) = a(x + 2)^2$
Equations and graphs of three members	$f(x) = (x - 4)(x - 7)$ ① $f(x) = 2(x - 4)(x - 7)$ ② $f(x) = 3(x - 4)(x - 7)$ ③	$f(x) = (x + 4)(x - 6)$ ① $f(x) = -(x + 4)(x - 6)$ ② $f(x) = 2(x + 4)(x - 6)$ ③	$f(x) = -(x + 2)^2$ ① $f(x) = (x + 2)^2$ ② $f(x) = 2(x + 2)^2$ ③

2. (-2) ; 5 ; -3 ; -3 ; 4 ; 4
$-3 = a(6)(-1)$
$a = \dfrac{1}{2}$
$\dfrac{1}{2}(x + 2)(x - 5)$
$\dfrac{1}{2}x^2 - \dfrac{3}{2}x - 5$

3. $f(x) = a(x + 1)(x - 4)$
$-6 = a(2 + 1)(2 - 4)$
$a = 1$
$(x + 1)(x - 4)$
$x^2 - 3x - 4$

4. $-20x(x - 1)$
$-20x^2 + 20x$

5. $-\dfrac{\sqrt{2}}{2}(x + \sqrt{2})(x - \sqrt{2})$
$-\dfrac{\sqrt{2}}{2}x^2 + \sqrt{2}$

6. $-(x - 1 - \sqrt{10})(x - 1 + \sqrt{10})$
$-x^2 + 2x + 9$

7. 4 ; 8
$7 = a(3 - 4)^2 + 8$
$a = -1$
$-(x - 4)^2 + 8$

8. $f(x) = a(x + 2)^2 - 5$
$4 = a(-5 + 2)^2 - 5$
$a = 1$
$(x + 2)^2 - 5$

9. $f(x) = a(x + \sqrt{2})^2 + \sqrt{2}$
$-\sqrt{2} = a(0 + \sqrt{2})^2 + \sqrt{2}$
$a = -\sqrt{2}$
$-\sqrt{2}(x + \sqrt{2})^2 + \sqrt{2}$

10a. 3.2 ; 35 ; 49
b. -24.5 ; 24.5 ; 10.5 ; 3.2 ; (-24.5) ; 24.5
$f(x) = a(x + 24.5)(x - 24.5)$
$3.2 = a(10.5 + 24.5)(10.5 - 24.5)$
$a \doteq -0.0065$
$f(x) \doteq -0.0065(x + 24.5)(x - 24.5)$
c. $f(0) = -0.0065(0 + 24.5)(0 - 24.5) = 3.90$
The maximum height is 3.9 m.
d. Distance away from P: 5.5
$f(5.5) = -0.0065(5.5 + 24.5)(5.5 - 24.5) \doteq 3.71$
The Frisbee would be at a height of 3.71 m.

11a. $f(x) = a(x + 30)(x - 30)$
$42 = a(0 + 30)(0 - 30)$
$a \doteq -0.0467$
$f(x) \doteq -0.0467(x + 30)(x - 30)$
b. Distance away from the centre: $30 - 8.5 = 21.5$
$f(x) = -0.0467(x + 30)(x - 30)$
$f(21.5) = -0.0467(21.5 + 30)(21.5 - 30) \doteq 20.44$
The height is 20.44 m.

3.7 Solving Linear-quadratic Systems

1. $2x - 5$
$x^2 - 9x + 20$
$(x - 5)(x - 4) = 0$
$x = 5$ or $x = 4$
$x = 5$, $y = 2(5) - 5 = 5$
$x = 4$, $y = 2(4) - 5 = 3$
$(5,5)$; $(4,3)$

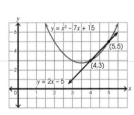

2. $-x^2 - 5x - 4 = -x - 4$
$x^2 + 4x = 0$
$x(x + 4) = 0$
$x = 0$ or $x = -4$
$x = 0$, $y = -0 - 4 = -4$
$x = -4$, $y = -(-4) - 4 = 0$
$(0,-4)$ and $(-4,0)$

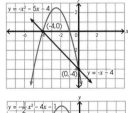

3. $-\dfrac{1}{2}x^2 - 4x - 1 = -x - \dfrac{9}{2}$
$-\dfrac{1}{2}x^2 - 3x + \dfrac{7}{2} = 0$
$-\dfrac{1}{2}(x + 7)(x - 1) = 0$
$x = -7$ or $x = 1$
$x = -7$, $y = -(-7) - \dfrac{9}{2} = \dfrac{5}{2}$
$x = 1$, $y = -1 - \dfrac{9}{2} = -\dfrac{11}{2}$
$(-7, \dfrac{5}{2})$ and $(1, -\dfrac{11}{2})$

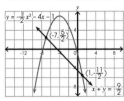

ISBN: 978-1-77149-222-5

4. $-\frac{1}{2}x^2 - 3x + 4 = -\frac{11}{4}x + \frac{5}{2}$

$-\frac{1}{2}x^2 - \frac{1}{4}x + \frac{3}{2} = 0$

$-\frac{1}{4}(2x - 3)(x + 2) = 0$

$x = \frac{3}{2}$ or $x = -2$

$x = \frac{3}{2}, y = -\frac{1}{2}(\frac{3}{2})^2 - 3(\frac{3}{2}) + 4 = -\frac{13}{8}$

$x = -2, y = -\frac{1}{2}(-2)^2 - 3(-2) + 4 = 8$

$(\frac{3}{2}, -\frac{13}{8})$ and $(-2, 8)$

5. $5x + 2$; 7 ; 1 ; $(-7)^2 - 4(3)(-1)$; 61 ; 2

6. $x^2 + 3x - 5 = -x - 1$

$x^2 + 4x - 4 = 0$

$b^2 - 4ac = 4^2 - 4(1)(-4) = 32 > 0$

2

7. $\frac{1}{2}x^2 + 3x - 14 = x - 5$

$\frac{1}{2}x^2 + 2x - 9 = 0$

$b^2 - 4ac = 2^2 - 4(\frac{1}{2})(-9) = 22 > 0$

2

8. $2x^2 - 2x + 1 = 3x - 5$

$2x^2 - 5x + 6 = 0$

$b^2 - 4ac = (-5)^2 - 4(2)(6) = -23 < 0$

0

9. $3x^2 - 2x - 4 = 3x + 5$

$3x^2 - 5x - 9 = 0$

$b^2 - 4ac = (-5)^2 - 4(3)(-9) = 133 > 0$

2

10. $x^2 - 5x + 7 = -x + 3$

$x^2 - 4x + 4 = 0$

$b^2 - 4ac = (-4)^2 - 4(1)(4) = 0$

1

11. $\frac{1}{3}x^2 + x - 2 = -x - 6$

$\frac{1}{3}x^2 + 2x + 4 = 0$

$b^2 - 4ac = 2^2 - 4(\frac{1}{3})(4) = -\frac{4}{3} < 0$

0

12. $x^2 + 2x - 4 = 8x - 13$

$x^2 - 6x + 9 = 0$

$b^2 - 4ac = (-6)^2 - 4(1)(9) = 0$

1

13. $0.2x^2 - 0.4x - 3.8 = 0.5x - 2$

$0.2x^2 - 0.9x - 1.8 = 0$

$b^2 - 4ac = (-0.9)^2 - 4(0.2)(-1.8) = 2.25 > 0$

2

14. linear equation: $y = -3x + b$

$-x^2 - 5x - 5 = -3x + b$

$-x^2 - 2x - 5 - b = 0$

$(-2)^2 - 4(-1)(-5 - b) = 0$

$4(-5 - b) = -4$

$b = -4$

$y = -3x - 4$

15. linear equation: $y = 2x + b$

$-2x^2 + 4x + 3 = 2x + b$

$-2x^2 + 2x + 3 - b = 0$

$2^2 - 4(-2)(3 - b) = 0$

$8(3 - b) = -4$

$b = \frac{7}{2}$

$y = 2x + \frac{7}{2}$

16. $2x^2 - 3x + 1 = kx - 2$

$2x^2 - (3 + k)x + 3 = 0$

$(-(3 + k))^2 - 4(2)(3) = 0$

$(3 + k)^2 = 24$

$k = -3 \pm 2\sqrt{6}$

17. $-2x^2 - x + 4 = kx + 5$

$-2x^2 - (1 + k)x - 1 = 0$

$(-(1 + k))^2 - 4(-2)(-1) = 0$

$(1 + k)^2 = 8$

$k = -1 \pm 2\sqrt{2}$

18. $0.5x^2 - 2x - 0.75 = -kx - 2.25$

$0.5x^2 - (2 - k)x + 1.5 = 0$

$(-(2 - k))^2 - 4(0.5)(1.5) = 0$

$(2 - k)^2 = 3$

$k = 2 \pm \sqrt{3}$

19. $x^2 - 6x + 3 = kx + \frac{1}{2}$

$x^2 - (6 + k)x + 2\frac{1}{2} = 0$

$(-(6 + k))^2 - 4(1)(2\frac{1}{2}) = 0$

$(6 + k)^2 = 10$

$k = -6 \pm \sqrt{10}$

20. $-0.7x^2 - 2x - 1 = \frac{k}{2}x + \frac{0.5}{2}$

$-1.4x^2 - (4 + k)x - 2.5 = 0$

$(-(4 + k))^2 - 4(-1.4)(-2.5) = 0$

$(4 + k)^2 = 14$

$k = -4 \pm \sqrt{14}$

21. $\sqrt{2}x^2 - 2x + \sqrt{2} = -kx - \sqrt{2}$

$\sqrt{2}x^2 - (2 - k)x + 2\sqrt{2} = 0$

$(-(2 - k))^2 - 4(\sqrt{2})(2\sqrt{2}) = 0$

$(2 - k)^2 = 16$

$k = 2 \pm 4$

$k = 6$ or $k = -2$

22a. $-x^2 - x + 1 = 2x + k$

$x^2 + 3x + k - 1 = 0$

$b^2 - 4ac = 0$

$3^2 - 4(1)(k - 1) = 0$

$k = \frac{13}{4}$

$g(x) = 2x + \frac{13}{4}$

b. $b^2 - 4ac > 0$ c. $b^2 - 4ac < 0$

$3^2 - 4(1)(k - 1) > 0$ $3^2 - 4(1)(k - 1) < 0$

$k < \frac{13}{4}$ $k > \frac{13}{4}$

$g(x) = 2x + 2$ $g(x) = 2x + 4$

23. Break even: $R = C$

$-4x^2 + 30x = 24 + 2x$

$-4x^2 + 28x - 24 = 0$

$-4(x^2 - 7x + 6) = 0$

$-4(x - 6)(x - 1) = 0$

$x = 6$ or $x = 1$

$x = 6, y = 24 + 2(6) = 36$

$x = 1, y = 24 + 2(1) = 26$

The functions intersect at $(1,26)$ and $(6,36)$.

The company is expected to break even after 1 year and 6 years.

24. rocket: $y = -x^2 + 9x$

flare: $y = -x + 9$

$-x^2 + 9x = -x + 9$

$-(x^2 - 10x + 9) = 0$

$-(x - 9)(x - 1) = 0$

$x = 9$ or $x = 1$

$x = 9, y = -9 + 9 = 0$

$x = 1, y = -1 + 9 = 8$

The paths intersect at $(9,0)$ and $(1,8)$.

3.8 Transformations

1. A ; D

2.

x	f(x)
-3	13
-2	8
-1	5
0	4
1	5
2	8
3	13

x	g(x)
-3	15
-2	10
-1	7
0	6
1	7
2	10
3	15

x	h(x)
0	13
1	8
2	5
3	4
4	5
5	8
6	13

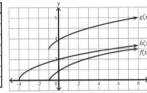

$g(x)$: translated 2 units up
$h(x)$: translated 3 units to the right

3.

x	f(x)
-1	0
0	1
1	1.4
2	1.7
3	2
4	2.2
5	2.4

x	g(x)
-1	3
0	4
1	4.4
2	4.7
3	5
4	5.2
5	5.4

x	h(x)
-4	0
-3	1
-2	1.4
-1	1.7
0	2
1	2.2
2	2.4

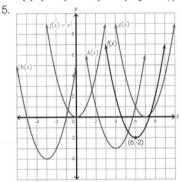

$g(x)$: translated 3 units up
$h(x)$: translated 3 units to the left

4. $g(x)$: $(x-7)^2$; $\{x \in \mathbb{R}\}$; $\{y \in \mathbb{R} \mid y \geq 0\}$
$h(x)$: $(x+3)^2 - 4$; $\{x \in \mathbb{R}\}$; $\{y \in \mathbb{R} \mid y \geq -4\}$
$k(x)$: $(x-4)^2 - 3$; $\{x \in \mathbb{R}\}$; $\{y \in \mathbb{R} \mid y \geq -3\}$

5.

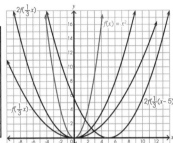

The translated function will be $l(x) = (x-6)^2 - 2$. Its vertex is (6,-2).

6a. $f(x) = (x-5)^2$
b. $f(x) = x^2 + 10$
c. $f(x) = (x+3)^2 - 10$
d. $f(x) = (x-12)^2 - 40$
e. $f(x) = x^2 - 12$

7.

the reflected function	numerical representation	how to reflect	graphical representation
$g(x) = f(-x) = \sqrt{-x}$	$(x,y) \rightarrow (-x,y)$	in the y-axis	
$h(x) = -f(x) = -\sqrt{x}$	$(x,y) \rightarrow (x,-y)$	in the x-axis	
$k(x) = -f(-x) = -\sqrt{-x}$	$(x,y) \rightarrow (-x,-y)$	in the x-axis and y-axis	

8.

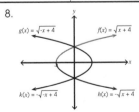

$g(x) = \sqrt{-x+4}$ $f(x) = \sqrt{x+4}$
$k(x) = -\sqrt{-x+4}$ $h(x) = -\sqrt{x+4}$

9.

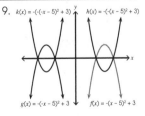

$k(x) = -(-(x-5)^2 + 3)$ $h(x) = -(-(x-5)^2 + 3)$
$g(x) = -(-x-5)^2 + 3$ $f(x) = -(x-5)^2 + 3$

10. vertical ; stretch ; $2f(x)$; 2

vertical ; compression ; $\frac{1}{5}f(x)$; $\frac{1}{5}$

horizontal ; stretch ; $f(\frac{1}{2}x)$; 2

horizontal ; compression ; $f(3x)$; $\frac{1}{3}$

11a. a vertical compression ; $\frac{1}{2}$; $(1, \frac{1}{2})$
b. a horizontal compression ; $\frac{1}{4}$; $(\frac{1}{4}, 1)$
c. a horizontal stretch ; 3 ; (3,1)
d. a vertical stretch ; 5 ; (1,5)

12. The equation will be $y = f(\frac{1}{2}x)$. (2,8) will be (4,8).

Try This (p. 68)
x-axis ; stretched by a factor of 2 ;
horizontally compressed by a factor of $\frac{1}{4}$;
translated 3 units up ; translated 1 unit to the left

13. 3 ; 2 ; 5 ; right

f(x)	$f(\frac{1}{3}x)$	$2f(\frac{1}{3}x)$	$2f(\frac{1}{3}(x-5))$
(-3,9)	(-9,9)	(-9,18)	(-4,18)
(-2,4)	(-6,4)	(-6,8)	(-1,8)
(-1,1)	(-3,1)	(-3,2)	(2,2)
(0,0)	(0,0)	(0,0)	(5,0)
(1,1)	(3,1)	(3,2)	(8,2)
(2,4)	(6,4)	(6,8)	(11,8)
(3,9)	(9,9)	(9,18)	(14,18)

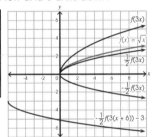

14. horizontally compressed by a factor of $\frac{1}{3}$
vertically compressed by a factor of $\frac{1}{2}$
reflected in the x-axis
translated 6 units to the left and 3 units down

f(x)	f(3x)	$\frac{1}{2}f(3x)$	$-\frac{1}{2}f(3x)$	$-\frac{1}{2}f(3(x+6))-3$
(0,0)	(0,0)	(0,0)	(0,0)	(-6,-3)
(1,1)	$(\frac{1}{3},1)$	$(\frac{1}{3},\frac{1}{2})$	$(\frac{1}{3},-\frac{1}{2})$	$(-5\frac{2}{3},-3\frac{1}{2})$
(4,2)	$(\frac{4}{3},2)$	$(\frac{4}{3},1)$	$(\frac{4}{3},-1)$	$(-4\frac{2}{3},-4)$
(9,3)	(3,3)	$(3,\frac{3}{2})$	$(3,-\frac{3}{2})$	$(-3,-4\frac{1}{2})$

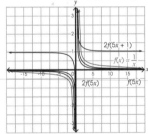

15. horizontally compressed by a factor of $\frac{1}{5}$
vertically stretched by a factor of 2
translated 1 unit up

f(x)	f(5x)	2f(5x)	2f(5x) + 1
$(-10,-\frac{1}{10})$	$(-2,-\frac{1}{10})$	$(-2,-\frac{1}{5})$	$(-2,\frac{4}{5})$
$(-5,-\frac{1}{5})$	$(-1,-\frac{1}{5})$	$(-1,-\frac{2}{5})$	$(-1,\frac{3}{5})$
$(5,\frac{1}{5})$	$(1,\frac{1}{5})$	$(1,\frac{2}{5})$	$(1,1\frac{2}{5})$
$(10,\frac{1}{10})$	$(2,\frac{1}{10})$	$(2,\frac{1}{5})$	$(2,1\frac{1}{5})$

16. $d_A(t) = 150 - 3(t+6)^2$
D: $\{t \in \mathbb{R} \mid t \geq 0\}$
R: $\{d \in \mathbb{R} \mid 0 \leq d \leq 42\}$

$d_B(t) = 150 - 3t^2$
D: $\{t \in \mathbb{R} \mid t \geq 0\}$
R: $\{d \in \mathbb{R} \mid 0 \leq d \leq 150\}$

The graphs of the functions do not intersect. So, they will not meet.

3.9 The Inverse of a Function

1.

$f(x)$	$f^{-1}(x)$
(2,7)	(7,2)
(1,5)	(5,1)
(0,3)	(3,0)
(-2,-4)	(-4,-2)
(-4,-2)	(-2,-4)
(-6,-3)	(-3,-6)

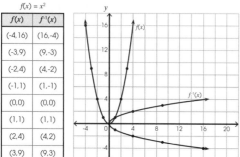

2A: $f(x) = x^2$

$f(x)$	$f^{-1}(x)$
(-4,16)	(16,-4)
(-3,9)	(9,-3)
(-2,4)	(4,-2)
(-1,1)	(1,-1)
(0,0)	(0,0)
(1,1)	(1,1)
(2,4)	(4,2)
(3,9)	(9,3)

B: $f(x) = -x^2 - x$

$f(x)$	$f^{-1}(x)$
(-4,-12)	(-12,-4)
(-3,-6)	(-6,-3)
(-2,-2)	(-2,-2)
(-1,0)	(0,-1)
(0,0)	(0,0)
(1,-2)	(-2,1)
(2,-6)	(-6,2)
(3,-12)	(-12,3)

3.

4.

5. ; ✔ 6. 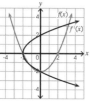 ; ✔

7. 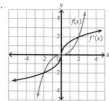 8.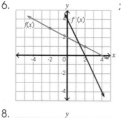

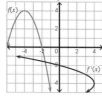

9. $\pm\sqrt{x-6}$; $\pm\sqrt{x-6}$

10. $y = 3x + 7$
$x = 3y + 7$
$y = \dfrac{1}{3}x - \dfrac{7}{3}$
$f^{-1}(x) = \dfrac{1}{3}x - \dfrac{7}{3}$

11. $f^{-1}(x) = \pm\sqrt{\dfrac{1}{5}x + \dfrac{3}{5}}$

12. $f^{-1}(x) = -\dfrac{1}{2}x + 5$

13. $f^{-1}(x) = -1 \pm\sqrt{x-1}$

14. $f^{-1}(x) = (x-1)^2$

15. $f^{-1}(x) = 1 \pm\sqrt{2x}$

16. $f^{-1}(x) = \dfrac{1}{5}x - \dfrac{4}{5}$

17. 5 ; 10 ; 5 ; 10 ; $5 \pm\sqrt{x+10}$;
5 ; 10 ; $\{x \in \mathbb{R}\}$; $\{y \in \mathbb{R} \mid y \geq -10\}$
$5 + \sqrt{x+10}$; $\{x \in \mathbb{R} \mid x \geq -10\}$; $\{y \in \mathbb{R} \mid y \geq 5\}$
$5 - \sqrt{x+10}$; $\{x \in \mathbb{R} \mid x \geq -10\}$; $\{y \in \mathbb{R} \mid y < 5\}$

18. $y = (x+2.5)^2 - 5.25$
$x = (y+2.5)^2 - 5.25$
$x = -2.5 \pm\sqrt{x+5.25}$
$(x+2.5)^2 - 5.25$
$\{x \in \mathbb{R}\}$; $\{y \in \mathbb{R} \mid y \geq -5.25\}$
$x \geq -2.5$; $-2.5 + \sqrt{x+5.25}$; $\{x \in \mathbb{R} \mid x \geq -5.25\}$; $\{y \in \mathbb{R} \mid y \geq -2.5\}$
$x < -2.5$; $-2.5 - \sqrt{x+5.25}$; $\{x \in \mathbb{R} \mid x \geq -5.25\}$; $\{y \in \mathbb{R} \mid y < -2.5\}$

19. $y = -(x+1)^2 - 3$
$x = -(y+1)^2 - 3$
$y = -1 \pm\sqrt{-x-3}$
$-(x+1)^2 - 3$
$\{x \in \mathbb{R}\}$; $\{y \in \mathbb{R} \mid y \leq -3\}$
$x \geq -1$; $-1 + \sqrt{-x-3}$; $\{x \in \mathbb{R} \mid x \leq -3\}$; $\{y \in \mathbb{R} \mid y \geq -1\}$
$x < -1$; $-1 - \sqrt{-x-3}$; $\{x \in \mathbb{R} \mid x \leq -3\}$; $\{y \in \mathbb{R} \mid y < -1\}$

20a. $f(x) = -\dfrac{1}{2}(x+3)^2 + \dfrac{9}{2}$
Domain: $\{x \in \mathbb{R}\}$
Range: $\{y \in \mathbb{R} \mid y \leq \dfrac{9}{2}\}$

b. For $f(x)$ restricted to $x \geq -3$,   For $f(x)$ restricted to $x < -3$,
$f^{-1}(x) = -3 + \sqrt{9-2x}$. $f^{-1}(x) = -3 - \sqrt{9-2x}$.
Domain: $\{x \in \mathbb{R} \mid x \leq \dfrac{9}{2}\}$ Domain: $\{x \in \mathbb{R} \mid x \leq \dfrac{9}{2}\}$
Range: $\{y \in \mathbb{R} \mid y \geq -3\}$ Range: $\{y \in \mathbb{R} \mid y < -3\}$

21a.

x	$d(x)$
0	0
4	2
12	18
20	50
28	98
36	162
44	242
52	338
60	450

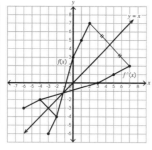

b. Range: $\{y \in \mathbb{R} \mid y \geq 0\}$
The range must be greater than or equal to 0 because the distance travelled cannot be negative.

c. The model is $f(x) = 2\sqrt{2x}$, where $f(x)$ is the force exerted in newtons and x is the distance travelled in metres. Both x and $f(x)$ are greater than or equal to 0.

d. Yes

4 Exponential Functions

4.1 Exponents

Try This (p. 74)

$\dfrac{1}{5^2}$; $\dfrac{1}{25}$ $(\dfrac{3}{2})^3$; $\dfrac{27}{8}$

1. $= \dfrac{1}{2^2}$
  $= \dfrac{1}{4}$

2. $= \dfrac{1}{4^3}$
  $= \dfrac{1}{64}$

3. $= -\dfrac{1}{3^3}$
  $= -\dfrac{1}{27}$

4. $= \dfrac{1}{(-5)^2}$
  $= \dfrac{1}{25}$

5. $= (\dfrac{4}{1})^2$
  $= 16$

6. $= (\dfrac{2}{3})^3$
  $= \dfrac{8}{27}$

ISBN: 978-1-77149-222-5

7. $= (-\frac{5}{4})^1$
   $= -\frac{5}{4}$

8. $= -(\frac{4}{3})^2$
   $= -\frac{16}{9}$

9. $= \frac{1}{2^1 \times 8}$
   $= \frac{1}{16}$

10. $= \frac{2 \times 8^1}{1}$
    $= 16$

11. $= \frac{2^3}{3^2}$
    $= \frac{8}{9}$

12. $= \frac{2^3 \times 2^1}{1}$
    $= 16$

Try This (p. 75)

$= 3^{4 + (-1)}$
$= 3^3$
$= 27$

$= 4^{2 + 3 - 4}$
$= 4^1$
$= 4$

13. $= 2^{5 + (-1) + (-2)}$
    $= 2^2$
    $= 4$

14. $= 8^{-9 + 8 + (-2)}$
    $= 8^{-3}$
    $= \frac{1}{512}$

15. $= 10^{2 - 3 - (-1)}$
    $= 10^0$
    $= 1$

16. $= 9^{3 + (-1) - (-2) - 3}$
    $= 9^1$
    $= 9$

17. $= 3^{-1 + 4 + (-3) - (-2) - 3}$
    $= 3^{-1}$
    $= \frac{1}{3}$

18. $= 14^{10 + (-5) - (-2) - 7 - 1}$
    $= 14^{-1}$
    $= \frac{1}{14}$

19. $= \frac{1}{4} + \frac{1}{16}$
    $= \frac{5}{16}$

20. $= 9 - \frac{1}{3}$
    $= \frac{26}{3}$

21. $= (\frac{1}{9} + \frac{1}{6}) \times 36$
    $= \frac{5}{18} \times 36$
    $= 10$

22. $= \frac{(2^4)^2}{2^{-1 + 5 + 4}}$
    $= \frac{2^8}{2^8}$
    $= 1$

23. $= \frac{5}{5^2} + \frac{1}{5}$
    $= \frac{2}{5}$

24. $\frac{4^{-1} \times 4^3}{4}$
    $= 4^{-1} \times 4^3 \times 4^{-1}$
    $= 4$

25. $\frac{(2^{-4})^{-2}}{2^3}$
    $= 2^{8 - 3}$
    $= 2^5$
    $= 32$

26. $\frac{8^2 \times (-8^{-1})^2}{8^{-1} + 8}$
    $= \frac{1}{\frac{1}{8} + 8}$
    $= \frac{8}{65}$

27. $(2^3 \times 3^{-4}) \times (2 \times 3)^2$
    $= 2^{-3 + 2} \times 3^{-4 + 2}$
    $= 2^{-1} \times 3^{-2}$
    $= \frac{1}{2 \times 3^2}$
    $= \frac{1}{18}$

28. $(2 \times (-1))^{-3} (\frac{2^{-1}}{(-1)^2})^{-1}$
    $= \frac{(-1)^2}{2^3 \times (-1)^3 \times 2^{-1}}$
    $= \frac{1}{2^2 \times (-1)}$
    $= -\frac{1}{4}$

29. $(\frac{(-2)^{-1}}{3})^2 \times (\frac{1}{-2})^{-1}$
    $= (\frac{1}{(-2) \times 3})^2 \times (-2)$
    $= -\frac{1}{18}$

30. $10^{6 - 3} \times (\frac{1}{10})^3$
    $= \frac{10^3}{10^3}$
    $= 1$

31. $\frac{(-3)^{3(-2) + 2(7)}}{-3^{-(-2) + 7}}$
    $= (-3)^{8 - 9}$
    $= (-3)^{-1}$
    $= -\frac{1}{3}$

32. $((-2)^2 \times 3)^1 (-(-2)(3))^{-2(1)}$
    $= (-2)^{2 + (-2)} (3)^{1 + (-2)} (-1)^{-2}$
    $= \frac{1}{3}$

33. $(5^2)^{-1} = 5^{-2} = \frac{1}{25}$
    $5^2 \times 5^{-1} = 5^{2 + (-1)} = 5$
    No, they are not equal.

34. $(\frac{2}{5})^{-2} = (\frac{5}{2})^2 = \frac{25}{4}$
    $((\frac{5}{2})^{-1})^{-2} = (\frac{5}{2})^2 = \frac{25}{4}$
    Yes, Lucas is correct.

35. He should not have cancelled out the terms.
    $2x^{-2} \times \frac{1}{x^2}$
    $= \frac{2}{x^2} \times \frac{1}{x^2}$
    $= \frac{2}{x^4}$

36. No, she should not have combined the terms.
    $(\frac{1}{y^{-2}})(y^{-1})^0$
    $= (y^2)(1)$
    $= y^2$

4.2 Rational Exponents

Try This (p. 77)

$\sqrt[4]{81} ; 3$ $(\sqrt[5]{32})^4 ; 2^4 ; 16$

1. $= \sqrt[4]{\frac{1}{10\,000}}$
   $= \frac{1}{10}$

2. $= \sqrt[3]{-8}$
   $= -2$

3. $= \sqrt{\frac{1}{16}}$
   $= \frac{1}{4}$

4. $= \sqrt[3]{-\frac{1}{27}}$
   $= -\frac{1}{3}$

5. $= \sqrt{49}$
   $= 7$

6. $= \sqrt[5]{-32}$
   $= -2$

7. $= 4^2$
   $= 16$

8. $= \sqrt{9}$
   $= 3$

9. $= -\frac{4}{5}$

10. $= \frac{6}{(-6)^2}$
    $= \frac{1}{6}$

11. $= (\sqrt[3]{-\frac{64}{27}})^2$
    $= (-\frac{4}{3})^2$
    $= \frac{16}{9}$

12. $= \sqrt[4]{\frac{81}{16}}$
    $= \frac{3}{2}$

13. $= \frac{(\sqrt[3]{-\frac{1}{8}})^4}{(\sqrt[7]{-\frac{1}{128}})^3}$
    $= \frac{(-\frac{1}{2})^4}{(-\frac{1}{2})^3}$
    $= -\frac{1}{2}$

14. $= \frac{(\sqrt{9})^5}{3^4 \times 3}$
    $= 3^{5 - 4 - 1}$
    $= 1$

15. $= \frac{(\sqrt{25})^3}{\sqrt{81} - \sqrt{16}}$
    $= \frac{125}{9 - 4}$
    $= 25$

16. $= \frac{\sqrt[3]{\frac{1}{8}} + 4}{\sqrt[4]{\frac{1}{16}}}$
    $= \frac{\frac{9}{2}}{\frac{1}{2}}$
    $= 9$

Try This (p. 78)

$= 5^{\frac{2}{3} + (-2)}$
$= 5^{-\frac{4}{3}}$

$= 6^{\frac{2}{3} - (-1)}$
$= 6^{\frac{5}{3}}$

17. $= 10^{\frac{1}{4} - (-1)}$
    $= 10^{\frac{5}{4}}$

18. $= 8^{\frac{5}{2} + (-\frac{3}{5})}$
    $= 8^{\frac{19}{10}}$

19. $= (-5)^{\frac{3}{2}}(-5)^{\frac{1}{3}}$
    $= (-5)^{\frac{3}{2} + \frac{1}{3}}$
    $= (-5)^{\frac{7}{6}}$

20. $= (7^{-6})(7^1)$
    $= 7^{-6 + 1}$
    $= 7^{-5}$

21. $= (-6)^{\frac{3}{2}}(-6)^{-\frac{1}{5}}$
    $= (-6)^{\frac{3}{2} + (-\frac{1}{5})}$
    $= (-6)^{\frac{17}{10}}$

22. $= (\frac{2}{3})^3(\frac{2}{3})^3$
    $= (\frac{2}{3})^6$

23. $= 2^{-3}(8)$
    $= 1$

24. $= \frac{2^{12} \times 5^{\frac{5}{2}}}{2 \times 5^{\frac{1}{2}}}$
    $= 2^{11} \times 5$

25. $= \frac{3^2 \times 3}{(-3)^2}$
    $= 3$

26. $= \dfrac{4^{2+0.5+(-3.5)}}{4^{-1}}$

   $= 1$

27. $= 3^2 + 3^3 - 3$

   $= 33$

28. $= \dfrac{2.5^3}{10+1.5}$

   $= \dfrac{2.5^3}{11.5}$

29a. $(9^{\frac{1}{2}}16^{\frac{1}{4}})^2$

   $= ((3)(2))^2$

   $= 36$

b. $(\dfrac{9}{16})^2(\dfrac{9}{16})^{-0.5}$

   $= (\dfrac{9}{16})^{2+(-0.5)}$

   $= \dfrac{27}{64}$

c. $(\dfrac{1}{9^{-1}})^{0.5}(\sqrt{9\times16})^{\frac{1}{2}}$

   $= 3\sqrt{12}$

   $= 6\sqrt{3}$

30a. $(\dfrac{4(-3)}{\sqrt{4}})^{0.5}(2(-3))^{\frac{1}{2}}$

   $= (-6)^{0.5}(-6)^{0.5}$

   $= -6$

b. $2^{2-(-3)}4^{-3}(\dfrac{4}{(-3)^2})^{\frac{1}{2}}$

   $= \dfrac{2^5 \times 2^{-6} \times 2}{3}$

   $= \dfrac{1}{3}$

c. $\sqrt{4}\,(4)^{0.5}(-3)^2(\dfrac{4^2(-3)}{2^{-1}})^{-1}$

   $= \dfrac{2 \times 2 \times 9}{16 \times -3 \times 2}$

   $= -\dfrac{3}{8}$

31a. $\dfrac{\sqrt[3]{27(-1)}}{(27(-1)^2)^{\frac{1}{3}}}$

   $= -3 \times 3$

   $= -9$

b. $\sqrt[4]{\dfrac{27}{3(-1)^2}}^2\left(\sqrt{\dfrac{1}{3} \times 27}\right)^{-3}$

   $= 3 \times \dfrac{1}{3^3}$

   $= \dfrac{1}{9}$

c. $\dfrac{\left(-\dfrac{1}{27}\right)^{\frac{2}{3}}\left(-\dfrac{27}{1}\right)^{-\frac{1}{3}}}{(\sqrt{27+2(-1)})^{-1}}$

   $= \dfrac{-\dfrac{1}{27}}{\sqrt{25}^{-1}}$

   $= -\dfrac{5}{27}$

32. Yes, it can be.
   $(\sqrt{25})^3 = 5^3 = 125$

33. Yes, it is true. This is because a negative integer raised to the power of 3 is negative, e.g. $\sqrt[3]{-8} = -2$.

34. She is incorrect. $(\sqrt[3]{4})^{\frac{3}{2}} = 4^{\frac{1}{3} \times \frac{3}{2}} = 4^{\frac{1}{2}} = 2$

35. It is not true. Even roots can only have positive real bases because any number raised to an even exponent is never negative.

4.3 Algebraic Expressions Involving Exponents

Try This (p. 80)

$= y^{-1+\frac{1}{2}}$ $= m^{-2 \times \frac{3}{4}}$

$= y^{-\frac{1}{2}}$ $= m^{-\frac{3}{2}}$

$= \dfrac{1}{y^{\frac{1}{2}}}$ $= \dfrac{1}{m^{\frac{3}{2}}}$

1. $= x^{-2+\frac{1}{3}+\frac{3}{4}}$
   $= x^{-\frac{11}{12}}$
   $= \dfrac{1}{x^{\frac{11}{12}}}$

2. $= y^{-\frac{3}{4}+2}$
   $= y^{\frac{5}{4}}$

3. $= \dfrac{1}{k^{-6}}$

4. $= (x^{-5})^{-\frac{1}{2}}$
   $= x^{\frac{5}{2}}$

5. $= m^{-2+\frac{3}{2}-(-1)}$
   $= m^{\frac{1}{2}}$

6. $= a^{4+(-0.75)-(-6)}$
   $= a^{9.25}$

7. $= b^{-5 \times 0.5 + 5 \times 0.2}$
   $= b^{-1.5}$
   $= \dfrac{1}{b^{1.5}}$

8. $= d^{(0.5+(-3)-(-1)) \times \frac{5}{3}}$
   $= d^{-2.5}$
   $= \dfrac{1}{d^{2.5}}$

9. $= n^{6+(2-(-0.25)-\frac{1}{4}) \times -1}$
   $= n^4$

10. $= x^{-1+(1+(-0.2)-(-2)) \times 2}$
   $= x^{4.6}$

11. $= \dfrac{9x^{-4}y^2}{x^{-1}y^3}$
   $= \dfrac{9}{x^3 y}$

12. $= \dfrac{5^2 a^2 b^{-1}}{5 a^{-2} b^{-1}}$
   $= 5a^4$

13. $= \dfrac{-2m^2 \times 3^2 m^{-4} n^2}{m^{-2} \times n^{-2}}$
   $= -18n^4$

14. $= x^{-n+(-3)-(-n)}$
   $= \dfrac{1}{x^3}$

15. $= i^{0.25-(n+1)-(-0.5n)}$

   $= i^{-0.5n-0.75}$

   $= \dfrac{1}{i^{0.5n+0.75}}$

16. $= b^{(\frac{2}{3}n+(-n)-0.2n) \times 2}$

   $= b^{-\frac{16}{15}n}$

   $= \dfrac{1}{b^{\frac{16}{15}n}}$

Try This (p. 81)

$= (\dfrac{b^{\frac{3}{4}}}{b^{\frac{2}{3}}})^6$ $= \dfrac{(x^{\frac{4}{2}})^{-1}}{(x^{\frac{4}{4}})^{-2}}$

$= b^{(\frac{3}{4}-\frac{2}{3}) \times 6}$ $= x^{\frac{4}{2}(-1)-(\frac{2}{4})(-2)}$

$= b^{\frac{1}{2}}$ $= \dfrac{1}{x}$

17. $= (x^{\frac{5}{2}})^{-3}(x^{\frac{3}{2}})^2$
   $= x^{(\frac{5}{2})(-3)+(\frac{3}{2})(2)}$
   $= x^{-\frac{9}{2}}$
   $= \dfrac{1}{x^{\frac{9}{2}}}$

18. $= y^{-1.5+\frac{1}{2}-(\frac{1}{4})(-2)}$
   $= y^{-\frac{1}{2}}$
   $= \dfrac{1}{y^{\frac{1}{2}}}$

19. $= a^{-0.3+\frac{4}{5}-1}$
   $= a^{-\frac{1}{2}}$
   $= \dfrac{1}{a^{\frac{1}{2}}}$

20. $= (-x)^{\frac{3}{2}+\frac{1}{5}}$
   $= \dfrac{1}{(-x)^{\frac{17}{10}}}$

21. $= (\dfrac{a}{b})^{\frac{3}{2}}(\dfrac{4a}{3b})^{\frac{3}{4}}$
   $= (\dfrac{4}{3})^{\frac{3}{4}}(\dfrac{a}{b})^{\frac{9}{4}}$

22. $= m^{1.5-0.5}\, n^{6-0.5}$
   $= mn^{5.5}$

23. $= a^{\frac{1}{2}}b^{-1}$
   $= \dfrac{a^{\frac{1}{2}}}{b}$
   $\dfrac{9^{\frac{1}{2}}}{16} = \dfrac{3}{16}$

24. $= x^{3+(-\frac{3}{4})-\frac{1}{4}}y^3$
   $= x^2 y^3$
   $4^2(-1)^3 = -16$

25. $= m^{5 \times 0.2}\, n^{5 \times 0.5}$
   $= mn^{2.5}$
   $(-1)8^{\frac{5}{2}} = -8^{\frac{5}{2}}$

26. $= d^{(\frac{3}{8})(4)}\, e^{(\frac{10}{5})(\frac{1}{2})}$
   $= d^{\frac{3}{2}}e$
   $9^{\frac{3}{2}}(-5) = -135$

27. $= \sqrt[10]{p^5 q^{10}}$
   $= p^{\frac{1}{2}} q$
   $25^{\frac{1}{2}}(-\dfrac{1}{2}) = -\dfrac{5}{2}$

28a. $= (\dfrac{x+y}{x-y})^2$ undefined when $x = y$

b. $= x^{\frac{x+y}{2}}$ undefined when $x = 0$ and $y \le 0$

c. $= (xy)^{x+2}$ undefined when $x \le -2$ and $y = 0$

4.4 Exponential Functions

1.

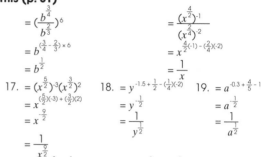

2. linear
   quadratic function
   exponential function

3a. $y = 2x$
b. $y = x^2$
c. $y = 2^x$

4. B ; C

5. horizontal ; 0 ; 1 ; 1
   greater ; faster
   greater ; less ; faster

6.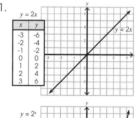

7. It represents an exponential decay because
   $2^{-x} = (\dfrac{1}{2})^x$, and $\dfrac{1}{2}$ is between 0 and 1.

8. $f(x) = (\dfrac{1}{3})^x$ 9. $f(x) = 2^x$ 10. $f(x) = 3^x$

11. $f(x) = (\dfrac{1}{2})^x$ 12. $f(x) = 10^x$ 13. $f(x) = (\dfrac{1}{10})^x$

14.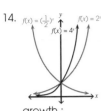
$f(x) = (\frac{1}{2})^x$ $f(x) = 2^x$ $f(x) = 4^x$

growth ;
$\{x \in \mathbb{R}\}$;
$\{y \in \mathbb{R} \mid y > 0\}$;
1 ; $y = 0$

15.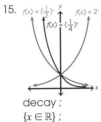
$f(x) = (\frac{1}{2})^x$ $f(x) = 2^x$ $f(x) = (\frac{1}{4})^x$

decay ;
$\{x \in \mathbb{R}\}$;
$\{y \in \mathbb{R} \mid y > 0\}$;
1 ; $y = 0$

16.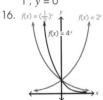
$f(x) = (\frac{1}{2})^x$ $f(x) = 2^x$ $f(x) = 4^x$

decay ;
$\{x \in \mathbb{R}\}$;
$\{y \in \mathbb{R} \mid y > 0\}$;
1 ; $y = 0$

17. Yes, they do. x has no restrictions, $\{x \in \mathbb{R}\}$. y is always greater than 0, $\{y \in \mathbb{R} \mid y > 0\}$. The y-intercept is always 1 and the horizontal asymptote is always $y = 0$.

18. She is incorrect. If n is a positive number that is less than 1, then the function is an exponential growth.

19. She is incorrect. If a is greater than 1, then the function is an exponential growth regardless of what value of x is.

20a. As x gets very big, y approaches infinity.
   b. As x gets very small, y approaches 0.

4.5 Transformations of Exponential Functions

1.

$f(x) = 2^x$	$f(x) = 2^x + 1$	$f(x) = 2^x - 1$
$(-2, \frac{1}{4})$	$(-2, 1\frac{1}{4})$	$(-2, -\frac{3}{4})$
$(-1, \frac{1}{2})$	$(-1, 1\frac{1}{2})$	$(-1, -\frac{1}{2})$
$(0, 1)$	$(0, 2)$	$(0, 0)$
$(1, 2)$	$(1, 3)$	$(1, 1)$
$(2, 4)$	$(2, 5)$	$(2, 3)$

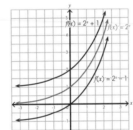

a. up
b. down

2. a translation of 3 units up ; 4
   a translation of 1 unit down ; 0
   a translation of 2 units down ; -1
   a translation of 1 unit up ; 2
   $f(x) = 3^x - 2$; $f(x) = 3^x + 1$; $f(x) = 3^x + 3$; $f(x) = 3^x - 1$

3.

$f(x) = 2^x$	$f(x) = 2^{(x-1)}$	$f(x) = 2^{(x+1)}$
$(-2, \frac{1}{4})$	$(-2, \frac{1}{8})$	$(-2, \frac{1}{2})$
$(-1, \frac{1}{2})$	$(-1, \frac{1}{4})$	$(-1, 1)$
$(0, 1)$	$(0, \frac{1}{2})$	$(0, 2)$
$(1, 2)$	$(1, 1)$	$(1, 4)$
$(2, 4)$	$(2, 2)$	$(2, 8)$

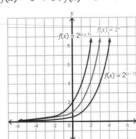

a. right ; left
b. $y = 0$
   $y = 0$
   $y = 0$
c. No, shifting a graph horizontally causes no change in the horizontal asymptote.

4.
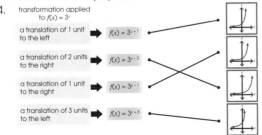
transformation applied to $f(x) = 3^x$

a translation of 1 unit to the left → $f(x) = 3^{x+1}$
a translation of 2 units to the right → $f(x) = 3^{x-2}$
a translation of 1 unit to the right → $f(x) = 3^{x-1}$
a translation of 3 units to the left → $f(x) = 3^{x+3}$

5a. stretch   b. compression   c. reflection

6A:
y $f(x) = 4^x$

a vertical stretch by a factor of 3

B:
y $f(x) = 4^x$

a vertical compression by a factor of $\frac{1}{2}$

C:
y $f(x) = 4^x$

a vertical stretch by a factor of 3 and a reflection in the x-axis

D:
y $f(x) = 4^x$

a vertical compression by a factor of $\frac{1}{2}$ and a reflection in the x-axis

7. He is correct. It can be shown that they are the same using exponential rules: $4^x = (2^2)^x = 2^{2x}$.

8. a horizontal compression by a factor of $\frac{1}{2}$;
   a horizontal compression by a factor of $\frac{1}{2}$ and a reflection in the y-axis ;
   a horizontal stretch by a factor of 2 ;
   a horizontal stretch by a factor of 2 and a reflection in the y-axis

9a. compression   b. stretch   c. y-axis

10. a horizontal compression by a factor of $\frac{1}{2}$;
    a horizontal stretch by a factor of 3 and a reflection in the y-axis ;
    a horizontal compression by a factor of $\frac{1}{2}$ and a reflection in the y-axis ;
    a horizontal stretch by a factor of 3

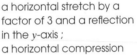
$f(x) = 3^{\frac{1}{3}x}$ $f(x) = 3^{2x}$ $f(x) = 3^{2x}$ $f(x) = 3^x$ $f(x) = 3^{\frac{1}{3}x}$

11. Parameter c:
    a translation of c units up ;
    a translation of c units down
    Parameter d:
    a translation of d units to the right ;
    a translation of d units to the left
    Parameter a:
    a vertical stretch by a factor of $|a|$;
    a vertical compression by a factor of $|a|$;
    a reflection in the x-axis
    Parameter k:
    a horizontal compression by a factor of $|\frac{1}{k}|$;
    a horizontal stretch by a factor of $|\frac{1}{k}|$;
    a reflection in the y-axis

12. Changing c will change the asymptote because it represents vertical translations.

13. A ; C ; G

14. $f(x) = \frac{1}{3}(5^{\frac{1}{4}(x+2)}) + 3$

15. $f(x) = 4(3^{2(x-1)}) - 4$

16. $f(x) = -4(2^{x+3})$

17. $f(x) = 4^{-3x} + 2$
    $\{x \in \mathbb{R}\}$;
    $\{y \in \mathbb{R} \mid y > 2\}$;
    $\frac{8}{3}$; $y = 2$

18.
$f(x) = \frac{1}{3}(2^{x+1}) + 2$
$(0, \frac{8}{3})$
$y = 2$

19.
$f(x) = 5(2^{x-1}) - 4$
$(0, -1.5)$
$y = -4$
    $\{x \in \mathbb{R}\}$;
    $\{y \in \mathbb{R} \mid y > -4\}$;
    -1.5 ; $y = -4$

20. Yes, it does affect the result. The order is similar to the order of operations for numerical expressions; apply the stretches and compressions (multiplications) before applying the translations (additions and subtractions).

4.6 Applications of Exponential Functions

1. $y = 4800$
2. $k = 23.1525$
3. $p \doteq 1508.99$
4. $i = \dfrac{13.44}{0.4^3}$ $i = 210$
5. $a = \dfrac{25}{5^4}$ $a = 0.04$
6. $h = \dfrac{12.15}{3^4}$ $h = 0.15$

7.

exponential growth	exponential growth	exponential decay
2	0.5	$n = 25$
0.5	2	$\dfrac{1}{5}$
4	$t \doteq 4.66$	2
$g = \dfrac{81}{8}$	84	16

8. $y = 5(1.2)^3$
   8.64
9. $96 = m(2)^5$ $m = \dfrac{96}{2^5}$
10. $d = 4(0.75)^2$
    2.25

11. growth ; 20 ; 100% ; 3 ; $p = 20(2^3)$
12. decay ; 90 000 ; -25% ; 5 ; $V = 90\,000(0.75)^5$
13. growth ; 210 ; 6% ; 6.5 ; $d = 210(1.06)^{6.5}$
14. decay ; 300 ; -0.5 ; 75 ; $75 = 300(0.5)^{\frac{t}{2.5}}$
15. growth ; 180 ; 25% ; $\dfrac{5}{2}$; $c = 180(1.25)^{\frac{5}{2}}$
16. decay ; 100 ; 8 ; 42 ; $42 = 100(1 - r)^8$
17a. $P(1) = 1425(1.04)^1 \doteq 1482$
    1482 people voted initially.
  b. The growth rate is 4%. It implies that 4% more people vote in every election.
  c. $P(5) = 1425(1.04)^5 \doteq 1734$
    About 1734 people will vote.
18a. $T(0) = 25(0.94)^0 - 4 = 21$
    The temperature is 21°C.
  b. $T(15) = 25(0.94)^{15} - 4 \doteq 5.88$
    The temperature will be 5.88°C.
  c. $T(t) = -4$ is the horizontal asymptote.
    The lowest temperature will be -4°C.
19a. This is an exponential decay.
  b. $P(5) = 115(\dfrac{5}{8})^5 \doteq 11$
    The goose population will be 1100.
20a. The initial investment is $2500 and the interest rate is 8%.
  b. $I(3) = 2500(1.08)^{2(3)} \doteq 3967.19$
    The value of the investment will be $3967.19.
21a. Yeast A: $A(t) = 200(2)^t$
    Yeast B: $B(t) = 50(3)^t$
  b. Yeast A: $A(3) = 200(2)^3 = 1600$
    Yeast B: $B(3) = 50(3)^3 = 1350$
    The population will be 1600 for Yeast A and 1350 for Yeast B.
  c. Yeast A: $A(5) = 200(2)^5 = 6400$
    Yeast B: $B(5) = 50(3)^5 = 12\,150$
    Yes, the population of Yeast B will be greater than that of Yeast A.
22. $I(t) = 15\,000(1 + \dfrac{0.06}{2})^{2t}$
    $I(10) = 15\,000(1.03)^{2(10)} \doteq 27\,091.67$
    The value will be $27 091.67.
23. $31.25 = a(0.5)^{24 \div 6}$
    $a = 500$
    The initial amount was 500 g.
24. $V(t) = 35\,000(0.8)^t$
    $V(5) = 35\,000(0.8)^5 = 11\,468.8$
    The value will be $11 468.80.

5 Trigonometry

5.1 Reciprocal Trigonometric Ratios

1. 0.31 ; 0.95 ; 0.32 ; 3.24 ; 1.05 ; 3.08
2. 0.24 ; 4.13
3. 0.14 ; 7.12
4. 0.79 ; 1.27
5. 0.87 ; 1.14
6. 1.13 ; $\cot 62° \doteq 0.53$
7. $\sec 31° \doteq 1.17$; $\csc 31° \doteq 1.94$
8. $\cot 43° \doteq 1.07$; $\sec 43° \doteq 1.37$
9. 1.13
10. $\csc 63° \doteq 1.12$
11. $\cot 47° \doteq 0.93$
12. $\csc 61° \doteq 1.14$
13. $\cot 72° \doteq 0.32$
14. $\sec 15° \doteq 1.04$
15. $\sec 7° \doteq 1.01$
16. $\cot 22° \doteq 2.48$
17. $\csc 86° \doteq 1.00$
18. $\dfrac{4}{11}$; 21°
19. $\tan \beta = \dfrac{9}{4}$ $\beta \doteq 66°$
20. $\cos \alpha = \dfrac{5}{7}$ $\alpha \doteq 44°$
21. $\tan \theta = \dfrac{7}{2}$ $\theta \doteq 74°$
22. $\cos \alpha = \dfrac{5}{8}$ $\alpha \doteq 51°$
23. $\sin \beta = \dfrac{3}{5}$ $\beta \doteq 37°$
24. $\cos 55° = \dfrac{x}{8}$ $\sec 55° = \dfrac{8}{x}$
    $x = 8 \cos 55°$ $x = \dfrac{8}{\sec 55°}$
    $x \doteq 4.59$ $x \doteq 4.59$
25. $\cos 52° = \dfrac{7}{x}$ $\sec 52° = \dfrac{x}{7}$
    $x = \dfrac{7}{\cos 52°}$ $x = 7 \sec 52°$
    $x \doteq 11.37$ $x \doteq 11.37$
26. $\sin 60° = \dfrac{x}{1.5}$ $\csc 60° = \dfrac{1.5}{x}$
    $x = 1.5 \sin 60°$ $x = \dfrac{1.5}{\csc 60°}$
    $x \doteq 1.30$ $x \doteq 1.30$
27. $\tan 43° = \dfrac{x}{5}$ $\cot 43° = \dfrac{5}{x}$
    $x = 5 \tan 43°$ $x = \dfrac{5}{\cot 43°}$
    $x \doteq 4.66$ $x \doteq 4.66$
28. F
29. F
30. T
31. F
32. T
33. $\sec 65° = \dfrac{30}{x}$
    $x = \dfrac{30}{\sec 65°}$
    $x \doteq 12.68$
    It is 12.68 m away from the wall.

34. $\csc 37° = \dfrac{y}{1.3}$
    $y = 1.3 \csc 37°$
    $y \doteq 2.16$
    The cable is 2.16 m long.

35. Toby: Kate:
    $\cot 30° = \dfrac{20}{t}$ $\cot 65° = \dfrac{20}{k}$
    $t = \dfrac{20}{\cot 30°}$ $k = \dfrac{20}{\cot 65°}$
    $t \doteq 11.55$ $k \doteq 42.89$
    Difference: 42.89 – 11.55 = 31.34
    His friends are 31.34 m apart.

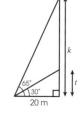

5.2 Special Angles

1. $\sqrt{2}$
   $\dfrac{1}{\sqrt{2}}$; $\dfrac{1}{\sqrt{2}}$; 1
2. $\sqrt{3}$
   $\dfrac{1}{2}$; $\dfrac{\sqrt{3}}{2}$; $\dfrac{1}{\sqrt{3}}$
   $\dfrac{\sqrt{3}}{2}$; $\dfrac{1}{2}$; $\sqrt{3}$

3. $\frac{1}{\sqrt{2}} ; \frac{1}{\sqrt{2}} ; 1$

Yes, the triangles are similar and they have the same trigonometric ratios.

4. $\frac{1}{2} ; \frac{\sqrt{3}}{2} ; \frac{1}{\sqrt{3}} ; \frac{\sqrt{3}}{2} ; \frac{1}{2} ; \sqrt{3}$

Yes, the triangles are similar and they have the same trigonometric ratios.

5. Regardless of the size of a triangle, as long as it is a right triangle with two 45° angles, or one 30° angle and one 60° angle, the exact values of its trigonometric ratios can be found.

6. $\frac{1}{\sqrt{2}} ; \frac{\sqrt{3}}{2} ; \frac{\sqrt{3}}{2} ; \frac{1}{\sqrt{2}} ; 1$

7. $\frac{1}{\sqrt{2}} ; \frac{1}{\sqrt{2}} ; 1$

8. $\frac{1}{2} ; \frac{1}{2} ; \sqrt{3}$

Try This (p. 100)

$= \frac{1}{2} \times \frac{1}{2} ; = \frac{1}{4}$

9. $= \frac{1}{\sqrt{2}} + \frac{1}{\sqrt{2}}$

$= \frac{2}{\sqrt{2}}$

10. $= \frac{\sqrt{3}}{2} \div \frac{1}{\sqrt{3}} + 1$

$= 2\frac{1}{2}$

11. $= 1 + \frac{1}{\sqrt{2}} \times \frac{1}{\sqrt{2}}$

$= 1\frac{1}{2}$

12. $= \frac{1}{\sqrt{2}} \times \frac{1}{\sqrt{2}} + \frac{1}{2}$

$= 1$

13. $= \frac{\sqrt{3}}{2} \times \frac{\sqrt{3}}{2} + 1 \div (\frac{\sqrt{3}}{2} \times \frac{\sqrt{3}}{2})$

$= 2\frac{1}{12}$

14. $\sin 45° \cos 45° = \frac{1}{\sqrt{2}} \times \frac{1}{\sqrt{2}} = \frac{1}{2}$

$\sin 30° \tan 45° = \frac{1}{2} \times 1 = \frac{1}{2}$

equivalent

15. $\tan 30° \tan 60° = \frac{1}{\sqrt{3}} \times \sqrt{3} = 1$

$\sin 60° \cos 30° = \frac{\sqrt{3}}{2} \times \frac{\sqrt{3}}{2} = \frac{3}{4}$

not equivalent

16. $(\tan^2 60°)(\cos 60°) = \sqrt{3} \times \sqrt{3} \times \frac{1}{2} = \frac{3}{2}$

$\sin 60° \tan 30° = \frac{\sqrt{3}}{2} \times \frac{1}{\sqrt{3}} = \frac{1}{2}$

not equivalent

17. $\frac{\sin 30°}{\sin 60° \tan 30°} = \frac{1}{2} \div (\frac{\sqrt{3}}{2} \times \frac{1}{\sqrt{3}}) = 1$

$\tan^2 30° = \frac{1}{\sqrt{3}} \times \frac{1}{\sqrt{3}} = \frac{1}{3}$

not equivalent

18. $\sin \theta = \frac{1}{2}$

$\theta = 30°$

$\sin 30° = \frac{2\sqrt{3}}{x}$

$x = \frac{2\sqrt{3}}{\sin 30°}$

$x = 4\sqrt{3}$

x is $4\sqrt{3}$ m.

$\tan 30° = \frac{2}{a}$

$a = \frac{2}{\tan 30°}$

$a = 2\sqrt{3}$

19. $\cos \beta = \frac{3\sqrt{2}}{h}$

$\frac{\sqrt{2}}{2} = \frac{3\sqrt{2}}{h}$

$h = 6$

Perimeter: $6 + 6 + 3\sqrt{2} + 3\sqrt{2} = 12 + 6\sqrt{2}$

The perimeter is $12 + 6\sqrt{2}$ cm.

20. $\sin \theta = \frac{\frac{\sqrt{2}}{2}}{h}$

$\frac{\sqrt{2}}{2} = \frac{\sqrt{2}}{2h}$

$h = 1$

$\cos 60° = \frac{1}{y}$

$y = \frac{1}{\cos 60°}$

$y = 2$

y is 2 m.

$\tan \alpha = \sqrt{3}$

$\alpha = 60°$

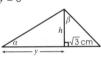

21. $\tan \beta = \frac{\sqrt{3}}{h}$

$1 = \frac{\sqrt{3}}{h}$

$h = \sqrt{3}$

$\tan \alpha = \frac{\sqrt{3}}{y}$

$\frac{\sqrt{3}}{3} = \frac{\sqrt{3}}{y}$

$y = 3$

Area: $\frac{(3 + \sqrt{3}) \times \sqrt{3}}{2} = \frac{3\sqrt{3} + 3}{2}$

The area is $\frac{3\sqrt{3} + 3}{2}$ cm².

22. $\tan 30° = \frac{b}{25}$

$b = 25 \tan 30°$

$b = 25 \times \frac{1}{\sqrt{3}}$

$b = \frac{25}{\sqrt{3}}$

The bear is $\frac{25}{\sqrt{3}}$ m away from the base of the tower.

23a. $\tan 30° = \frac{t}{10}$

$t = 10 \tan 30°$

$t = 10 \times \frac{1}{\sqrt{3}}$

$t = \frac{10}{\sqrt{3}}$

The building is $\frac{10}{\sqrt{3}}$ m tall.

b. $\tan 45° = \frac{l}{10}$

$10 \tan 45° = l$

$l = 10$

The height of the rod is 10 m.

5.3 Angles in the Cartesian Plane

1. =, =, =, A ; =, =, =, B ; =, =, =, A ; =, =, =, B
2. Quadrants 1 and 2 ; Quadrants 1 and 4 ; Quadrants 1 and 3
3. B ; C
4. C
5. A ; B
6. A ; B
7. A ; C
8. A
9. A

Try This (p. 103)

$r = \sqrt{(-3)^2 + (-4)^2} = 5$

$\sin \beta = \frac{4}{5}$

$\cos \beta = \frac{3}{5}$

$\tan \beta = \frac{4}{3}$

$\sin \theta = -\frac{4}{5}$

$\cos \theta = -\frac{3}{5}$

$\tan \theta = \frac{4}{3}$

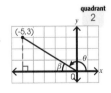

10. $r = \sqrt{(-5)^2 + 3^2} \doteq 5.83$

$\sin \beta = \frac{3}{5.83}$

$\cos \beta = \frac{5}{5.83}$

$\tan \beta = \frac{3}{5}$

$\sin \theta = \frac{3}{5.83}$

$\cos \theta = -\frac{5}{5.83}$

$\tan \theta = -\frac{3}{5}$

11. $r = \sqrt{4^2 + (-2)^2} \doteq 4.47$

$\sin \beta = \dfrac{2}{4.47}$ $\sin \theta = -\dfrac{2}{4.47}$

$\cos \beta = \dfrac{4}{4.47}$ $\cos \theta = \dfrac{4}{4.47}$

$\tan \beta = \dfrac{2}{4}$ $\tan \theta = -\dfrac{1}{2}$

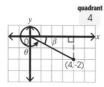

12. $r = \sqrt{(-3)^2 + 3^2} \doteq 4.24$

$\sin \beta = \dfrac{3}{4.24}$ $\sin \theta = \dfrac{3}{4.24}$

$\cos \beta = \dfrac{3}{4.24}$ $\cos \theta = -\dfrac{3}{4.24}$

$\tan \beta = \dfrac{3}{3}$ $\tan \theta = -1$

Try This (p. 104)

$\tan \beta = \dfrac{3}{5}$
$\beta \doteq 31°$
counterclockwise:
$\theta = 180° + 31° = 211°$
clockwise:
$\theta = -149°$

$\tan \beta = \dfrac{3}{4}$
$\beta \doteq 37°$
counterclockwise:
$\theta = 180° - 37° = 143°$
clockwise:
$\theta = -217°$

13.

$\tan \beta = \dfrac{3}{2}$
$\beta \doteq 56°$
counterclockwise:
$\theta = 180° + 56° = 236°$
clockwise:
$\theta = -124°$

14.

$\tan \beta = \dfrac{4}{3}$
$\beta \doteq 53°$
counterclockwise:
$\theta = 360° - 53° = 307°$
clockwise:
$\theta = -53°$

15.

$\tan \beta = \dfrac{4}{4}$
$\beta \doteq 45°$
counterclockwise:
$\theta = 180° + 45° = 225°$
clockwise:
$\theta = -135°$

16.

$\tan \beta = \dfrac{2}{5}$
$\beta \doteq 22°$
counterclockwise:
$\theta = 360° - 22° = 338°$
clockwise:
$\theta = -22°$

17.

$\tan \beta = \dfrac{1}{4}$
$\beta \doteq 14°$
counterclockwise:
$\theta = 180° + 14° = 194°$
clockwise:
$\theta = -166°$

18.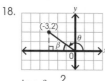

$\tan \beta = \dfrac{2}{3}$
$\beta \doteq 34°$
counterclockwise:
$\theta = 180° - 34° = 146°$
clockwise:
$\theta = -214°$

Try This (p. 105)

• quadrant 1:
$\theta = \cos^{-1} 0.866$
$\theta \doteq 30°$
θ can be either 30° or 330°.

• quadrant 4:
$\theta = 360° - 30°$
$\theta = 330°$

19. • quadrant 1:
$\theta = \sin^{-1} 0.8192$
$\theta \doteq 55°$
θ can be either 55° or 125°.

• quadrant 2:
$\theta = 180° - 55°$
$\theta = 125°$

20. • quadrant 1:
$\theta = \tan^{-1} 2.4751$
$\theta \doteq 68°$
θ can be either 68° or 248°.

• quadrant 3:
$\theta = 180° + 68°$
$\theta = 248°$

21. • quadrant 1:
$\theta = \cos^{-1} 0.766$
$\theta \doteq 40°$
θ can be either 40° or 320°.

• quadrant 4:
$\theta = 360° - 40°$
$\theta = 320°$

22. • quadrant 2:
$\theta = \cos^{-1} -0.9135$
$\theta \doteq 156°$
θ can be either 156° or 204°.

• quadrant 3:
$\theta = 180° + (180° - 156°)$
$\theta = 204°$

23. $\sin \theta = \dfrac{1}{1.1547}$

• quadrant 1:
$\theta = \sin^{-1} \left(\dfrac{1}{1.1547}\right)$
$\theta \doteq 60°$
θ can be either 60° or 120°.

• quadrant 2:
$\theta = 180° - 60°$
$\theta = 120°$

24. • quadrant 4:
$\theta = \sin^{-1} -0.5736$
$\theta \doteq -35°$
$\theta = 360° - 35° = 325°$
θ can be either 215° or 325°.

• quadrant 3:
$\theta = 180° + 35°$
$\theta = 215°$

25. • quadrant 4:
$\theta = \tan^{-1} -0.4663$
$\theta \doteq -25°$
$\theta = 360° - 25° = 335°$
θ can be either 155° or 335°.

• quadrant 2:
$\theta = 180° - 25°$
$\theta = 155°$

26. $\tan \theta = -\dfrac{1}{0.0875}$

• quadrant 4:
$\theta = \tan^{-1} \left(-\dfrac{1}{0.0875}\right)$
$\theta \doteq -85°$
$\theta \doteq 360° - 85° = 275°$
θ can be either 95° or 275°.

• quadrant 2:
$\theta = 180° - 85°$
$\theta = 95°$

27. $\cos \theta = \dfrac{1}{1.0154}$

• quadrant 1:
$\theta = \cos^{-1} \left(\dfrac{1}{1.0154}\right)$
$\theta \doteq 10°$
θ can be either 10° or 350°.

• quadrant 4:
$\theta = 360° - 10°$
$\theta = 350°$

28. It is necessary to determine the quadrants because each ratio corresponds to 2 angles in different quadrants.

5.4 Trigonometric Identities

1. $= \sin \theta \cdot \dfrac{1}{\cos \theta}$
$= \tan \theta$

2. $= \dfrac{1}{\tan \theta} \cdot \sin \theta \cdot \dfrac{1}{\cos \theta}$
$= \dfrac{\tan \theta}{\tan \theta}$
$= 1$

3. $= \sin^2 \theta - \sin^2 \theta$
$= 0$

4. $= \dfrac{\sin \theta}{1}$
$= \sin \theta$

5. $= \tan^2 \theta \cdot \dfrac{1}{\tan \theta}$
$= \tan \theta$

6. $= (2 \cos \theta - \cos \theta)\left(\dfrac{1}{\cos \theta}\right)$
$= \cos \theta \cdot \dfrac{1}{\cos \theta}$
$= 1$

Try This (p. 106)

$LS = \sec \theta$ $\qquad$ $RS = \csc \theta \tan \theta$

$\quad = \dfrac{r}{x}$ $\qquad\qquad\qquad = \dfrac{r}{y} \times \dfrac{y}{x}$

$\qquad\qquad\qquad\qquad\qquad = \dfrac{r}{x}$

$\qquad\qquad\qquad\qquad\qquad = LS$

$\therefore \sec \theta = \csc \theta \tan \theta$ for all angles θ where $0° \le \theta \le 360°$ except $0°$, $90°$, $180°$, $270°$, and $360°$.

7. $LS = \sin^2 \theta + \cos^2 \theta$ $\qquad RS = 1$

$\quad = (\dfrac{y}{r})^2 + (\dfrac{x}{r})^2$ $\qquad\qquad = LS$

$\quad = \dfrac{y^2 + x^2}{r^2}$

$\quad = \dfrac{r^2}{r^2}$

$\quad = 1$

$\therefore \sin^2 \theta + \cos^2 \theta = 1$ for all angles θ where $0° \le \theta \le 360°$.

8. $LS = 1 + \tan^2 \theta$ $\qquad RS = \sec^2 \theta$

$\quad = 1 + (\dfrac{y}{x})^2$ $\qquad\qquad = (\dfrac{r}{x})^2$

$\quad = \dfrac{x^2 + y^2}{x^2}$ $\qquad\qquad = \dfrac{r^2}{x^2}$

$\quad = \dfrac{r^2}{x^2}$ $\qquad\qquad\qquad = LS$

$\therefore 1 + \tan^2 \theta = \sec^2 \theta$ for all angles θ where $0° \le \theta \le 360°$ except $90°$ and $270°$.

9. $LS = 1 + \cot^2 \theta$ $\qquad RS = \csc^2 \theta$

$\quad = 1 + (\dfrac{x}{y})^2$ $\qquad\qquad = (\dfrac{r}{y})^2$

$\quad = \dfrac{y^2 + x^2}{y^2}$ $\qquad\qquad = \dfrac{r^2}{y^2}$

$\quad = \dfrac{r^2}{y^2}$ $\qquad\qquad\qquad = LS$

$\therefore 1 + \cot^2 \theta = \csc^2 \theta$ for all angles θ where $0° \le \theta \le 360°$ except $0°$, $180°$, and $360°$.

Try This (p. 107)

$LS = \csc \theta$ $\qquad$ $RS = \sec \theta \cot \theta$

$\quad = \dfrac{1}{\sin \theta}$ $\qquad\qquad = \dfrac{1}{\cos \theta} \times \dfrac{\cos \theta}{\sin \theta}$

$\qquad\qquad\qquad\qquad\quad = \dfrac{1}{\sin \theta}$

$\qquad\qquad\qquad\qquad\quad = LS$

When $\sin \theta = 0$, $\csc \theta$ is undefined. This occurs when $\theta = 0°$, $180°$, or $360°$.

When $\cos \theta = 0$, $\sec \theta$ is undefined. This occurs when $\theta = 90°$ or $270°$.

$\therefore \csc \theta = \sec \theta \cot \theta$ for all angles θ where $0° \le \theta \le 360°$ except $0°$, $90°$, $180°$, $270°$, and $360°$.

10. $LS = \sin \theta (1 + \csc \theta)$ $\qquad RS = \sin \theta + 1$

$\quad = \sin \theta (1 + \dfrac{1}{\sin \theta})$ $\qquad\qquad = LS$

$\quad = \sin \theta + 1$

When $\sin \theta = 0$, $\csc \theta$ is undefined. This occurs when $\theta = 0°$, $180°$, or $360°$.

$\therefore \sin \theta (1 + \csc \theta) = \sin \theta + 1$ for all angles θ where $0° \le \theta \le 360°$ except $0°$, $180°$, and $360°$.

11. $LS = \csc^2 \theta$ $\qquad RS = \cot^2 \theta (1 + \tan^2 \theta)$

$\quad = (\dfrac{1}{\sin \theta})^2$ $\qquad\qquad = \dfrac{1}{\tan^2 \theta} (\sec^2 \theta)$

$\quad = \dfrac{1}{\sin^2 \theta}$ $\qquad\qquad = \dfrac{1}{\tan^2 \theta} \times \dfrac{1}{\cos^2 \theta}$

$\qquad\qquad\qquad\qquad\qquad = \dfrac{1}{\sin^2 \theta}$

$\qquad\qquad\qquad\qquad\qquad = LS$

When $\sin \theta = 0$, $\csc \theta$ is undefined. This occurs when $\theta = 0°$, $180°$, or $360°$.

When $\cos \theta = 0$, $\tan^2 \theta$ is undefined. This occurs when $\theta = 90°$ or $270°$.

$\therefore \csc^2 \theta = \cot^2 \theta (1 + \tan^2 \theta)$ for all angles θ where $0° \le \theta \le 360°$ except $0°$, $90°$, $180°$, $270°$, and $360°$.

12. $LS = \cot^2 \theta + 1$ $\qquad RS = \csc^2 \theta$

$\quad = 1 + \cot^2 \theta$ $\qquad\qquad = LS$

$\quad = \csc^2 \theta$

When $\sin \theta = 0$, $\csc^2 \theta$ is undefined. This occurs when $\theta = 0°$, $180°$, or $360°$.

$\therefore \cot^2 \theta + 1 = \csc^2 \theta$ for all angles θ where $0° \le \theta \le 360°$ except $0°$, $180°$, and $360°$.

13. $LS = \dfrac{\sec \theta}{\sin \theta}$ $\qquad RS = \cot \theta + \tan \theta$

$\quad = \dfrac{\frac{1}{\cos \theta}}{\sin \theta}$ $\qquad\qquad = \dfrac{\cos \theta}{\sin \theta} + \dfrac{\sin \theta}{\cos \theta}$

$\quad = \dfrac{1}{\cos \theta \sin \theta}$ $\qquad\qquad = \dfrac{\cos^2 \theta + \sin^2 \theta}{\sin \theta \cos \theta}$

$\qquad\qquad\qquad\qquad\qquad = \dfrac{1}{\cos \theta \sin \theta}$

$\qquad\qquad\qquad\qquad\qquad = LS$

When $\sin \theta = 0$, $\dfrac{\sec \theta}{\sin \theta}$ is undefined. This occurs when $\theta = 0°$, $180°$, or $360°$.

When $\cos \theta = 0$, $\tan \theta$ is undefined. This occurs when $\theta = 90°$ or $270°$.

$\therefore \dfrac{\sec \theta}{\sin \theta} = \cot \theta + \tan \theta$ for all angles θ where $0° \le \theta \le 360°$ except $0°$, $90°$, $180°$, $270°$, and $360°$.

Try This (p. 108)

$LS = \dfrac{\sin \alpha \cot \alpha \cos \alpha}{\cos \alpha}$ $\qquad RS = \cos \alpha$

$\quad = \sin \alpha \cot \alpha$ $\qquad\qquad\qquad = LS$

$\quad = \sin \alpha \cdot \dfrac{\cos \alpha}{\sin \alpha}$

$\quad = \cos \alpha$

When $\cos \alpha = 0$, $\dfrac{\sin \alpha \cot \alpha \cos \alpha}{\cos \alpha}$ is undefined.

When $\sin \alpha = 0$, $\cot \alpha$ is undefined.

$\therefore \dfrac{\sin \alpha \cot \alpha \cos \alpha}{\cos \alpha} = \cos \alpha$ where $\sin \alpha \neq 0$ and $\cos \alpha \neq 0$.

14. $LS = \dfrac{1 - \sin \theta}{\cos \theta}$ $\qquad RS = \dfrac{\cos \theta}{1 + \sin \theta}$

$\quad = \dfrac{1 - \sin \theta}{\cos \theta} \times \dfrac{1 + \sin \theta}{1 + \sin \theta}$ $\qquad = LS$

$\quad = \dfrac{1 - \sin^2 \theta}{\cos \theta (1 + \sin \theta)}$

$\quad = \dfrac{\cos^2 \theta}{\cos \theta (1 + \sin \theta)}$

$\quad = \dfrac{\cos \theta}{1 + \sin \theta}$

$\therefore \dfrac{1 - \sin \theta}{\cos \theta} = \dfrac{\cos \theta}{1 + \sin \theta}$ where $\cos \theta \neq 0$ and $\sin \theta \neq -1$.

15. $LS = 1 - \cos \alpha$ $\qquad RS = \dfrac{\sin^2 \alpha}{1 + \cos \alpha}$

$\qquad\qquad\qquad\qquad\qquad = \dfrac{1 - \cos^2 \alpha}{1 + \cos \alpha}$

$\qquad\qquad\qquad\qquad\qquad = \dfrac{(1 - \cos \alpha)(1 + \cos \alpha)}{1 + \cos \alpha}$

$\qquad\qquad\qquad\qquad\qquad = 1 - \cos \alpha$

$\qquad\qquad\qquad\qquad\qquad = LS$

$\therefore 1 - \cos \alpha = \dfrac{\sin^2 \alpha}{1 + \cos \alpha}$ where $\cos \alpha \neq 1$.

16. $LS = \sin^4 \alpha - \cos^4 \alpha$

$\quad = (\sin^2 \alpha)^2 - (\cos^2 \alpha)^2$

$\quad = (\sin^2 \alpha - \cos^2 \alpha)(\sin^2 \alpha + \cos^2 \alpha)$

$\quad = (\sin^2 \alpha - \cos^2 \alpha)(1)$

$\quad = (1 - \cos^2 \alpha - \cos^2 \alpha)$

$\quad = 1 - 2\cos^2 \alpha$

$RS = 1 - 2\cos^2 \alpha$

$\quad = LS$

$\therefore \sin^4 \alpha - \cos^4 \alpha = 1 - 2\cos^2 \alpha$.

17. LS $= \dfrac{\cos\beta}{1-\sin\beta} + \dfrac{\cos\beta}{1+\sin\beta}$

$= \dfrac{\cos\beta(1+\sin\beta) + \cos\beta(1-\sin\beta)}{(1-\sin\beta)(1+\sin\beta)}$

$= \dfrac{\cos\beta(1+\sin\beta + 1 - \sin\beta)}{1-\sin^2\beta}$

$= \dfrac{2\cos\beta}{\cos^2\beta}$

$= \dfrac{2}{\cos\beta}$

RS $= \dfrac{2}{\cos\beta}$

$=$ LS

$\therefore \dfrac{\cos\beta}{1-\sin\beta} + \dfrac{\cos\beta}{1+\sin\beta} = \dfrac{2}{\cos\beta}$ where $\sin\beta \neq 1$, $\sin\beta \neq -1$, and $\cos\beta \neq 0$.

5.5 The Sine Law and Cosine Law

1. 2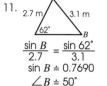

2. 1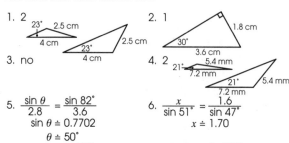

3. no

4. 2

5. $\dfrac{\sin\theta}{2.8} = \dfrac{\sin 82°}{3.6}$
$\sin\theta \doteq 0.7702$
$\theta \doteq 50°$

6. $\dfrac{x}{\sin 51°} = \dfrac{1.6}{\sin 47°}$
$x \doteq 1.70$

7. $\dfrac{x}{\sin 75°} = \dfrac{4.53}{\sin 70°}$
$x \doteq 4.66$

8. $\dfrac{\sin\theta}{2.85} = \dfrac{\sin 120°}{5.25}$
$\sin\theta \doteq 0.4701$
$\theta \doteq 28°$

9. $\dfrac{\sin\theta}{1.01} = \dfrac{\sin 53°}{0.98}$
$\sin\theta \doteq 0.8231$
$\theta \doteq 55°$

10. $\dfrac{x}{\sin 37°} = \dfrac{10.2}{\sin 103°}$
$x \doteq 6.30$

11. $\dfrac{\sin B}{2.7} = \dfrac{\sin 62°}{3.1}$
$\sin B \doteq 0.7690$
$\angle B \doteq 50°$

12. $\dfrac{\sin B}{3.6} = \dfrac{\sin 134°}{5.1}$
$\sin B \doteq 0.5078$
$\angle B \doteq 31°$

13. $\dfrac{\sin B}{4.1} = \dfrac{\sin 32°}{3.5}$
$\sin B \doteq 0.6208$
$\angle B \doteq 38°$

$\dfrac{\sin B}{4.1} = \dfrac{\sin 32°}{3.5}$
$\sin B \doteq 0.6208$
$\angle B \doteq 38°$
$\angle B = 180° - 38° = 142°$

14. $\dfrac{\sin B}{0.95} = \dfrac{\sin 81°}{0.94}$
$\sin B \doteq 0.9982$
$\angle B \doteq 87°$

$\dfrac{\sin B}{0.95} = \dfrac{\sin 81°}{0.94}$
$\sin B \doteq 0.9982$
$\angle B \doteq 87°$
$\angle B = 180° - 87° = 93°$

15. $x^2 = 2.61^2 + 3.44^2 - 2(2.61)(3.44)\cos 100°$
$x \doteq 4.67$

16. $x^2 = 1.01^2 + 0.82^2 - 2(1.01)(0.82)\cos 30°$
$x \doteq 0.51$

17. $4.2^2 = 6.5^2 + 7.1^2 - 2(6.5)(7.1)\cos\theta$
$\cos\theta \doteq 0.8128$
$\theta \doteq 36°$

18. $4^2 = 7.2^2 + 9.1^2 - 2(7.2)(9.1)\cos\theta$
$\cos\theta \doteq 0.9054$
$\theta \doteq 25°$

19. $x^2 = 4.21^2 + 6.3^2 - 2(4.21)(6.3)\cos 68°$
$x \doteq 6.13$

20. $a^2 = 20^2 + 60^2 - 2(20)(60)\cos 47°$
$a \doteq 48.61$

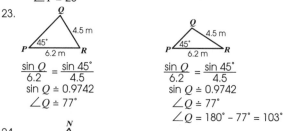

21. $\dfrac{e}{\sin 75°} = \dfrac{2}{\sin 25°}$
$e \doteq 4.57$

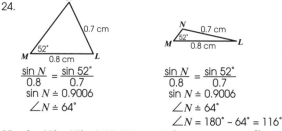

22. $\dfrac{\sin Y}{0.82} = \dfrac{\sin 141°}{1.1}$
$\sin Y \doteq 0.4691$
$\angle Y \doteq 28°$

23.

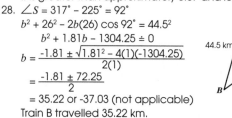

$\dfrac{\sin Q}{6.2} = \dfrac{\sin 45°}{4.5}$
$\sin Q \doteq 0.9742$
$\angle Q \doteq 77°$

$\dfrac{\sin Q}{6.2} = \dfrac{\sin 45°}{4.5}$
$\sin Q \doteq 0.9742$
$\angle Q \doteq 77°$
$\angle Q = 180° - 77° = 103°$

24.

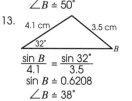

$\dfrac{\sin N}{0.8} = \dfrac{\sin 52°}{0.7}$
$\sin N \doteq 0.9006$
$\angle N \doteq 64°$

$\dfrac{\sin N}{0.8} = \dfrac{\sin 52°}{0.7}$
$\sin N \doteq 0.9006$
$\angle N \doteq 64°$
$\angle N = 180° - 64° = 116°$

25. $u^2 = 28^2 + 37^2 - 2(28)(37)\cos 84°$
$u \doteq 44$

26. $3 < 4\sin I$
$0.75 < \sin I$
$\sin^{-1} 0.75 < \angle I$
$49° < \angle I$
$\angle I$ is greater than approximately 49°.

27. $1.1\sin 31° < d < 1.1$
$0.57 < d < 1.1$
d is greater than approximately 0.57 and less than 1.1.

28. $\angle S = 317° - 225° = 92°$
$b^2 + 26^2 - 2b(26)\cos 92° = 44.5^2$
$b^2 + 1.81b - 1304.25 \doteq 0$
$b = \dfrac{-1.81 \pm \sqrt{1.81^2 - 4(1)(-1304.25)}}{2(1)}$
$= \dfrac{-1.81 \pm 72.25}{2}$
$= 35.22$ or -37.03 (not applicable)
Train B travelled 35.22 km.

29. $2.5^2 = 10^2 + 9.44^2 - 2(10)(9.44)\cos\theta$
$\cos\theta \doteq 0.9686$
$\theta \doteq 14°$
bearing: $270° + 14° = 284°$
The bearing of the fire from Tower B is 284°.

30. $1.4^2 = k^2 + 1.5^2 - 2k(1.5)\cos 56°$
$k^2 - 1.68k + 0.29 \doteq 0$
$k = \dfrac{-(-1.68) \pm \sqrt{(-1.68)^2 - 4(1)(0.29)}}{2(1)}$
$= 1.485$ or 0.195

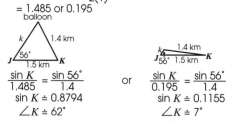

$\dfrac{\sin K}{1.485} = \dfrac{\sin 56°}{1.4}$
$\sin K \doteq 0.8794$
$\angle K \doteq 62°$

or

$\dfrac{\sin K}{0.195} = \dfrac{\sin 56°}{1.4}$
$\sin K \doteq 0.1155$
$\angle K \doteq 7°$

Kenneth's angle of elevation is 7° or 62°.

ISBN: 978-1-77149-222-5

31. $\angle A = (360° - 245°) + 39° = 154°$
$d^2 = 18^2 + 24^2 - 2(18)(24) \cos 154°$
$d \doteq 40.95$
Ship B sailed 40.95 km.

5.6 Solving 3-D Problems Using Trigonometry

Try This (p. 113)
$WY = \sqrt{33^2 - 30^2} \doteq 13.75$
$\dfrac{\sin W}{19.8} = \dfrac{\sin 42°}{13.75}$
$\sin W \doteq 0.9635$
$\angle W \doteq 74°$
The measure of $\angle YWZ$ is 74°.

1. $\dfrac{MO}{\sin 21°} = \dfrac{1.4}{\sin 129°}$ $\dfrac{\sin N}{0.65} = \dfrac{\sin 43°}{0.8}$
$MO \doteq 0.65$ $\sin N \doteq 0.5541$
                                   $\angle N \doteq 34°$
The measure of $\angle MNO$ is 34°.

2. $\dfrac{SR}{\sin 56°} = \dfrac{10.6}{\sin 96°}$ $\dfrac{SQ}{\sin 28°} = \dfrac{10.6}{\sin 96°}$
$SR \doteq 8.84$ $SQ \doteq 5.00$
$\angle SRQ = 180° - 96° - 56° = 28°$
$PS = SQ = 5$
$PR = \sqrt{5^2 + 8.84^2} \doteq 10.16$
The length of PR is 10.16 cm.

3. $\angle DCE = 180° - 40° - 43° = 97°$
$\dfrac{DE}{\sin 97°} = \dfrac{7.2}{\sin 43°}$
$DE \doteq 10.48$
$16.1^2 = 9.42^2 + 10.48^2 - 2(9.42)(10.48) \cos D$
$\cos D \doteq -0.3071$
$\angle D \doteq 108°$
The measure of $\angle EDF$ is 108°.

4. $\angle NFO = 180° - 90° - 24° = 66°$
$\angle RFO = 180° - 90° - 36° = 54°$
$\dfrac{NO}{\sin 66°} = \dfrac{18}{\sin 24°}$ $\dfrac{RO}{\sin 54°} = \dfrac{18}{\sin 36°}$
$NO \doteq 40.43$ $RO \doteq 24.77$
$65^2 = 24.77^2 + 40.43^2 - 2(24.77)(40.43) \cos O$
$\cos O \doteq -0.9870$
$\angle O \doteq 171°$
The measure of the angle is 171°.

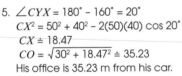

5. $\angle CYX = 180° - 160° = 20°$
$CX^2 = 50^2 + 40^2 - 2(50)(40) \cos 20°$
$CX \doteq 18.47$
$CO = \sqrt{30^2 + 18.47^2} \doteq 35.23$
His office is 35.23 m from his car.

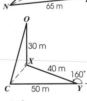

6. $\angle TAO = 12°$ $\angle TBO = 19°$
$\angle ATO = 180° - 90° - 12°$ $\angle BTO = 180° - 90° - 19°$
$\quad = 78°$ $\quad = 71°$
$\dfrac{AO}{\sin 78°} = \dfrac{22}{\sin 12°}$ $\dfrac{BO}{\sin 71°} = \dfrac{22}{\sin 19°}$
$AO \doteq 103.50$ $BO \doteq 63.89$
$AB^2 = 103.5^2 + 63.89^2 - 2(103.5)(63.89) \cos 78°$
$AB \doteq 109.75$
The distance is 109.75 m.

7. $\dfrac{a}{\sin 51°} = \dfrac{3.2}{\sin 39°}$ $\dfrac{b}{\sin 35°} = \dfrac{3.2}{\sin 55°}$
$a \doteq 3.95$ $b \doteq 2.24$
$c^2 = 3.95^2 + 2.24^2 - 2(3.95)(2.24) \cos 76°$
$c \doteq 4.04$
Agnes and Brian are 4.04 m apart.

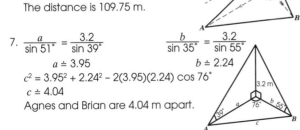

8. $\angle ETG = 75° + (360° - 328°) = 107°$
$\qquad 50^2 = 35^2 + TG^2 - 2(35)(TG) \cos 107°$
$TG^2 + 20.47TG - 1275 = 0$
$\qquad TG \doteq 26.91$ or -47.38 (not applicable)
$\tan 11.7° = \dfrac{h}{26.91}$
$\qquad h \doteq 5.57$
The giraffe was 5.57 m tall.

9. $\tan 29° = \dfrac{315}{AO}$
$\quad AO \doteq 568.28$
$\tan 36° = \dfrac{315}{BO}$
$\quad BO \doteq 433.56$
$\angle AOB = 32° + (360° - 322°) = 70°$
$AB^2 = 568.28^2 + 433.56^2 - 2(568.28)(433.56) \cos 70°$
$AB \doteq 585.13$
The boats were 585.13 m apart.

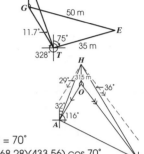

6 Sinusoidal Functions

6.1 Properties of Periodic Functions

1. A ; B ; E ; F
2. Table A represents the values of a periodic function. Its y-values show a repeating cycle over regular intervals.

Try This (p. 117)
2. $4 ; 3 ; -1 ; \{y \in \mathbb{R} \mid -1 \le y \le 3\} ; y = 1 ; 2$
3. $10\,s ; 110\,m ; 50\,m ; 30\,m ; \{y \in \mathbb{R} \mid 50 \le y \le 110\} ; y = 80$
4. $24\,h ; 28°C ; 18°C ; 5°C ; \{y \in \mathbb{R} \mid 18 \le y \le 28\} ; y = 23$
5. $2\,s ; 3\,m ; 0.5\,m ; 1.25\,m ; \{y \in \mathbb{R} \mid 0.5 \le y \le 3\} ; y = 1.75$
6. $2.5 ; y = 2 ; 1 ; y = 0.5$
   B ; D
   A ; C
7. periodic ; time ; height jumped
8. periodic ; time ; water level
9. nonperiodic
10A.

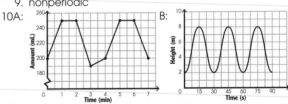

11. Graph B is periodic. Its period is 30 s, peak is 8 m, trough is 2 m, range is $\{y \in \mathbb{R} \mid 2 \le y \le 8\}$, equation of the axis is $y = 5$, and amplitude is 3 m.

6.2 Properties of Sinusoidal Functions

1. periodic
2. neither
3. periodic
4. sinusoidal
5. sinusoidal
6. sinusoidal
7. It is not true because having repeating cycles in a periodic graph does not imply that the cycles resemble smooth and symmetrical curves.
8. neither   9. sinusoidal   10. periodic
11. sinusoidal   12. neither   13. sinusoidal
14A. $\sin x$
$360° ; 1 ; \{x \in \mathbb{R} \mid 0° \le x \le 90°, 270° \le x \le 360°\} ;$
$\{x \in \mathbb{R} \mid 90° \le x \le 270°\}$

B: $f(x) = \cos 2x$
180° ; 1 ; $\{x \in \mathbb{R} \mid 90° \le x \le 180°, 270° \le x \le 360°\}$;
$\{x \in \mathbb{R} \mid 0° \le x \le 90°, 180° \le x \le 270°\}$

C: $f(x) = \sin (2x) - 1$
180° ; 1 ; $\{x \in \mathbb{R} \mid 0° \le x \le 45°, 135° \le x \le 225°, 315° \le x \le 360°\}$;
$\{x \in \mathbb{R} \mid 45° \le x \le 135°, 225° \le x \le 315°\}$

D: $f(x) = \cos (3x) + 1$
120° ; 1 ; $\{x \in \mathbb{R} \mid 60° \le x \le 120°, 180° \le x \le 240°, 300° \le x \le 360°\}$;
$\{x \in \mathbb{R} \mid 0° \le x \le 60°, 120° \le x \le 180°, 240° \le x \le 300°\}$

15a. $h = 15$; the height of the centre of the gear
$a = 3$; the radius of the gear

b. The gear covers 18.84 cm for each rotation every 12.5 s. So the speed is 1.5072 cm/s.

16a. $h = 0$; the height of the turbine's centre

b. The turbine is installed perpendicularly to the base of the river because the height of the blade is not constant.

17a. $p = 2$; the time it takes for the pendulum to swing 1 cycle

b. Since the pendulum returns to the centre every second, the clock probably tells time accurately.

18.

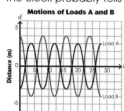

Motions of Loads A and B

a. • period:
Load A: 8 s   Load B: 8 s
It represents the amount of time it takes for each load to complete a swing back and forth.

• amplitude:
Load A: $\dfrac{3 - (-3)}{2} = 3$ Load B: $\dfrac{4 - (-4)}{2} = 4$
It represents each load's maximum distance from its resting position.

• equation of the axis:
Load A: $y = \dfrac{3 + (-3)}{2} = 0$ Load B: $y = \dfrac{4 + (-4)}{2} = 0$
$\therefore y = 0$ $\therefore y = 0$
It represents the resting position of each load.

b. Both loads arrive at their resting positions at the same time. Therefore, Load B will be farther away since it has a greater amplitude.

c. When Load A is increasing, Load B is decreasing, and vice versa. This implies that the loads are on the opposite sides of their resting positions of each other.

Try This (p. 124)

$A(x,y) = (4 \cos 48°, 4 \sin 48°) \doteq (2.68, 2.97)$

19a. $(x,y) = (2 \cos 75°, 2 \sin 75°) \doteq (0.52, 1.93)$

b. $(x,y) = (4 \cos 98°, 4 \sin 98°) \doteq (-0.56, 3.96)$

c. $(x,y) = (3 \cos 127°, 3 \sin 127°) \doteq (-1.81, 2.40)$

20a. $(x,y) = (2 \cos 140°, 2 \sin 140°) \doteq (-1.53, 1.29)$

b. $(x,y) = (5 \cos 326°, 5 \sin 326°) \doteq (4.15, -2.80)$

21a. $\pi r^2 = 28.26$
$r = 3$
$(x,y) = (3 \cos 86°, 3 \sin 86°) \doteq (0.21, 2.99)$

b. $\pi r^2 = 50.24$
$r = 4$
$(x,y) = (4 \cos 86°, 4 \sin 86°) \doteq (0.28, 3.99)$

6.3 Transformations of Sinusoidal Functions

1. Sine Functions:
$\sin x + 1$; a translation of 1 unit up
$1.5 \sin x$; a vertical stretch by a factor of 1.5
$\sin (x + 60°)$; a translation of 60° to the left
Cosine Functions:
$\cos (x - 90°)$; a translation of 90° to the right
$\dfrac{1}{2} \cos x$; a vertical compression by a factor of $\dfrac{1}{2}$
$\cos x - 1$; a translation of 1 unit down

Function	Range	Max. / Min. Value	Period	Amplitude	Equation of the Axis
$f(x) = 1.5 \sin x$	✔	✔		✔	
$f(x) = \sin x + 1$	✔	✔			✔
$f(x) = \sin (x + 60°)$					
$f(x) = \frac{1}{2} \cos x$	✔	✔		✔	
$f(x) = \cos x - 1$	✔	✔			✔
$f(x) = \cos (x - 90°)$					

2. a vertical stretch by a factor of 3 and a translation of 45° to the left

3. a reflection in the x-axis, a vertical compression by a factor of 0.5, a translation of 30° to the right and 5 units down

4. a vertical compression by a factor of $\dfrac{1}{3}$ and a translation of 180° to the right and 4 units up

5. a reflection in the x-axis, a vertical stretch by a factor of 2, a horizontal compression by a factor of $\dfrac{1}{4}$, and a translation of 120° to the left and 1 unit up

	$f(x)$	$g(x)$	$h(x)$	$k(x)$
domain	$\{x \in \mathbb{R}\}$	$\{x \in \mathbb{R}\}$	$\{x \in \mathbb{R}\}$	$\{x \in \mathbb{R}\}$
range	$\{y \in \mathbb{R} \mid -3 \le y \le 3\}$	$\{y \in \mathbb{R} \mid -5.5 \le y \le -4.5\}$	$\{y \in \mathbb{R} \mid 3\frac{2}{3} \le y \le 4\frac{1}{3}\}$	$\{y \in \mathbb{R} \mid -1 \le y \le 3\}$
period	360°	360°	360°	90°
amplitude	3	0.5	$\frac{1}{3}$	2
max./min. value	max. = 3 min. = -3	max. = -4.5 min. = -5.5	max. = $4\frac{1}{3}$ min. = $3\frac{2}{3}$	max. = 3 min. = -1
equation of the axis	$y = 0$	$y = -5$	$y = 4$	$y = 1$

6.

x	$\sin x$	$\cos (x - 90°)$
0°	0	0
90°	1	1
180°	0	0
270°	-1	-1
360°	0	0

x	$\cos x$	$\sin (x + 90°)$
0°	1	1
90°	0	0
180°	-1	-1
270°	0	0
360°	1	1

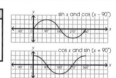

The graphs of $\sin x$ and $\cos x$ are horizontal translations of each other.

Try This (p. 127)

• a reflection in the x-axis

• a horizontal compression by a factor of $\dfrac{1}{2}$

• a translation of 60° to the right and 1 unit down

7. a reflection in the x-axis, a vertical stretch by a factor of 2, and a translation of 180° to the right and 0.5 units up

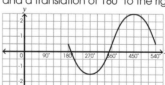

$\{y \in \mathbb{R} \mid -1.5 \le y \le 2.5\}$ 2
360°   max. = 2.5, min. = -1.5
$y = 0.5$

ISBN: 978-1-77149-222-5

8. a vertical compression by a factor of 0.5, a horizontal compression by a factor of $\frac{1}{2}$, and a translation of 120° to the left and 1 unit down

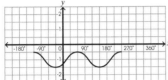

$\{y \in \mathbb{R} \mid -1.5 \le y \le -0.5\}$; 180° ; max. = -0.5, min. = -1.5
0.5 ; $y = -1$

9. a vertical compression by a factor of $\frac{3}{4}$, a horizontal stretch by a factor of 2, and a translation of 60° to the right and $\frac{1}{2}$ units down

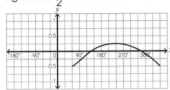

$\{y \in \mathbb{R} \mid -1\frac{1}{4} \le y \le \frac{1}{4}\}$; 720° ; max. = $\frac{1}{4}$, min. = $-1\frac{1}{4}$
$\frac{3}{4}$; $y = -\frac{1}{2}$

10a. T   b. T   c. F
11a. F   b. T

6.4 Graphing and Modelling

Try This (p. 129)

(Suggested answers)
$a: \frac{0.5 - (-2.5)}{2} = 1.5$

$k: 180° = \frac{360°}{|k|}$
     $k = 2$

$d: 90°$

$c: y = -1$

$1.5 \cos (2(x - 90°)) - 1$

1-7. (Suggested answers)

1. $a: \frac{2 - (-2)}{2} = 2$

$k: 120° = \frac{360°}{|k|}$
     $k = 3$

$d: 60°$

$f(x) = 2 \sin (3(x - 60°))$

2. $a: \frac{0.5 - (-0.5)}{2} = \frac{1}{2}$

$k: 90° = \frac{360°}{|k|}$
     $k = 4$

$d: -30°$

$f(x) = \frac{1}{2} \sin (4(x + 30°))$

3. $a: \frac{4 - (-2)}{2} = 3$

$k: 10 = \frac{360°}{|k|}$
     $k = 36°$

$c: 1$

$f(x) = 3 \cos (36x)° + 1$

4. $a: = \frac{1.5 - (-1.5)}{2} = \frac{3}{2}$

$k: 4 = \frac{360°}{|k|}$
     $k = 90°$

$d: 0.5$

$f(x) = \frac{3}{2} \sin (90(x - 0.5))°$

5.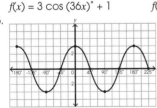

$f(x) = 3 \cos (2x)$ $f(x) = 3 \sin (2(x + 45°))$

6.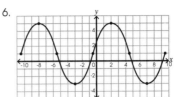

$f(x) = 4 \cos (36(x - 2))° + 1$ $f(x) = 4 \sin (36(x + 0.5))° + 1$

7.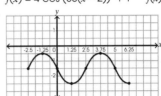

$f(x) = \sin (72(x - 2.5))° - 1.5$ $f(x) = \cos (72(x + 1.25))° - 1.5$

8. $f(x) = 5 \sin (x + 90°) + 2$ or $f(x) = 5 \cos (x + 90°) + 2$
9. $f(x) = 3 \sin (6(x - 180°)) - 5$ or $f(x) = 3 \cos (6(x - 180°)) - 5$
10. $f(x) = 4 \sin (\frac{3}{2}(x + 100°)) - 1$ or $f(x) = 4 \cos (\frac{3}{2}(x + 100°)) - 1$
11. $f(x) = 3 \sin (2x)° - 1$ or $f(x) = 3 \cos (2x)° - 1$
12. $f(x) = -\frac{1}{8} \sin (x - 3) + 5$ or $f(x) = -\frac{1}{8} \cos (x - 3) + 5$
13. $f(x) = \sin (-\frac{1}{7}(x - 2.5))$ or $f(x) = \cos (-\frac{1}{7}(x - 2.5))$
14. B ; A ; D ; C
15. Yes. A sinusoidal function that has $y = -7$ as the equation of the axis has its maximum at 0.
16-17. (Suggested answers)
16. $f(x) = -4 \sin (6x)°$ 17. $f(x) = 6 \cos (3x)° - 12$
18. $-2 - (-5) = 3$
Its amplitude is 3.

19.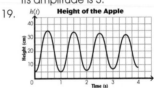

a. (Suggested answer) $h(t) = 15 \sin (360(t - 0.25))° + 20$
b. $h(6) = 15 \sin (360(6 - 0.25))° + 20 = 5$
The height at 6 s will be about 5 cm.

20.

a. (Suggested answer) $h(t) = 1.25 \sin (360(t - 0.4))° - 0.75$
b. $h(5) = 1.25 \sin (360(5 - 0.4))° - 0.75 \doteq -1.48$
The height of the blade will be about -1.48 m.

6.5 Applications of Sinusoidal Models

Try This (p. 133)

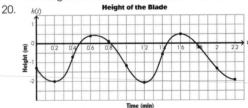

$a = 2$
$k = 60°$
$d = 1$
$c = 1$
$f(x) = 2 \cos (60(x - 1))° + 1$

1-8. (Suggested answers)
1.

$a = 1.5$
$k = 60°$
$d = 3$
$c = -2.5$
$f(x) = 1.5 \cos (60(x - 3))° - 2.5$

ISBN: 978-1-77149-222-5

2.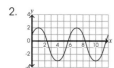

$a = 2.5$
$k = 60°$
$d = 1$
$c = -0.5$
$f(x) = 2.5 \cos (60(x - 1))° - 0.5$

3.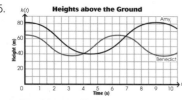

$a = 5.5$
$k = 22.5°$
$d = -1$
$c = 4.5$
$f(x) = -5.5 \sin (22.5(x + 1))° + 4.5$

4.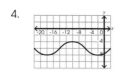

$a = 2$
$k = 22.5°$
$d = -10$
$c = -6$
$f(x) = 2 \cos (22.5(x + 10))° - 6$

5.

Heights above the Ground

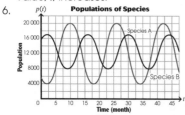

a. $h(t) = 21 \cos (40t)° + 61$
b. $h(t) = 13.5 \cos (56.25t)° + 51.5$
c. The heights are 82 m and 65 m, which are the heights when $t = 0$.
d. No. Although the model resembles a sinusoidal function, it is not. This is due to the fact that the "periods" will not be symmetrical as the independent value, t, increases.

6.

Populations of Species

a. $P(t) = 4500 \cos (\frac{180}{7}(t - 2))° + 12\,500$
b. $P(t) = 8000 \cos (22.5(t - 10))° + 12\,000$
c. Yes, the species demonstrated a predator-prey interaction. This is because as Species A's population increased, Species B's population tended to decrease, and vice versa.

7a. 15 ; the maximum distance from the resting position
3 ; the time needed to swing 1 cycle
$y = 0$; the location of the resting position
$\{x \in \mathbb{R} \mid x \geq 0\}$; the possible values of time
$\{y \in \mathbb{R} \mid -15 \leq y \leq 15\}$; the possible values of distance
b. $D(t) = 15 \cos (120(t - 2))°$
$D(10) = 15 \cos (120(10 - 2))° = -7.5$
He will be 7.5 m to the back of his resting position at 10 s.

8a. period: $2\pi r = \dfrac{360°}{|k|}$ $a = 30$
$k = \dfrac{360°}{2 \times 3.14 \times 30}$ $c = 30$
$k \doteq 1.91$
$h(x) = 30 \cos (1.91x)° + 30$
b. Total distance: $8 \times 2\pi(30) = 1507.2$
Domain: $\{x \in \mathbb{R} \mid 0 \leq x \leq 1507.2\}$
Range: $\{y \in \mathbb{R} \mid 0 \leq y \leq 60\}$
c. $h(1000) = 30 \cos (1.91 \times 1000)° + 30 \doteq 19.74$
The height of the scratch is 19.74 cm when the roller rolls a distance of 1000 cm.

7 Discrete Functions

7.1 Discrete Functions and Sequences

Try This (p. 136)

discrete function ; {-2, -1, 0, 1, 2} ; {0, 1, 2}
continuous function ; $\{x \in \mathbb{R}\}$; $\{y \in \mathbb{R} \mid y \leq 1\}$
1. discrete function ; {-3, -2, -1, 1, 3, 4} ; {-2, -1, 1, 2}
2. continuous function ; $\{x \in \mathbb{R}\}$; $\{y \in \mathbb{R} \mid y \geq -2\}$
3. discrete function ; {-4, -2, 0, 2, 4} ; {-2, -1, 0, 1, 2}

4.
No. of Tickets (x)	1	2	3	4	5
Cost (y)	25	50	75	100	125

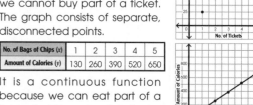

It is a discrete function because we cannot buy part of a ticket. The graph consists of separate, disconnected points.

5.
No. of Bags of Chips (x)	1	2	3	4	5
Amount of Calories (y)	130	260	390	520	650

It is a continuous function because we can eat part of a bag of chips, meaning that x can be any value greater than or equal to 0. The graph consists of connected points.

6.
No. of Storybooks (x)	1	2	3	4	5
Amount of Money Left (y)	41.5	33	24.5	16	7.5

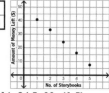

It is a discrete function because we cannot buy part of a storybook. The graph consists of separate, disconnected points.
a. {1, 2, 3, 4, 5}   b. {7.5, 16, 24.5, 33, 41.5}
c. No, it is not possible to buy -1 storybook.
d. She can buy a maximum of 5 books.
e. The initial amount was $50.

7.
Term No. n	Term t_n	First Difference	Second Difference
1	-1		
2	1	2	
3	3	2	
4	5	2	
5	7	2	

linear
$f(n) = 2n - 3$; 9

8.
Term No. n	Term t_n	First Difference	Second Difference
1	2	–	–
2	11	9	–
3	26	15	6
4	47	21	6
5	74	27	6

quadratic
$f(n) = 3n^2 - 1$; 107

9.
Term No. n	Term t_n	First Difference	Second Difference
1	1	–	–
2	3	2	–
3	6	3	1
4	10	4	1
5	15	5	1

quadratic
$f(n) = \frac{1}{2}(n^2 + n)$; 21

10.
Term No. n	Term t_n	First Difference	Second Difference
1	7	–	–
2	4	-3	–
3	1	-3	–
4	-2	-3	–
5	-5	-3	–

linear
$f(n) = 10 - 3n$; -8

11.
Term No. n	Term t_n	First Difference	Second Difference
1	0	–	–
2	2	2	–
3	6	4	2
4	12	6	2
5	20	8	2

quadratic
$f(n) = n^2 - n$; 30

12.
Term No. n	Term t_n	First Difference	Second Difference
1	1	–	–
2	4	3	–
3	7	3	–
4	10	3	–
5	13	3	–

linear
$f(n) = 3n - 2$; 16

13.

Term No. n	Term t_n	First Difference
1	1	–
2	4	3
3	7	3
4	10	3
5	13	3

$f(n) = 3n - 2$

14.

Term No. n	Term t_n	First Diff.	Second Diff.
1	0	–	–
2	3	3	–
3	8	5	2
4	15	7	2
5	24	9	2

$f(n) = n^2 - 1$

15. 5, 17, 37   **16.** 2, 4, 8   **17.** -1, -5, -9
18. $\frac{1}{2}, \frac{2}{3}, \frac{3}{4}$ **19.** $\frac{5}{3}, \frac{4}{3}, 1$ **20.** 5, 6, 9

7.2 Recursive Procedures

1. B ; C ; E ; H ; J

Try This (p. 140)

1 ; 2 ; = 8
$f(3) = 10 - f(2) = 10 - 8 = 2$
$f(4) = 10 - f(3) = 10 - 2 = 8$
2, 8, 2, 8

2. $t_2 = t_1 + 5 = 2 + 5 = 7$
$t_3 = t_2 + 5 = 7 + 5 = 12$
$t_4 = t_3 + 5 = 12 + 5 = 17$
The first four terms are
2, 7, 12, 17.

3. $t_2 = (t_1)^2 = (\frac{1}{2})^2 = \frac{1}{4}$
$t_3 = (t_2)^2 = (\frac{1}{4})^2 = \frac{1}{16}$
$t_4 = (t_3)^2 = (\frac{1}{16})^2 = \frac{1}{256}$
The first four terms are
$\frac{1}{2}, \frac{1}{4}, \frac{1}{16}, \frac{1}{256}$.

4. $t_2 = t_1 + 4y = x + 2y + 4y = x + 6y$
$t_3 = t_2 + 4y = x + 6y + 4y = x + 10y$
$t_4 = t_3 + 4y = x + 10y + 4y = x + 14y$
The first four terms are $x + 2y, x + 6y, x + 10y, x + 14y$.

5. $f(2) = 3f(1) = 3(-1) = -3$
$f(3) = 3f(2) = 3(-3) = -9$
$f(4) = 3f(3) = 3(-9) = -27$
The first four terms are
-1, -3, -9, -27.

6. $f(2) = 5 - f(1) = 5 - 0.5 = 4.5$
$f(3) = 5 - f(2) = 5 - 4.5 = 0.5$
$f(4) = 5 - f(3) = 5 - 0.5 = 4.5$
The first four terms are
0.5, 4.5, 0.5, 4.5.

7. $f(2) = f(1) + x = x - y + x = 2x - y$
$f(3) = f(2) + x = 2x - y + x = 3x - y$
$f(4) = f(3) + x = 3x - y + x = 4x - y$
The first four terms are $x - y, 2x - y, 3x - y, 4x - y$.

Try This (p. 141)

3 ; -2 ; $t_3 \times -2$; $t_4 = -24 = t_3 \times -2$
3 ; $t_{n-1} \times -2$

8. Pattern: + 2
$t_1 = 15$
$t_2 = 17 = t_1 + 2$
$t_3 = 19 = t_2 + 2$
$t_4 = 21 = t_3 + 2$
$t_1 = 15, t_n = t_{n-1} + 2$

9. Pattern: – 3
$t_1 = 7$
$t_2 = 4 = t_1 - 3$
$t_3 = 1 = t_2 - 3$
$t_4 = -2 = t_3 - 3$
$t_1 = 7, t_n = t_{n-1} - 3$

10. Pattern: × 2
$t_1 = -5$
$t_2 = -10 = t_1 \times 2$
$t_3 = -20 = t_2 \times 2$
$t_4 = -40 = t_3 \times 2$
$t_1 = -5, t_n = 2t_{n-1}$

11. -10, -5, 0, 5
$t_1 = -15$
$t_2 = -10 = t_1 + 5$
$t_3 = -5 = t_2 + 5$
$t_4 = 0 = t_3 + 5$
$t_1 = -15, t_n = t_{n-1} + 5$

12. -2, -4, -8, -16, -32
$t_1 = -2$
$t_2 = -4 = t_1 \times 2$
$t_3 = -8 = t_2 \times 2$
$t_4 = -16 = t_3 \times 2$
$t_1 = -2, t_n = 2t_{n-1}$

13. 2 ; 7 ; 3 ; 11 ; 4
$t_{n-1} + n$

14. $t_1 = 100$
$t_2 = 90 = t_1 - 10$
$t_3 = 81 = t_2 - 9$
$t_4 = 73 = t_3 - 8$
$t_1 = 100, t_n = t_{n-1} - 12 + n$

15a. $t_1 = 1.5$
$t_2 = 1.6 = 1.5 + 0.1 = t_1 + 0.1(2 - 1)$
$t_3 = 1.8 = 1.6 + 0.2 = t_2 + 0.1(3 - 1)$
$t_4 = 2.1 = 1.8 + 0.3 = t_3 + 0.1(4 - 1)$
$t_1 = 1.5, t_n = t_{n-1} + 0.1(n - 1)$

b. $t_6 = t_5 + 0.1(6 - 1) = 2.5 + 0.1(5) = 3$
He jogged 3 km on Saturday.

16a. 40, 44, 48, 52...

b. $t_1 = 40$
$t_2 = 44 = 40 + 4 = t_1 + 4$
$t_3 = 48 = 44 + 4 = t_2 + 4$
$t_4 = 52 = 48 + 4 = t_3 + 4$
$t_1 = 40, t_n = t_{n-1} + 4$

c. $t_5 = t_4 + 4 = 52 + 4 = 56$
$t_6 = t_5 + 4 = 56 + 4 = 60$
$t_7 = t_6 + 4 = 60 + 4 = 64$
$t_8 = t_7 + 4 = 64 + 4 = 68$
There are 68 seats in row 8.

17a.

Year	1st	2nd	3rd	4th	5th
Value ($)	850 000	935 000	1 028 500	1 131 350	1 244 485

b. $t_1 = 850\,000, t_n = t_{n-1} \times 1.1$

c. $t_6 = t_5 \times 1.1 = 1\,244\,485 \times 1.1 = 1\,368\,933.5$
The value is $1 368 933.50.

18a.

Year	1st	2nd	3rd	4th
Production (tonne/year)	2.4 million	2.16 million	1.944 million	1.7496 million

b. $t_1 = 2.4$ million, $t_n = t_{n-1} \times 0.9$

7.3 Pascal's Triangle and Expanding Binomial Powers

1.

$n = 0$	1 $r = 1$	$1 = 2^0$
$n = 1$	1 1 $r = 2$	$2 = 2^1$
$n = 2$	1 2 1 $r = 3$	$4 = 2^2$
$n = 3$	1 3 3 1 $r = 4$	$8 = 2^3$
$n = 4$	1 4 6 4 1 $r = 5$	$16 = 2^4$
$n = 5$	1 5 10 10 5 1 $r = 6$	$32 = 2^5$
$n = 6$	1 6 15 20 15 6 1	$64 = 2^6$

$t_{4,2}$ $t_{4,6}$

2a. 3   **b.** 15   **c.** 4   **d.** 10
3a. $t_{6,4}$ **b.** $t_{3,2}$ **c.** $t_{5,2}$
4a. $t_{4,2} + t_{4,3}$ **b.** $t_{2,2} + t_{2,3}$ **c.** $t_{5,3} + t_{5,4}$
5. 1, 7, 21, 35, 35, 21, 7, 1
1, 8, 28, 56, 70, 56, 28, 8, 1
6a. 2^4 ; 16   **b.** 2^6 ; 64   **c.** 2^n
7a. 3   **b.** 9   **c.** 7

8.

Value of n	$(a + b)^n$
0	$(a + b)^0 = 1$
1	$(a + b)^1 = 1\ a + 1\ b$
2	$(a + b)^2 = 1\ a^2 + 2\ ab + 1\ b^2$
3	$(a + b)^3 = 1\ a^3 + 3\ a^2b + 3\ ab^2 + 1\ b^3$
4	$(a + b)^4 = 1\ a^4 + 4\ a^3b + 6\ a^2b^2 + 4\ ab^3 + 1\ b^4$

Pascal's Triangle

n ; decreases ; increases ; equal to
9. 6 ; 15 ; 20 ; 15 ; 6
10. 6 ; 15 ; 20 ; 15 ; 6 ; 1
$m^6 - 6m^5n + 15m^4n^2 - 20m^3n^3 + 15m^2n^4 - 6mn^5 + n^6$

ISBN: 978-1-77149-222-5

11. $(x)^7(2y)^0 + 7(x)^6(2y)^1 + 21(x)^5(2y)^2 + 35(x)^4(2y)^3 + 35(x)^3(2y)^4$
$+ 21(x)^2(2y)^5 + 7(x)^1(2y)^6 + (x)^0(2y)^7$
$= x^7 + 14x^6y + 84x^5y^2 + 280x^4y^3 + 560x^3y^4 + 672x^2y^5 + 448xy^6$
$+ 128y^7$

12. $(a^2)^5(-2b)^0 + 5(a^2)^4(-2b)^1 + 10(a^2)^3(-2b)^2 + 10(a^2)^2(-2b)^3 +$
$5(a^2)^1(-2b)^4 + (a^2)^0(-2b)^5$
$= a^{10} - 10a^8b + 40a^6b^2 - 80a^4b^3 + 80a^2b^4 - 32b^5$

13. $(\frac{1}{2}x)^6(2y)^0 + 6(\frac{1}{2}x)^5(2y)^1 + 15(\frac{1}{2}x)^4(2y)^2 + 20(\frac{1}{2}x)^3(2y)^3$
$+ 15(\frac{1}{2}x)^2(2y)^4 + 6(\frac{1}{2}x)^1(2y)^5 + 1(\frac{1}{2}x)^0(2y)^6$
$= \frac{1}{64}x^6 + \frac{3}{8}x^5y + \frac{15}{4}x^4y^2 + 20x^3y^3 + 60x^2y^4 + 96xy^5 + 64y^6$

14a. $t_1 = 1$, $t_2 = 1$, $t_n = t_{n-1} + t_{n-2}$ C. $5 ; 8 ; 13$
   b. $t_8 = 8 + 13 = 21$ The numbers in the
      $t_9 = 13 + 21 = 34$ Fibonacci sequence are
      $t_{10} = 21 + 34 = 55$ the sums of the diagonals
                                   in Pascal's triangle.

15. $t_{7,4}$ is the number in horizontal row 7 and diagonal row 4 of Pascal's triangle.
    $t_{7,4}$ is 35. The terms $t_{7,5}$, $t_{35,2}$, and $t_{35,35}$ have the same value.

16. Distributive property:
$(-2x + \frac{1}{x})^3$
$= (4x^2 - 4 + \frac{1}{x^2})(-2x + \frac{1}{x})$
$= -8x^3 + 4x + 8x - \frac{4}{x} - \frac{2}{x} + \frac{1}{x^3}$
$= -8x^3 + 12x - \frac{6}{x} + \frac{1}{x^3}$

Pascal's triangle:
$(-2x)^3(\frac{1}{x})^0 + 3(-2x)^2(\frac{1}{x})^1 + 3(-2x)^1(\frac{1}{x})^2 + (-2x)^0(\frac{1}{x})^3$
$= -8x^3 + 12x - \frac{6}{x} + \frac{1}{x^3}$
The results are the same.

17a. There are 7 terms. Yes, there is a constant. It is 15.
   b. There are 9 terms. There are no constants.
   c. There are 5 terms. There are no constants.

7.4 Arithmetic Sequences

1. A ; C ; F ; I

Try This (p. 146)

$a = 16$ $a = 2.5$
$d = 19 - 16 = 3$ $d = 2 - 2.5 = -0.5$

2. $a = -10$ 3. $a = -0.5$
   $d = -3 - (-10) = 7$ $d = -1.5 - (-0.5) = -1$
   18, 25, 32   -4.5, -5.5, -6.5

4. $a = \frac{4}{10}$ 5. $a = 3$
   $d = \frac{3}{10} - \frac{4}{10} = -\frac{1}{10}$ $d = -1 - 3 = -4$
   $0, -\frac{1}{10}, -\frac{2}{10}$ -13, -17, -21

6. $a = 1\frac{1}{8}$ 7. $a = 6 \times 10^2$
   $d = 1\frac{1}{4} - 1\frac{1}{8} = \frac{1}{8}$ $d = 5 \times 10^2 - 6 \times 10^2 = -1 \times 10^2$
   $1\frac{5}{8}, 1\frac{3}{4}, 1\frac{7}{8}$ $2 \times 10^2, 1 \times 10^2, 0$

8. $2 ; 2 ; 4 ; 6 ; 6 + 4 = 10 ; 10 + 4 = 14$
   2, 6, 10, 14

9. $t_1 = 6$ 10. $t_1 = \frac{1}{2}$
   $t_2 = 6 + (-2) = 4$ $t_2 = \frac{1}{2} + \frac{1}{4} = \frac{3}{4}$
   $t_3 = 4 + (-2) = 2$ $t_3 = \frac{3}{4} + \frac{1}{4} = 1$
   $t_4 = 2 + (-2) = 0$ $t_4 = 1 + \frac{1}{4} = 1\frac{1}{4}$
   6, 4, 2, 0 $\frac{1}{2}, \frac{3}{4}, 1, 1\frac{1}{4}$

11. $t_1 = 1$ 12. $t_1 = y$
    $t_2 = 1 + (-0.5) = 0.5$ $t_2 = y + 2$
    $t_3 = 0.5 + (-0.5) = 0$ $t_3 = y + 2 + 2 = y + 4$
    $t_4 = 0 + (-0.5) = -0.5$ $t_4 = y + 4 + 2 = y + 6$
    1, 0.5, 0, -0.5 $y, y + 2, y + 4, y + 6$

13. $t_1 = 5 - x$
    $t_2 = 5 - x + (-x) = 5 - 2x$
    $t_3 = 5 - 2x + (-x) = 5 - 3x$
    $t_4 = 5 - 3x + (-x) = 5 - 4x$
    $5 - x, 5 - 2x, 5 - 3x, 5 - 4x$

14. $t_2 = t_1 + (-2)$ 15. $t_2 = t_1 + d$
    $4 = t_1 - 2$ $-3 = 1 + d$
    $t_1 = 6$ $d = -4$
    $t_3 = t_2 + (-2) = 4 - 2 = 2$ $t_3 = t_2 - 4 = -3 - 4 = -7$
    $t_4 = t_3 + (-2) = 2 - 2 = 0$ $t_4 = t_3 - 4 = -7 - 4 = -11$
    6, 4, 2, 0   1, -3, -7, -11
    $6 ; -2 ; t_1 = 6, t_n = t_{n-1} - 2$ $1 ; -4 ; t_1 = 1, t_n = t_{n-1} - 4$

16. -20, -10, 0, 10
    $-20 ; 10 ; t_1 = -20, t_n = t_{n-1} + 10$

17. 90, 60, 30, 0
    $90 ; -30 ; t_1 = 90, t_n = t_{n-1} - 30$

18. $3 - 2(n - 1) ; -15 ; -25 ; -195$

19. $-5 + \frac{1}{2}(n - 1) ; -1\frac{1}{2} ; 4\frac{1}{2} ; 19\frac{1}{2}$

20. $-0.5 - 0.25(n - 1) ; -2.25 ; -5.25$

21. $12.5(n - 1) ; 112.5 ; 612.5$

22. $-7 + x(n - 1) ; 4x - 7 ; 9x - 7$

23. $x + y - y(n - 1) ; x - 5y ; x - 10y$

24. $t_n = 2 + 2(n - 1)$ 25. $t_n = 40 + 10(n - 1)$
    $60 = 2 + 2(n - 1)$ $170 = 40 + 10(n - 1)$
    $n = 30$ $n = 14$
    30   the 14th term: 170

26. $t_n = \frac{1}{2} + (n - 1)$
    $\frac{19}{2} = \frac{1}{2} + (n - 1)$
    $n = 10$
    the 10th term: $\frac{19}{2}$

27. $0 = a + (15 - 1)d$ $8 = a + (31 - 1)d$
    $0 = a + 14d$ ① $8 = a + 30d$ ②
    $8 = 16d$ ② – ①
    $d = \frac{1}{2}$ $0 = a + 14(\frac{1}{2})$
                                    $a = -7$
    $-7 ; \frac{1}{2} ; -7 + (n - 1)\frac{1}{2} = -7\frac{1}{2} + \frac{1}{2}n$

28. $21.5 = a + (7 - 1)d$ $65.5 = a + (18 - 1)d$
    $21.5 = a + 6d$ ① $65.5 = a + 17d$ ②
    $44 = 11d$ ② – ①
    $d = 4$ $21.5 = a + 6(4)$
                                    $a = -2.5$
    $-2.5 ; 4 ; 4n - 6.5$

29. $x + 6y = a + (8 - 1)d$ $x + 19y = a + (21 - 1)d$
    $x + 6y = a + 7d$ ① $x + 19y = a + 20d$ ②
    $13y = 13d$ ② – ①
    $d = y$ $x + 6y = a + 7y$
                                      $a = x - y$
    $x - y ; y ; x + (n - 2)y$

30a. 20 terms   b. 16 terms
   c. 467 terms   d. 52 terms

31. $t_{11} = a + (11 - 1)d = -360$
    $t_{20} = a + (20 - 1)d = -576$
    $a = -120$
    $d = -24$
    $t_n = -120 + (n - 1)(-24) = -24n - 96$
    $t_1 = -120, t_n = t_{n-1} - 24$

32a. 30, 32, 34, 36...

  b. $t_n = 30 + 2(n-1) = 2n + 28$
    3 days = 72 hours
    $t_{72} = 2(72) + 28 = 172$
    The cost of renting the chainsaw for 3 days is $172.

33. "L" is the 12th letter.
    Billy will place the letter "L" in the 12th stack.

34a. $t_5 = 58\,000 + 3800(5-1) = 73\,200$
    A teacher earns $73 200 in Year 5.

  b. $84\,600 = 58\,000 + 3800(n-1)$
          $n = 8$
    It will take 8 years.

7.5 Geometric Sequences

1. $\frac{4}{2} = 2, \frac{8}{4} = 2, \frac{16}{8} = 2$
   It is a geometric sequence.

2. $5 - 1 = 4, 9 - 5 = 4, 13 - 9 = 4$
   It is an arithmetic sequence.

3. $\frac{2}{1} = 2, \frac{4}{2} = 2, \frac{16}{4} = 4$
   $2 - 1 = 1, 4 - 2 = 2, 16 - 4 = 12$
   It is neither.

4. $\frac{-9}{-3} = 3, \frac{-27}{-9} = 3, \frac{-81}{-27} = 3$
   It is a geometric sequence.

5. $\frac{\frac{5}{2}}{\frac{1}{2}} = 5, \frac{\frac{25}{2}}{\frac{5}{2}} = 5, \frac{\frac{125}{2}}{\frac{25}{2}} = 5$
   It is a geometric sequence.

6. $\frac{7}{8} - \frac{5}{8} = \frac{1}{4}, \frac{9}{8} - \frac{7}{8} = \frac{1}{4}, \frac{11}{8} - \frac{9}{8} = \frac{1}{4}$
   It is an arithmetic sequence.

7. -2 ; 192, -384

8. 0.2 ; 0.16, 0.032

9. $\frac{1}{3}$; $\frac{1}{162}, \frac{1}{486}$

10. -1 ; $\frac{1}{4}, -\frac{1}{4}$

11. $2a$; $64a^5, 128a^6$

12. $\frac{\sqrt{y}}{2}$; $\frac{y^{\frac{5}{2}}}{32}, \frac{y^3}{64}$

13. $\frac{1}{x+y}$; 1, $\frac{1}{x+y}$

Try This (p. 151)

324 ; -108 ; 324 ; $-\frac{1}{3}$

324 ; $-\frac{1}{3}$

324 ; $-\frac{1}{3}$; 4

324 ; $-\frac{1}{3}$; $-\frac{4}{3}$

14. 6 ; 2 ; $6(2)^{n-1}$; 96, 192

15. $\frac{1}{3}$; $\frac{1}{2}$; $\frac{1}{3}(\frac{1}{2})^{n-1}$; $\frac{1}{48}, \frac{1}{96}$

16. 0.25 ; 10 ; $0.25(10)^{n-1}$; 2500, 25 000

17. $\frac{2x}{y}$; -2 ; $\frac{2x}{y}(-2)^{n-1}$; $\frac{32x}{y}, -\frac{64x}{y}$

18. $\frac{m}{u^2}$; u ; $\frac{m}{u^2}(u)^{n-1}$; mu^2, mu^3

19. $0.5a$; $2\sqrt{a}$; $0.5a(2\sqrt{a})^{n-1}$; $8a^3, 16a^{\frac{7}{2}}$

20. $f(1) = -2(3)^{1-1} = -2$
    $f(2) = -2(3)^{2-1} = -6$
    $f(3) = -2(3)^{3-1} = -18$
    -2, -6, -18

21. $t_1 = 24(\frac{1}{4})^{1-1} = 24$
    $t_2 = 24(\frac{1}{4})^{2-1} = 6$
    $t_3 = 24(\frac{1}{4})^{3-1} = \frac{3}{2}$
    24, 6, $\frac{3}{2}$

22. $\frac{1}{3}(-3)^{n-1}$
    $t_1 = \frac{1}{3}(-3)^{1-1} = \frac{1}{3}$
    $t_2 = \frac{1}{3}(-3)^{2-1} = -1$
    $t_3 = \frac{1}{3}(-3)^{3-1} = 3$
    $\frac{1}{3}$, -1, 3

23. 5 ; 2 ; $5(2)^{n-1}$
    20 480 ; 5 ; 2
    4096 ; 2
    $2^{12} = 2^{n-1}$
    $12 = n - 1$
    $n = 13$
    13

24. $a = 16, r = -\frac{1}{2}$
    $t_n = 16(-\frac{1}{2})^{n-1}$
    $\frac{1}{4} = 16(-\frac{1}{2})^{n-1}$
    $\frac{1}{64} = (-\frac{1}{2})^{n-1}$
    $(-\frac{1}{2})^6 = (-\frac{1}{2})^{n-1}$
    $6 = n - 1$
    $n = 7$
    7

25. $a = 5, r = \sqrt{5}$
    $t_n = 5(\sqrt{5})^{n-1}$
    $3125 = 5(\sqrt{5})^{n-1}$
    $625 = (\sqrt{5})^{n-1}$
    $(\sqrt{5})^8 = (\sqrt{5})^{n-1}$
    $8 = n - 1$
    $n = 9$
    9

26. $a = 0.1, r = 1000$
    $t_n = 0.1(1000)^{n-1}$
    $10^{11} = 0.1(1000)^{n-1}$
    $10^{12} = (1000)^{n-1}$
    $(1000)^4 = (1000)^{n-1}$
    $4 = n - 1$
    $n = 5$
    5

27. $a = \frac{3}{16}, r = 4$
    $t_n = \frac{3}{16}(4)^{n-1}$
    $768 = \frac{3}{16}(4)^{n-1}$
    $4096 = (4)^{n-1}$
    $(4)^6 = (4)^{n-1}$
    $6 = n - 1$
    $n = 7$
    7

28. $a = \frac{m^2}{n}, r = \frac{2}{m}$
    $t_n = \frac{m^2}{n}(\frac{2}{m})^{n-1}$
    $\frac{512}{m^7 n} = \frac{m^2}{n}(\frac{2}{m})^{n-1}$
    $\frac{512}{m^9} = (\frac{2}{m})^{n-1}$
    $(\frac{2}{m})^9 = (\frac{2}{m})^{n-1}$
    $9 = n - 1$
    $n = 10$
    10

29. $80 = ar^{5-1}$
    $80 = ar^4$
    $\frac{ar^{11}}{ar^4} = \frac{-10\,240}{80}$
    $r^7 = -128$
    $r^7 = (-2)^7$
    $r = -2$

    $-10\,240 = ar^{12-1}$
    $-10\,240 = ar^{11}$
    $\therefore 80 = a(-2)^4$
    $80 = a(16)$
    $a = 5$

30. $\frac{27}{2} = ar^{4-1}$
    $\frac{27}{2} = ar^3$
    $\frac{ar^9}{ar^3} = \frac{\frac{1}{54}}{\frac{27}{2}}$
    $r^6 = \frac{1}{729}$
    $r^6 = (\frac{1}{3})^6$
    $r = \frac{1}{3}$

    $\frac{1}{54} = ar^{10-1}$
    $\frac{1}{54} = ar^9$
    $\therefore \frac{27}{2} = a(\frac{1}{3})^3$
    $a = \frac{729}{2}$

31. $9 = ar^{3-1}$
    $9 = ar^2$
    $\frac{ar^7}{ar^2} = \frac{\frac{2187}{32}}{9}$
    $r^5 = \frac{243}{32}$
    $r^5 = (\frac{3}{2})^5$
    $r = \frac{3}{2}$

    $\frac{2187}{32} = ar^{8-1}$
    $\frac{2187}{32} = ar^7$
    $\therefore 9 = a(\frac{3}{2})^2$
    $9 = \frac{9}{4}a$
    $a = 4$

32. A: geometric sequence ; The common ratio is -2.
    $t_n = (-1)(-2)^{n-1}$
   B: arithmetic sequence ; The common difference is -4.
    $t_n = 8 - 4(n-1)$
   C: geometric sequence ; The common ratio is 4.
    $t_n = 2(4)^{n-1}$

33a. no. of 20-min periods: $(3 \times 60) \div 20 = 9$
The number of bacteria after 3 hours is the 10th term.
$t_n = ar^{n-1} = (110)(2)^{10-1} = 56\,320$
There will be 56 320 bacteria.

b. $3520 = (110)(2)^{n-1}$
$32 = 2^{n-1}$
$2^5 = 2^{n-1}$
$5 = n - 1$
$n = 6$
The 6th term has 3520 bacteria, so it has doubled 5 times.
five 20-min period: 100 min
It will take 100 minutes.

34. $a = 3500$, $r = 0.98$
$t_n = 3500(0.98)^{n-1}$
$t_1 = 3500$ $t_2 = 3500(0.98)^{2-1} = 3430$
$t_3 = 3500(0.98)^{3-1} \doteq 3361$ $t_4 = 3500(0.98)^{4-1} \doteq 3294$
$t_5 = 3500(0.98)^{5-1} \doteq 3228$ $t_6 = 3500(0.98)^{6-1} \doteq 3164$

Year	2010	2014	2018	2022	2026	2030
No. of Votes	3500	3430	3361	3294	3228	3164

7.6 Arithmetic Series

Try This (p. 154)

$S_{15} = \frac{15}{2}(-8 + 62)$ $S_{15} = \frac{15}{2}(2(-8) + (15 - 1)5)$
$= 405$ $= 405$
405

1. $\frac{n}{2}(a + t_n)$

a. $S_9 = \frac{9}{2}(12 + 16) = 126$

b. $S_{10} = \frac{10}{2}(-2\sqrt{2} + 7\sqrt{2}) = 25\sqrt{2}$

c. $S_{19} = \frac{19}{2}(10^2 + 28) = 1216$

d. $S_{16} = \frac{16}{2}(-2x + 13x) = 88x$

e. $S_{12} = \frac{12}{2}(-7 + 11y - 7) = 66y - 84$

f. $S_8 = \frac{8}{2}(x + y + x - 5y) = 8x - 16y$

2. $\frac{n}{2}(2a + (n - 1)d)$

a. $S_9 = \frac{9}{2}(2(-2) + (9 - 1)\frac{3}{2}) = 36$

b. $S_{45} = \frac{45}{2}(2(\frac{1}{2}) + (45 - 1)(-\frac{5}{2})) = -2452.5$

c. $S_{20} = \frac{20}{2}(2(-8) + (20 - 1)(-6)) = -1300$

d. $S_{10} = \frac{10}{2}(2(3x) + (10 - 1)(-x)) = -15x$

e. $S_{32} = \frac{32}{2}(2(x - y) + (32 - 1)y) = 32x + 464y$

f. $S_{16} = \frac{16}{2}(2(1 - m) + (16 - 1)2m) = 16 + 224m$

3. $S_{12} = \frac{12}{2}(2(3) + (12 - 1)(-2)) = -96$

4. $S_{12} = \frac{12}{2}(2(-2) + (12 - 1)y) = 66y - 24$

5. $S_{12} = \frac{12}{2}(2(\sqrt{5}) + (12 - 1)(-\sqrt{5})) = -54\sqrt{5}$

6. $S_{12} = \frac{12}{2}(2(\frac{2}{9}) + (12 - 1)(-\frac{5}{9})) = -34$

7. $S_{12} = \frac{12}{2}(2(2x^2) + (12 - 1)(-x^2)) = -42x^2$

8. $S_{12} = \frac{12}{2}(2(-x + 5) + (12 - 1)(x + 1)) = 54x + 126$

9. $S_{12} = \frac{12}{2}(2(3 - x) + (12 - 1)x) = 54x + 36$

10. $\frac{1}{2}$; $\frac{1}{4}$; $\frac{20}{2}(2(\frac{1}{2}) + (20 - 1)(\frac{1}{4})) = 57\frac{1}{2}$

11. 3 ; -5 ; $\frac{20}{2}(2(3) + (20 - 1)(-5)) = -890$

12. $\sqrt{2}x$; $-\sqrt{2}x$; $\frac{20}{2}(2(\sqrt{2}x) + (20 - 1)(-\sqrt{2}x)) = -170\sqrt{2}x$

13. $\frac{5}{9}$; $\frac{6}{9}$; $\frac{20}{2}(2(\frac{5}{9}) + (20 - 1)(\frac{6}{9})) = 137\frac{7}{9}$

14. $x + y$; $x - y$; $\frac{20}{2}(2(x + y) + (20 - 1)(x - y)) = 210x - 170y$

15. $-\frac{3}{y}$; $-\frac{2}{y}$; $\frac{20}{2}(2(-\frac{3}{y}) + (20 - 1)(-\frac{2}{y})) = -\frac{440}{y}$

16. $\frac{57}{5} = \frac{1}{5} + \frac{2}{5}(n - 1)$
$n = 29$
$S_{29} = \frac{29}{2}(\frac{1}{5} + \frac{57}{5}) = 168\frac{1}{5}$

17. $83\sqrt{3} = 2\sqrt{3} + 3\sqrt{3}(n - 1)$
$n = 28$
$S_{28} = \frac{28}{2}(2\sqrt{3} + 83\sqrt{3}) = 1190\sqrt{3}$

18. $-107x = x + (n - 1)(-4x)$
$27 = n - 1$
$n = 28$
$S_{28} = \frac{28}{2}(x - 107x) = -1484x$

19. $(-5a + 7b) = (5a - 3b) + (-a + b)(n - 1)$
$n = 11$
$S_{11} = \frac{11}{2}((5a - 3b) + (-5a + 7b)) = 22b$

20. $4x + 1 - (2x + 4) = 40 - x - (4x + 1)$
$2x - 3 = 39 - 5x$
$7x = 42$
$x = 6$
The first 3 terms are 16, 25, 34.
$S_{10} = \frac{10}{2}(2(16) + (10 - 1)9) = 565$

21. $t_7 = 5x = a + (7 - 1)d$ $3d = \frac{37}{5}x - 5x$
     $5x = a + 6d$
$t_{10} = \frac{37}{5}x = a + (10 - 1)d$ $d = \frac{4}{5}x$
     $\frac{37}{5}x = a + 9d$
$a = \frac{1}{5}x$
$S_{20} = \frac{20}{2}(2(\frac{1}{5}x) + (20 - 1)\frac{4}{5}x) = 156x$

22. 3, 4, 5, ... , 15
$15 = 3 + 1(n - 1)$
$n = 13$
$S_{13} = \frac{13}{2}(3 + 15) = 117$
There are 117 cans in total.

23a. $d = 2.75 - 2.25 = 0.5$
$S_{20} = \frac{20}{2}(2(2.25) + 0.5(20 - 1)) = 140$
Kevin will have $140 on May 20.

b. There are 31 days in May.
$S_{31} = \frac{31}{2}(2(2.25) + 0.5(31 - 1)) = 302.25$
His total savings will be $302.25.

24a. $d = 72 - 68 = 4$
$t_{15} = 68 + 4(15 - 1) = 124$
There are 124 seats in the 15th row.

b. $S_{18} = \frac{18}{2}(2(68) + 4(18 - 1)) = 1836$
Total sales: $85 \times 1836 = 156\,060$
The total sales will be $156 060.

7.7 Geometric Series

1. ar^2 ; r
S_n ; a
r ; 1 ; r^n ; 1
r^n ; 1 ; r ; 1

2. 6 ; 3 ; $\dfrac{6(3^6 - 1)}{3 - 1} = 2184$; $\dfrac{6(3^{10} - 1)}{3 - 1} = 177\ 144$

3. 12 ; $-\dfrac{1}{2}$; $\dfrac{12((-\frac{1}{2})^8 - 1)}{(-\frac{1}{2}) - 1} = \dfrac{255}{32}$; $\dfrac{12((-\frac{1}{2})^{20} - 1)}{(-\frac{1}{2}) - 1} = 8 - \dfrac{1}{2^{17}}$

4. 0.1 ; 10 ; $\dfrac{0.1(10^7 - 1)}{10 - 1} = 111\ 111.1$;

   $\dfrac{0.1(10^{10} - 1)}{10 - 1} = 111\ 111\ 111.1$

5. 5 ; -1 ; $\dfrac{5((-1)^{18} - 1)}{(-1) - 1} = 0$; $\dfrac{5((-1)^{27} - 1)}{(-1) - 1} = 5$

6. $\sqrt{3}x$; $\sqrt{3}$; $\dfrac{\sqrt{3}x((\sqrt{3})^8 - 1)}{\sqrt{3} - 1} = 120x + 40\sqrt{3}x$;

   $\dfrac{\sqrt{3}x((\sqrt{3})^{11} - 1)}{\sqrt{3} - 1} = 363x + 364\sqrt{3}x$

7. 2 ; $-x$; $\dfrac{2((-x)^{15} - 1)}{-x - 1} = \dfrac{2(x^{15} + 1)}{x + 1}$; $\dfrac{2((-x)^{30} - 1)}{-x - 1} = \dfrac{-2(x^{30} - 1)}{x + 1}$

8. $\dfrac{1}{3x}$; $-\dfrac{3}{2}$; $\dfrac{\frac{1}{3x}((-\frac{3}{2})^6 - 1)}{-\frac{3}{2} - 1} = -\dfrac{133}{96x}$; $\dfrac{\frac{1}{3x}((-\frac{3}{2})^{11} - 1)}{-\frac{3}{2} - 1} = \dfrac{35\ 839}{3072x}$

9. 128 ; $\dfrac{1}{2x}$; $\dfrac{128((\frac{1}{2x})^5 - 1)}{\frac{1}{2x} - 1} = \dfrac{8(1 - 32x^5)}{(1 - 2x)x^4}$;

   $\dfrac{128((\frac{1}{2x})^8 - 1)}{\frac{1}{2x} - 1} = \dfrac{1 - 256x^8}{(1 - 2x)x^7}$

Try This (p. 158)

81 ; $\dfrac{1}{3}$

$\dfrac{1}{243}$; 81 ; $\dfrac{1}{3}$

$\dfrac{1}{19\ 683} = (\dfrac{1}{3})^{n-1}$

$(\dfrac{1}{3})^9 = (\dfrac{1}{3})^{n-1}$

$\quad 9 = n - 1$

$\quad n = 10$

$S_{10} = \dfrac{81((\frac{1}{3})^{10} - 1)}{\frac{1}{3} - 1} = 121\dfrac{121}{243}$

10. $a = 10$, $r = \dfrac{1}{2}$

    $\dfrac{5}{128} = 10(\dfrac{1}{2})^{n-1}$

    $\dfrac{1}{256} = (\dfrac{1}{2})^{n-1}$

    $(\dfrac{1}{2})^8 = (\dfrac{1}{2})^{n-1}$

    $\quad n = 9$

    $S_9 = \dfrac{10((\frac{1}{2})^9 - 1)}{\frac{1}{2} - 1} = 19\dfrac{123}{128}$

11. $a = 4$, $r = 4$

    $65\ 536 = 4(4)^{n-1}$

    $16\ 384 = 4^{n-1}$

    $\quad 4^7 = 4^{n-1}$

    $\quad n = 8$

    $S_8 = \dfrac{4(4^8 - 1)}{4 - 1} = 87\ 380$

12. $a = -59\ 049$, $r = -\dfrac{1}{3}$

    $\quad 3 = -59\ 049(-\dfrac{1}{3})^{n-1}$

    $-\dfrac{1}{19\ 683} = (-\dfrac{1}{3})^{n-1}$

    $(-\dfrac{1}{3})^9 = (-\dfrac{1}{3})^{n-1}$

    $\quad n = 10$

    $S_{10} = \dfrac{-59\ 049((-\frac{1}{3})^{10} - 1)}{-\frac{1}{3} - 1} = -44\ 286$

13. $a = 1$, $r = -\dfrac{3}{4}$

    $\dfrac{729}{4096} = 1(-\dfrac{3}{4})^{n-1}$

    $(-\dfrac{3}{4})^6 = (-\dfrac{3}{4})^{n-1}$

    $\quad n = 7$

    $S_7 = \dfrac{1((-\frac{3}{4})^7 - 1)}{-\frac{3}{4} - 1} = \dfrac{2653}{4096}$

14. $a = -2$, $r = -\dfrac{1}{4}$

    $-\dfrac{1}{32\ 768} = -2(-\dfrac{1}{4})^{n-1}$

    $\dfrac{1}{65\ 536} = (-\dfrac{1}{4})^{n-1}$

    $(-\dfrac{1}{4})^8 = (-\dfrac{1}{4})^{n-1}$

    $\quad n = 9$

    $S_9 = \dfrac{-2((-\frac{1}{4})^9 - 1)}{-\frac{1}{4} - 1} = -\dfrac{52\ 429}{32\ 768}$

15. $a = 3$, $r = a$

    $3a^x = 3(a)^{n-1}$

    $\quad a^x = a^{n-1}$

    $\quad n = x + 1$

    $S_{x+1} = \dfrac{3(a^{x+1} - 1)}{a - 1}$

16. $a = 2$, $r = 5$

    $\dfrac{2(5^n - 1)}{5 - 1} = 7812$

    $\quad 5^n - 1 = 15\ 624$

    $\quad 5^n = 15\ 625$

    $\quad 5^n = 5^6$

    $\quad n = 6$

    The value of n is 6.

17. $\quad \dfrac{7x - 2}{x + 1} = \dfrac{50 - x}{7x - 2}$

    $49x^2 - 28x + 4 = -x^2 + 49x + 50$

    $50x^2 - 77x - 46 = 0$

    $(50x + 23)(x - 2) = 0$

    $\quad\quad x = 2$ or $x = -0.46$ (not applicable)

    The first three terms are 3, 12, 48.

    $S_5 = \dfrac{3(4^5 - 1)}{4 - 1} = 1023$

    The sum of the first five terms is 1023.

18. $t_{10} = ar^{10-1} = \dfrac{3}{512}$

    $t_{15} = ar^{15-1} = \dfrac{3}{16\ 384}$

    $\dfrac{ar^{14}}{ar^9} = \dfrac{3}{16\ 384} \times \dfrac{512}{3}$

    $\quad r^5 = \dfrac{1}{32}$

    $\quad r^5 = (2^{-1})^5$

    $\quad r = \dfrac{1}{2}$

    $\quad a = 3$

    $S_{10} = \dfrac{3((\frac{1}{2})^{10} - 1)}{\frac{1}{2} - 1} = \dfrac{3069}{512}$

    The sum of the first ten terms is $\dfrac{3069}{512}$.

19a. $a = 1$, $r = 4$

    $t_5 = 1(4)^{5-1} = 256$

    There will be 256 small equilateral triangles in Design 5.

  b. $S_6 = \dfrac{1(4^6 - 1)}{4 - 1} = 1365$

    There will be 1365 equilateral triangles in total.

ISBN: 978-1-77149-222-5

ANSWERS

8 Financial Applications

8.1 Simple Interest

Try This (p. 160)

$700(0.06)(\frac{1}{2})$; 21 ; $21

1. $1680 ; ✔
2. $1600
3. $266.67
4. $52.31
5a. $1800 ; $16 800
b. 4% ; $3000
c. 3 months ; $8050
d. $7500 ; 4.5 years
e. 4.5% ; $6750
f. $1200 ; $1230.40
6. $66 ; $66 ; $66 ; $66 ; $66

a. They represent the interest earned each year.
b. 1266 – 66 = 1200
The initial principal is $1200.

c. $I = Prt$
$66 = 1200r(1)$
$r = 0.055$
The interest rate is 5.5%.

d.

e. $\frac{1332 - 1266}{2 - 1} = 66$
The slope of the line represents the interest.

f. $A = 1200(1 + 0.055t)$

7. $7840 = 14\,000(0.08)t$
$t = 7$
It took her 7 years to pay back the loan.

8. $495 = 2400(0.055)t$
$t = 3.75$
It took Samuel 3.75 years.

9. $I = 1800(0.032)(7) = 403.2$
$403.20 is earned.

10a. $403.2 = 1800r(5)$
$r = 0.0448$
The interest rate must be 4.48%.

b. $403.2 \times 2 = 1800r(2\frac{1}{2})$
$r = 0.1792$
The interest rate must be 17.92%.

11a. $A = 600 + 600(0.038)t$

b. $A = 600 + 600(0.038)(\frac{1}{4}) = 605.7$
Harry will have $605.70.

c. $670 = 600 + 600(0.038)t$
$t \doteq 3.07$
It will take 3.07 years.

12. A: $I = 6200(0.1)(5) = 3100$
B: $I = 300 + 6200(0.089)(5) = 3059$
B is a better option.

8.2 Compound Interest

1.

Compounding Period	Principal for the Period	Amount Calculation	Amount at the End of the Period
1	P	$A = P(1 + i)$	$P(1 + i)$
2	$P(1 + i)$	$A = P(1 + i)(1 + i) = P(1 + i)^2$	$P(1 + i)^2$
3	$P(1 + i)^2$	$A = P(1 + i)^2(1 + i) = P(1 + i)^3$	$P(1 + i)^3$
4	$P(1 + i)^3$	$A = P(1 + i)^3(1 + i) = P(1 + i)^4$	$P(1 + i)^4$
⋮	⋮	⋮	⋮
n	$P(1 + i)^{n-1}$	$A = P(1 + i)^{n-1}(1 + i) = P(1 + i)^n$	$P(1 + i)^n$

Compound Interest Formula: $A = P(1 + i)^n$

2. $A = 2000(1 + 0.025)^6$
$\doteq 2319.39$
$I = 2319.39 - 2000$
$= 319.39$

3. $A = 5000(1 + 0.0325)^3$
$\doteq 5503.52$
$I = 5503.52 - 5000$
$= 503.52$

4. $A = 600(1 + 0.06)^5$
$\doteq 802.94$
$I = 802.94 - 600$
$= 202.94$

5. $A = 3000(1 + 0.018)^2$
$\doteq 3108.97$
$I = 3108.97 - 3000$
$= 108.97$

6. 0.025 ; 6
4 ; 0.0125 ; 4 ; 12
$\frac{0.05}{12} \doteq 0.00417$; $12 \times 3 = 36$
$26 ; \frac{0.05}{26} \doteq 0.00192$; $26 \times 3 = 78$
$365 ; \frac{0.05}{365} \doteq 0.000137$; $365 \times 3 = 1095$

7a. 0.03 ; 0.0025 ; 12 ; 36
$A = 600(1 + 0.0025)^{36} \doteq 656.43$
$I = 656.43 - 600 = 56.43$

b. $i = \frac{0.026}{4} = 0.0065$ $n = 1.5 \times 4 = 6$
$A = 5000(1 + 0.0065)^6 \doteq 5198.20$
$I = 5198.2 - 5000 = 198.2$

c. $i = \frac{0.04}{26} \doteq 0.00154$ $n = \frac{6}{12} \times 26 = 13$
$A = 1200(1 + 0.00154)^{13} \doteq 1224.25$
$I = 1224.25 - 1200 = 24.25$

d. $i = \frac{0.032}{365} \doteq 0.0000877$ $n = \frac{30}{365} \times 365 = 30$
$A = 2800(1 + 0.0000877)^{30} \doteq 2807.38$
$I = 2807.38 - 2800 = 7.38$

8. $i = \frac{0.0325}{2} = 0.01625$ $n = \frac{30}{12} \times 2 = 5$
$A = 8000(1 + 0.01625)^5 \doteq 8671.47$
$I = 8671.47 - 8000 = 671.47$
The amount is $8671.47 and the interest is $671.47.

9a. $i = \frac{0.013}{365} \doteq 0.0000356$ $n = \frac{45}{365} \times 365 = 45$
$A = 4800(1 + 0.0000356)^{45} \doteq 4807.70$
$I = 4807.7 - 4800 = 7.7$
Zoe will earn $7.70.

b. $n = 31 + 28 = 59$
$A = 4800(1 + 0.0000356)^{59} \doteq 4810.09$
$I = 4810.09 - 4800 = 10.09$
Zoe will earn $10.09.

10. A: $I = 800(0.11)(5) = 440$
B: $A = 800(1 + 0.11)^5 \doteq 1348.05$
$I = 1348.05 - 800 = 548.05$

C: $i = \frac{0.11}{4} = 0.0275$ $n = 5 \times 4 = 20$
$A = 800(1 + 0.0275)^{20} \doteq 1376.34$
$I = 1376.34 - 800 = 576.34$

D: $i = \frac{0.11}{12} \doteq 0.00917$ $n = 5 \times 12 = 60$
$A = 800(1 + 0.00917)^{60} \doteq 1383.41$
$I = 1383.41 - 800 = 583.41$
Simple interest is the best and compounding monthly is the worst.

11. $A = P(1 + i)^n$
$842 = 550(1 + \frac{r}{2})^{12}$
$r \doteq 0.0723$
The annual interest rate charged was 7.23%.

12. KM Bank:
$A = 3200(1 + \frac{0.04}{2})^{5 \times 2}$
$\doteq 3900.78$

Direct Bank:
$A = 3200(1 + \frac{0.038}{12})^{5 \times 12}$
$= 3868.44$

Kayla should invest in KM Bank.

228   COMPLETE MATHSMART (GRADE 11)   ISBN: 978-1-77149-222-5

8.3 Present Value

1. Compound Interest Formula: $A = P(1 + i)^n$

   Present Value Formula: $PV = \dfrac{FV}{(1 + i)^n}$

2. $PV = \dfrac{10\,000}{(1 + 0.05)^6} \doteq 7462.15$

   The present value is $7462.15.

3. $2000 = \dfrac{4317.85}{(1 + r)^{10}}$

   $r = 0.08$

   The interest rate is 8%.

4. $PV = \dfrac{900}{(1 + 0.06)^4} \doteq 712.88$

   The invested amount is $712.88.

5. $PV = \dfrac{2PV}{(1 + r)^{15}}$

   $(1 + r)^{15} = 2$

   $r \doteq 0.0473$

   The interest rate is 4.73%.

6. $PV = \dfrac{1.69}{(1 + 0.025)^{20}} = 1.03$

   The price of a similar packet was $1.03.

7. $1.69 - 1.03 = 0.66$

   The price difference was $0.66.

8. A

   The interest is compounded monthly.

   $i = \dfrac{0.04}{12} \doteq 0.0033$ $n = 3\dfrac{1}{2} \times 12 = 42$

   $PV = 8707.75$

   Mr. Smith must invest $8707.75.

9. B

   The interest is compounded quarterly.

   $i = \dfrac{0.05}{4} = 0.0125$ $n = 6 \times 4 = 24$

   $PV \doteq 6200$

   $I = 8353.58 - 6200 = 2153.58$

   $6200 was borrowed. $2153.58 is the interest charged.

10. A

    $PV = 600, FV = 695$

    $(1 + \dfrac{r}{12})^{24} = \dfrac{695}{600}$

    $r \doteq 0.0737$

    The annual interest rate is 7.37%.

11. C

    $n = 4 \times 2 = 8$

    $PV \doteq 1200$

    $I = 1592.43 - 1200 = 392.43$

    The scholarship was $1200. Hannah earned $392.43 of interest.

12. $PV = \dfrac{26\,924.20}{(1 + \dfrac{0.051}{12})^{12 \times 12}} \doteq 14\,619$

    The present value is $14\,619.

13a. $PV = \dfrac{2.69}{(1 + 0.02)^{17}} \doteq 1.92$

    The milk cost $1.92 in 2000.

   b. $2.69 = \dfrac{FV}{(1 + 0.02)^8}$

      $FV = 3.15$

      The milk will cost $3.15 in 2025.

14a. $PV = \dfrac{3600}{(1 + 0.04)^3} \doteq 3200.39$

   b. $PV = \dfrac{3600}{(1 + \dfrac{0.04}{4})^{3 \times 4}} \doteq 3194.82$

   c. $PV = \dfrac{3600}{(1 + \dfrac{0.04}{26})^{3 \times 26}} \doteq 3193.21$

   d. $PV = \dfrac{3600}{(1 + \dfrac{0.04}{365})^{3 \times 365}} \doteq 3192.93$

15. Plan A: $PV = \dfrac{8000}{(1 + \dfrac{0.058}{4})^{3 \times 4}} \doteq 6730.78$

    Plan B: $PV = \dfrac{8000}{(1 + \dfrac{0.055}{12})^{3 \times 12}} \doteq 6785.71$

    They should choose Plan A because less investment is needed for the same return.

16.
```
    $4000   $4000   $3000
  |----|------|-------|
  0    2      3       6
```

    $PV \text{ (payment 3)} = \dfrac{3000}{(1 + \dfrac{0.068}{4})^{12}} \doteq 2450.59$

    $PV \text{ (payment 2)} = \dfrac{2450.59 + 4000}{(1 + \dfrac{0.068}{4})^4} \doteq 6029.98$

    $PV \text{ (payment 1)} = \dfrac{6029.98 + 4000}{(1 + \dfrac{0.068}{4})^8} \doteq 8764.61$

    Sam originally borrowed $8764.61.

8.4 Annuities

1. $400(1 + 0.06)^3 + 400(1 + 0.06)^4$

   $1 + 0.06 ; 5 ; 1 ; 1 + 0.06$

   $1.06 ; 5 ; 1 ; 0.06$

   2254.84

   $2254.84

2. $R(1 + i)^{n-2} ; R(1 + i)^{n-1}$

   $R(1 + i) + R(1 + i)^2 + ... + R(1 + i)^{n-2} + R(1 + i)^{n-1}$

   $1 + i ; n ; 1 + i$

   $\dfrac{R((1 + i)^n - 1)}{i}$

3. $FV = \dfrac{3000((1 + 0.05)^4 - 1)}{0.05} \doteq 12\,930.38$

4. $FV = \dfrac{500((1.0075)^{48} - 1)}{0.0075} \doteq 28\,760.36$

5. **Compounding Period**
```
Now    1      2      3      4
 |-----|------|------|------|
      150    150    150    150
              └→ 150(1 + 0.052)
              → 150(1 + 0.052)^2
              → 150(1 + 0.052)^3
```

   a. $A = \dfrac{150((1 + 0.052)^4 - 1)}{0.052} \doteq 648.44$

      The amount of annuity is $648.44.

   b. $648.44 - 150 \times 4 = 48.44$

      $48.44 of interest will be earned.

6. **Compounding Period**

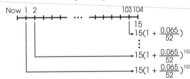

   a. $A = \dfrac{15((1 + \dfrac{0.065}{52})^{104} - 1)}{\dfrac{0.065}{52}} \doteq 1664.83$

      The amount of annuity is $1664.83.

   b. $1664.83 - 15 \times 104 = 104.83$

      $104.83 of interest will be earned.

7. **Compounding Period**

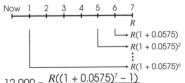

   $12\,000 = \dfrac{R((1 + 0.0575)^7 - 1)}{0.0575}$

   $R \doteq 1440.56$

   $1440.56 must be invested each year.

ISBN: 978-1-77149-222-5

8.

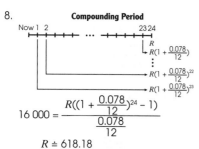

Compounding Period

$$16\,000 = \frac{R\left(\left(1 + \frac{0.078}{12}\right)^{24} - 1\right)}{\frac{0.078}{12}}$$

$R \doteq 618.18$

She should invest $618.18 each month.

9. $i = \frac{0.09}{12} = 0.0075$ $\qquad n = 12 \times 4 = 48$

$FV = \frac{350\left((1 + 0.0075)^{48} - 1\right)}{0.0075} \doteq 20\,132.25 > 20\,000$

Yes, Mrs. Remoto will have enough money to buy a car.

10a. $i = \frac{0.0325}{12} \doteq 0.0027$ $\qquad n = 12 \times 5 = 60$

$A = \frac{1200\left((1 + 0.0027)^{60} - 1\right)}{0.0027} \doteq 78\,046.03$

The amount of the annuity will be $78 046.03.

b. $I = 78\,046.03 - 5 \times 12 \times 1200 = 6046.03$

$6046.03 of interest will be earned.

c. $275\,000 = \frac{1200\left((1 + 0.0027)^{n} - 1\right)}{0.0027}$

$n \doteq 179$

They will have to save for 119 more months.

11. Option A:
$I = Prt$
$\quad = 6000(0.04)(5)$
$\quad = 1200$

Option B:
$A = P(1 + i)^n$
$\quad = 6000\left(1 + \frac{0.038}{12}\right)^{60}$
$\quad \doteq 7253.32$
$I = 7253.32 - 6000 = 1253.32$

Option C:
$A = \frac{100\left(\left(1 + \frac{0.07}{12}\right)^{60} - 1\right)}{\frac{0.07}{12}} \doteq 7159.29$

$I = 7159.29 - 100 \times 12 \times 5 = 1159.29$

Karen should choose Option B because it gives her the most interest.

12. $i = \frac{0.048}{52} \doteq 0.00092$ $\qquad n = 45 \times 52 = 2340$

$50\,000 = \frac{R\left((1 + 0.00092)^{2340} - 1\right)}{0.00092}$

$46 \doteq 7.6R$

$R \doteq 6.05$

Faisal should deposit $6.05 weekly.

8.5 Present Value of an Annuity

Try This (p. 172)

0.003 ; 12 ; 24
800 ; 0.003 ; 24
800 ; 0.003 ; 24 ; 0.003
18 498.35
$18 498.35

1. A: $\frac{5000(1 - 1.012^{-18})}{0.012} \doteq 80\,511.70$

B: $PV = \frac{800(1 - 1.053^{-6})}{0.053} \doteq 4021.89$

C: $PV = \frac{450(1 - 1.004^{-12})}{0.004} \doteq 5262.18$

D: $PV = \frac{1000(1 - 1.0025^{-10})}{0.0025} \doteq 9863.86$

2. $i = \frac{0.053}{12} \doteq 0.0044$ $\qquad n = 6 \times 12 = 72$

$PV = \frac{66.67(1 - 1.0044^{-72})}{0.0044} \doteq 4106.53$

3. $\frac{4000(1 - 1.062^{-6})}{0.062} \doteq 19\,546.30$

4. $PV = \frac{850\left(1 - \left(1 + \frac{0.093}{26}\right)^{-(5 \times 26)}\right)}{\frac{0.093}{26}} \doteq 88\,244.00$

5. $PV = \frac{225\left(1 - \left(1 + \frac{0.048}{4}\right)^{-(4 \times 4)}\right)}{\frac{0.048}{4}} \doteq 3257.80$

6. $PV = \frac{700\left(1 - \left(1 + \frac{0.028}{12}\right)^{-(2.5 \times 12)}\right)}{\frac{0.028}{12}} \doteq 20\,259.04$

7. $PV = \frac{1500(1 - (1 + 0.035)^{-3})}{0.035} \doteq 4202.46$

8. $PV = \frac{400\left(1 - \left(1 + \frac{0.05}{4}\right)^{-\left(\frac{18}{12} \times 4\right)}\right)}{\frac{0.05}{4}} \doteq 2298.40$

9. $i = 0.062$ $\qquad n = 8$

$7500 = \frac{R(1 - 1.062^{-8})}{0.062}$

$(1 - 1.062^{-8})R = 465$

$R \doteq 1217.35$

$1217.35 can be withdrawn at the end of each year.

10. $i = 0.072$ $\qquad n = 25$

$PV = \frac{18\,000(1 - 1.072^{-25})}{0.072} \doteq 206\,038.72$

Dawson should deposit $206 038.72 into his account today.

11a. $i = \frac{0.0375}{12} = 0.003125$ $\qquad n = 40 \times 12 = 480$

$PV = \frac{5500(1 - 1.003125^{-480})}{0.003125} \doteq 1\,366\,371.34 > 1\,000\,000$

No, Ernest cannot afford to live off his lottery winnings for 40 years.

b. $1\,000\,000 = \frac{R(1 - 1.003125^{-480})}{0.003125}$

$3125 \doteq R(0.776)$

$R \doteq 4027.06$

Ernest can withdraw $4027.06 monthly at most.

12a. Option 1: $7500 = \frac{R\left(1 - \left(1 + \frac{0.07}{4}\right)^{-16}\right)}{\frac{0.07}{4}}$

$R \doteq 541.50$

Option 2: $7500 = \frac{R\left(1 - \left(1 + \frac{0.0675}{12}\right)^{-48}\right)}{\frac{0.0675}{12}}$

$R \doteq 178.73$

The regular withdrawal for Option 1 is $541.50 and for Option 2 is $178.73.

b. Option 1: $541.50 \times 16 - 7500 = 1164$
Option 2: $178.73 \times 48 - 7500 = 1079.04$
The total interest earned for Option 1 is $1164 and for Option 2 is $1079.04.

c. (Individual answer)

13. $PV = \frac{30\,000(1 - (1 + 0.09)^{-25})}{0.09} \doteq 294\,677.39 < 300\,000$

Option 1 is worth $294 677.39 and Option 2 is worth $300 000. So Kelsey should accept Option 2.

Cumulative Review

1. C	2. A	3. A	4. D
5. B	6. C	7. D	8. D
9. C	10. A	11. B	12. B
13. C	14. C	15. D	16. C
17. A			

ISBN: 978-1-77149-222-5

18a. D   b. B   19. B

20. T   21. F   22. T   23. T

24. T   25. F   26. T

27. no points of intersection
28. two points of intersection
29. two points of intersection
30. no points of intersection
31. no points of intersection
32. one point of intersection

33a. D: {-4,-3,-2,-1} ; R: {0,3,6,9}
  b. D: $\{x \in \mathbb{R}\}$; R: $\{y \in \mathbb{R} \mid y \le 0\}$
  c. D: $\{x \in \mathbb{R} \mid x \ne -2\}$; R: $\{y \in \mathbb{R} \mid y \ne 0\}$

34a. $-8 < k < 8$ b. $k = \pm 8$
  c. $k > 8$ or $k < -8$

35. $k = \pm 7, \pm 11,$ or $\pm 2\sqrt{10}$

36. $\dfrac{1}{(x+5)(x+1)}$
    $x \ne -12, -5, -1,$ or 5

37. $\dfrac{(x-3)(x+5)}{(x+6)(x+1)}$
    $x \ne -6, -1,$ or 3

38a. $f^1(x) = \pm\sqrt{\dfrac{x+3}{2}} - 1$
  b. D: $\{x \in \mathbb{R} \mid x \ge -1\}$ or $\{x \in \mathbb{R} \mid x \le -1\}$

39. 5 new trees should be planted for a total of 20 trees. The maximum number of apples is 4000.

40a. LS $= \tan\theta + \dfrac{1}{\tan\theta}$ RS $= \dfrac{1}{\sin\theta\cos\theta}$
    $= \dfrac{\sin\theta}{\cos\theta} + \dfrac{\cos\theta}{\sin\theta}$ $=$ LS
    $= \dfrac{\sin^2\theta + \cos^2\theta}{\cos\theta\sin\theta}$
    $= \dfrac{1}{\sin\theta\cos\theta}$
    $\therefore \tan\theta + \dfrac{1}{\tan\theta} = \dfrac{1}{\sin\theta\cos\theta}$

  b. LS $= \csc\theta\left(\dfrac{1}{\cot\theta} + \dfrac{1}{\sec\theta}\right)$ RS $= \sec\theta + \cot\theta$
    $= \dfrac{1}{\sin\theta}(\tan\theta + \cos\theta)$ $=$ LS
    $= \dfrac{\tan\theta}{\sin\theta} + \dfrac{\cos\theta}{\sin\theta}$
    $= \dfrac{1}{\cos\theta} + \cot\theta$
    $= \sec\theta + \cot\theta$
    $\therefore \csc\theta\left(\dfrac{1}{\cot\theta} + \dfrac{1}{\sec\theta}\right) = \sec\theta + \cot\theta$

  c. LS $= \dfrac{\sin\theta\tan\theta}{1 - \cos\theta}$ RS $= 1 + \sec\theta$
    $= \dfrac{\sin\theta\tan\theta}{1 - \cos\theta} \times \dfrac{1 + \cos\theta}{1 + \cos\theta}$ $=$ LS
    $= \dfrac{\sin\theta\tan\theta(1 + \cos\theta)}{1 - \cos^2\theta}$
    $= \dfrac{\sin\theta\tan\theta(1 + \cos\theta)}{\sin^2\theta}$
    $= \dfrac{\tan\theta + \sin\theta}{\sin\theta}$
    $= \dfrac{\tan\theta}{\sin\theta} + \dfrac{\sin\theta}{\sin\theta}$
    $= \sec\theta + 1$
    $\therefore \dfrac{\sin\theta\tan\theta}{1 - \cos\theta} = 1 + \sec\theta$

d. LS $= \dfrac{1 + \sin\theta}{\cos\theta} + \dfrac{\cos\theta}{1 + \sin\theta}$ RS $= 2\sec\theta$
    $= \dfrac{(1 + \sin\theta)^2 + \cos^2\theta}{\cos\theta(1 + \sin\theta)}$ $=$ LS
    $= \dfrac{1 + 2\sin\theta + \sin^2\theta + \cos^2\theta}{\cos\theta(1 + \sin\theta)}$
    $= \dfrac{2 + 2\sin\theta}{\cos\theta(1 + \sin\theta)}$
    $= \dfrac{2(1 + \sin\theta)}{\cos\theta(1 + \sin\theta)}$
    $= \dfrac{2}{\cos\theta}$
    $= 2\sec\theta$
    $\therefore \dfrac{1 + \sin\theta}{\cos\theta} + \dfrac{\cos\theta}{1 + \sin\theta} = 2\sec\theta$

41. There will be $497.

42a. Amy should choose Option A because she will have a better return in the amount of $186 341.97.
  b. Amy will have saved $678 747.36 by age 65.

43a. This sequence is geometric. ; $t_n = 10(3^{n-1})$
  b. 11 tickets can be drawn at most.
  c. $114 270 is left.

44a. 3 ; 720° ; 45° to the left ; 1 unit down

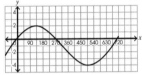

  b. 2 ; 90° ; 30° to the right ; 2 units up

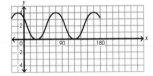

45a. $E = 300 + 0.07s$
  b. Erin needs to make $10 000 in sales.

46.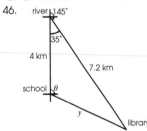

The school is 4.54 km from the library. The bearing of the library from the school is 115°.

47.

Row	Pascal's Triangle
0	1
1	1 1
2	1 2 1
3	1 3 3 1
4	1 4 6 4 1
5	1 5 10 10 5 1
6	1 6 15 20 15 6 1

Start with a^6b^0. The exponent of a decreases by 1 down to 0 and the exponent of b increases by 1 up to 6. The coefficient of the terms in the expansion of $(a + b)^6$ corresponds to the terms in row 6 of Pascal's triangle.
  a. $a^5 + 10a^4b + 40a^3b^2 + 80a^2b^3 + 80ab^4 + 32b^5$
  b. $\dfrac{1}{64}x^6 - \dfrac{3}{16}x^4 + \dfrac{15}{16}x^2 - \dfrac{5}{2} + \dfrac{15}{4x^2} - \dfrac{3}{x^4} + \dfrac{1}{x^6}$

48. It is an arithmetic series with $a = 150$ and $d = -3$. There are 3690 seats in total.

49. Helga should choose KC Bank because she only needs to invest $1576.99 today.

50a. $\sin \theta = \dfrac{4}{5}$ $\qquad \cos \theta = -\dfrac{3}{5}$ $\qquad \tan \theta = -\dfrac{4}{3}$

The sine ratio is positive in quadrants 1 and 2. The point that defines an angle with the same sine value is (3,4).

$\sin \beta = \dfrac{4}{5}$ $\qquad \cos \beta = \dfrac{3}{5}$ $\qquad \tan \beta = \dfrac{4}{3}$

b. $\sin \theta = -\dfrac{2}{\sqrt{5}}$ $\qquad \cos \theta = -\dfrac{1}{\sqrt{5}}$ $\qquad \tan \theta = 2$

The sine ratio is negative in quadrants 3 and 4. The point that defines an angle with the same sine value is (2,-4).

$\sin \beta = -\dfrac{2}{\sqrt{5}}$ $\qquad \cos \beta = \dfrac{1}{\sqrt{5}}$ $\qquad \tan \beta = -2$

51a. (Suggested answer)

$$h(t) = 49 \cos \left(-\dfrac{2\pi}{30}(t - 15)\right) + 50$$

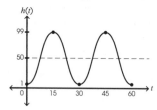

b. The times were 12.1 s and 17.9 s.

52a. A

$f(x) = 52\,500(1.021)^x$ is a function that represents an exponential growth.

b. 52 500 is the starting population and 1.021 is the growth rate.

c. The population will be about 97 934.

d. The population of Vistaville will reach 120 000 in 2055.

53. The height of the cliff is 342.17 m.

54. Julie can makes $1415.30 withdrawal every quarter for 4 years.

ISBN: 978-1-77149-222-5